The

Touring

Tandem

Clayton Pratt

2016 Pratt Publishing Paperback Edition

Portions of this book were previously written for
www.thetouringtandem.com

Cover: Highway 13, Southern Utah. Photo Credit: Holly Jo Hackett
Spine: near Wiesmath, Austria. Back: The Graian Alps, from Mont Blanc

ISBN-13: 978-0-9973198-0-4

1. Pratt, Clayton, 1985-   2. Bike Touring – International
3. Warmshowers – Hospitality 4. Food – Baklava – Yum!

Printed in the United States of America

10 9 8 7 6 5 4 3 2 1 – Liftoff

For Katy
My wife, my friend, my stoker

Forget not that the earth delights to feel your bare feet
and the wind longs to play with your hair
Gibran Khalil Gibran

And also for all the good men and women
we met along the road

For their food, for their friendship, for a good night's rest,
for their encouraging words and energetic enthusiasm

POSSIBLE PRAISE FOR
THE TOURING TANDEM

"The Touring Tandem is a compelling portrait of two souls traipsing across our Mother Earth searching to find the best food this planet has to offer. Before you set this heartwarming tale down, you'll be fixing up your bicycle and going for a ride to your nearest bakery."

-- The National Bakery

"Not a bad way to spend a year."

-- The Morning Herald

"Just when you think this adventure is coming to an end, it keeps on going – because the book isn't over yet."

-- Elijah Wollage Pratt

"They were on their bike for a really long time. The least you could do would be to put down your iPhone, skim a few pages of Pratt's riveting account and leave a decent review on Amazon."

-- The Paper

"Holy shit! My parents did what?"

-- George Wollage Pratt IV

"Every time that wheel turn round, bound to cover just a little more ground."

-- Jerome John Garcia

It is by riding a bicycle that you learn the contours of a country best, since you have to sweat up the hills and coast down them. Thus you remember them as they actually are, while in a motorcar only a high hill impresses you, and you have no such accurate remembrance of country you have driven through as you gain by riding a bicycle.

ERNEST HEMINGWAY

CONTENTS

PROLOGUE:
RAJASTHAN, INDIA

Dragging my feet down the desert highway, twenty meters behind my determined, enthusiastic wife, I dreamed of being somewhere else. Anywhere else. December's hot sun punched into my eyes and exacerbated a weeklong headache and my lungs burned with each cough of the dry air. Judging by my increasingly baggy and sweat-stained Pearl Izumi spandex shorts, I guessed I had lost ten pounds that week. My body was tired and weak, and my mind wanted to give up, and to quit.

A weak body can do incredible things when controlled by a strong mind. Six months earlier, on July 1st 2014, Katy and I left London, England headed for Southeast Asia on a tandem bicycle. Not your typical bicycle ride, but we were confident we could rely on strong legs and a love of cycling to easily overcome any obstacles along the road. We were wrong. The hills in England had tortured us, the rain in the Alps kept falling, the wind in Turkey howled and India just wouldn't go away, but our will and determination had prevailed. On this day, however, trapped between illness, India and arguments with my wife, I slogged down a remote highway in Western Rajasthan, dreaming and wishing that I was home, alone, in my quiet basement with a bowl of

Grape Nuts, some cold Winder Dairy milk, and nothing else.

My murmuring thoughts carried me deeper and deeper into the hole of hopelessness when a blaring horn shattered the silence. The horn shrieked for ten or twenty seconds as the car approached, as if to warn all those within earshot of impending disaster. But the road was empty, and the vast desert as well, except for an occasional goatherd and his flock or a stray herd of camels. Katy didn't acknowledge the driver, and neither did I.

The car passed me, hands waving and heads hanging out all four windows, but when the driver saw Katy walking our tandem down the highway he slammed on the brakes and left his car in the middle of the highway. Five middle-aged Indian gentlemen hopped out. Katy's pace slowed and she glanced back at me, *I'm not doing this one on my own.* I caught up to her just as the men approached and greeted us with a sideways wag of the head. The head wag is a unique Indian gesture with a myriad of interpretations – I had spent hours practicing the subtle lateral deviation of the head and the accompanying half eye blink – and I wagged my head in response.

"Ooh, lovely double cycle. Very nice," one of the men sang in the all too familiar Indian accent. He wore nice slacks, leather shoes and a long sleeve white dress shirt underneath a warm sweater. He was too old and dressed too professional to stop on the side of the road to ogle a bicycle. But, this was India.

"Yes, lovely double cycle," Katy responded, a bit of the Indian accent slipping into her own voice.

"From which country you are?" he asked.

"America, and my name's Clayton. We started in England and we're going to Thailand," I answered. It was a familiar routine so I answered his other questions before he asked them.

"Oh, nice long trip, isn't it?"

"Yes, very nice long trip."

"And you must be very strong, isn't it?"

"Yes, very strong."

"One photo please?"

"A photo? That's a great idea. Why didn't I think of it?" I remarked, with overflowing sarcasm. We often tried to resist these frequent photo requests, but how do you turn down strangers who smile as wide as the ocean and are friendlier than your friends?

"Thank you, thank you," the five men uttered with a slight bow of the head.

"Thank you, thank you." I replied, in my best Indian accent.

After the photos we shook hands before they crammed back into their car and sped off. The car disappeared into the haze, but before Katy and I returned to speaking terms, I marveled at what had just taken place. In a somewhat out-of-body experience, I relived the entire experience, but saw it from a distance. A foreigner, dragging his tired and battered body down a highway in rural India is arrested by the apparition of five fantastically energetic Indians, a short conversation follows, photos are taken, and then as quickly as they appeared, the Indians vanish. You could ride your bike across the entire United States and that might never happen, but for our six weeks in India it happened . . . *every . . . single . . . day*.

The contagious energy of those men crept into my body and lifted my spirits; their words echoed in my mind, "Nice long trip; you must be very strong, isn't it?" It was a long trip; we'd been gone for six months. And I suppose we were strong, or at least felt strong before that awful week of illness; we had seen twenty countries thus far and cycled almost 5,000 miles. I cheered up, and Katy felt it.

"Want to get back on the bike?" she asked.

"Sure. How much farther is it to the Desert Haveli?"

"Twenty-five more kilometers."

"Alright, let's go."

I lifted my right leg up and over the top tube of our bright red Co-Motion Primera tandem, as I had done a thousand times, sat down on my Brooks B-17 leather saddle and with my left foot lifted my left pedal into the starting position, "Ready?"

"Yep."

We were back on our bike. That's what we did that year; we just kept on getting back on our bike.

I've reflected many times on this day, and it seems fitting that when I had given up, it was the energy and enthusiasm of strangers that helped us through one more day of our journey. When our will to continue faltered, as it occasionally did, the goodness of others always picked us up and pushed us toward our destination.

*　*　*

Sauntering through the Indian desert while fighting off sickness and defeat, over the Christmas season no less, was not something I had planned on. Obviously. Normally, I would have been on the Collins chairlift at Alta Ski Resort, shredding fresh powder and answering questions from friends and family about life in medical school. But life doesn't always go as planned. This trip, cycling across the world, wasn't something we planned on. Like many of life's great events, it just kind of happened. One thing led to another, and all of a sudden we boarded a plane to England with a tandem bike, looking forward to a year of freedom and the hope that our love for each other would endure the trials of the road. England, however, with its quaint villages and rolling hills, is not where this story gets interesting.

Our journey began before that. To start our story in the Heathrow International Airport where we assembled our tandem with nothing more than an Allen wrench and a screwdriver would be incomplete. It also wouldn't address the question everyone had hurled at us before we left: "Katy's quitting Google and you're taking a year off medical school to go on a bike ride?"

This trip, then, began with a feeling, one that is shared by most people, because Katy and I are, in fact, just like most people. This feeling was that at some point in the future, maybe when our last child graduated from high school, or maybe not until we were old and wrinkled and life had run its course, Katy and I would look back at our life and wonder if we had missed out, if our good years were over, and if we had perhaps failed to live the life we should have. For me, this feeling came loud and clear when I was twenty eight years old, and only one year into medical school. And it happened, of all places, on a bicycle.

PART ONE

"Nothing compares to the simple pleasure of a bike ride."

John F. Kennedy

AN UNEXPECTED EMAIL

July 2013. Parkdale, Oregon. 5am.

Wake up you sleepy head. Put on some clothes, shake up your bed.
Put another log on the fire for me. I've made some breakfast and coffee.
Look out my window and what do I see?
Oh You Pretty Things – David Bowie

When my alarm goes off too early, especially on vacation, I wonder what on Earth I was thinking the night before. The productivity of the day, however, is often determined in the fifteen seconds after David Bowie starts singing. I can be lazy and roll over or I can leap out of bed. Do I approach life full of energy or do I hit the snooze and accept life as it comes at me? On that morning, like all mornings, I was pulled in conflicting directions.

My mother taught me to love the mountains, and to explore them. I grew up in Salt Lake City, Utah with the Wasatch Mountains in my backyard and spent my childhood in Albion Basin where my mother told me the stories she had heard from her father, Richard Nebeker, or Grandpa Dick – of exploring new valleys and peaks, getting lost in the process and always returning home before morning to tell someone about it. Grandpa Dick embodied the word wanderlust; he had a strong desire to wander or travel or explore. Nebeker genes are strong genes, and some might say I inherited the impulse to wander. In 1956 my Grandpa Dick built a cabin in Albion Basin and firmly planted a love for the mountains deep in his heart and in the hearts of his children and grandchildren. He built the cabin to have an outlet from his routine life, and to have a base from which to explore the Wasatch Mountains, because he, like me, would say that a day wandering in the mountains, well, that's just my kind of day.

When I think of my own dad, I think of routine and consistency. Throughout my childhood, in the early hours of the morning, a light would appear underneath the crack of my door, which meant my dad was awake, many hours before I needed to be, attending to his morning routine of sit-ups, push-ups and stretches before a long day in the office. When the spiritual side of his life picked up, his morning routine was considerably lengthened by morning prayers that lasted longer than a kid could ever understand.

My dad inherited these traits from his father, Grandpa Judge. My sister Elizabeth likes to tell a story which adequately sums up Grandpa Judge. During a conversation, my grandpa casually mentioned he suffered from some leg pain, but a new set of exercises from a therapist was really helping. Elizabeth asked, "I'm so sorry. When did you hurt your leg?"

My grandpa thought about it for a moment, and then replied, "I guess it happened back in the late 70s or so."

"What?" Elizabeth laughed in disbelief. "You've been doing the same exercises every morning for 40 years?"

"Yep. The exercises helped, so I just kept doing them."

I had plenty of reasons to get out of bed that morning. If I were more like my grandfathers, discipline and a love of the mountains would have been enough. But when the disciplined and energetic alarm-setting Clayton meets the sleepy and apathetic alarm-snoozing Clayton to fight the morning battle of, "Should we get up and get going?" there is no telling who will win. And as chance would have it, I pressed snooze, rolled over and fell back to sleep.

Some time later I heard my wife mumble, "Didn't you have a long ride planned today?" Katy's words electrified my mind, and within a moment I was looking for my Pearl Izumi cycling shorts.

My morning routine before an early ride is: get dressed, eat, go to the bathroom, fill two water bottles, stuff my jersey with Shot Blocks, Clif Bars and a couple bananas and head out the door. For some people, 100 or more miles seems too far for a bike ride. It's not. Just be sure to bring some calories for the road. I was scheduled for my first ultra cycling event in a couple of months, a 400-mile loop in central Ohio, and today was another day of training.

I love cycling, so much. It is my avenue to freedom, and a way to escape. It lets me explore new places and see the world from a different, slower perspective. I love when my quads burn and my lungs race. I prefer to cycle over mountains, rather than around them, because nothing compares to the 40mph descent that follows the pain and suffering of a relentless climb. I like to swerve through traffic, skip stop signs and race cars off the line when red lights turn green. And if I ride far enough and long enough my mind gets to wander and daydream.

I rolled out of Parkdale, Oregon on that crisp July morning and cycled south on Highway 35 towards Mt. Hood National Forest. Alone on my bike, I recalled a conversation from the previous night.

"Why do you want to ride your bike *four hundred* miles? Katy's uncle asked, confused at the thought of such self-inflicted physical punishment.

"Well, why not?" I responded.

My mind stopped there. "Why not?" It was a fake answer. A fake answer that evaded my deeper, more complicated, reasons. To be honest, there isn't an easy answer to that question. In simple terms, I like cycling and I like being different. Cycling four hundred miles is pretty different, so why not give it a try.

My wife also likes to be different. Katy and I have many differences, but our desire to be different is a unifying similarity. This helps to explain why we've been married for seven years and still don't have any children, and why I'm twenty nine and only halfway through medical school. Whatever it is, we like to run against the grain. We try to enjoy life one day at a time and I suppose we're in no hurry to be grownups. My greatest fear is that one day I will grow up. That would be normal, and normal is boring.

My desire to be different has not always been something I've aspired to; rather, it is a deeply rooted personality trait that has been positively reinforced throughout my life. A few years ago, a marriage counselor (every good marriage needs a counselor, right?) retraced my history and asked about times in my life I wanted to be different. Here are some of the stories I shared.

In high school I took AP Psychology with my best friend, Austin Hackett. We were good students, but in 2002, sitting in the corner of Chas Adams' psychology class at Skyline High School, you couldn't tell it by looking at us. We wore unwashed clothes (we were in the middle of a "sweat-bet," an ongoing competition among friends to see who could wear the same pair of sweat pants the longest – without washing them), prided ourselves in our long hair and spent our free time collecting couches, listening to Bob Dylan and Pink Floyd, and working on our hacky-sack skills. Dr. Adams got sick and a substitute teacher taught the last 3 months of the year. The first impressions we made must have been less than ideal and our new teacher wrote us off as "students who lack potential." It wasn't until our final exam scores came back that the substitute approached us and said, "I'm sorry, I really got you two wrong. More than any other students I've had, you two made me challenge my first impression."

When I was five and a half years old, my elementary school had designated one week as Spirit Week, and on Wednesday we could show our spirit by wearing backwards and mismatched clothes. Before school, my twin sister Elizabeth experimented with a closet-full of wardrobe options, which made me very upset. My options were limited to shorts and a t-shirt. Eventually, I broke down crying and screamed, "My wanna wear a dress." My mom consented and let me wear my sister's red and white polka dot dress with a striped shirt, because polka dots and stripes don't match. My older sister, Jessica, who was seven at the time, was mortified, but I skipped down the road to school and carried my head high. Later that month, at parent-teacher conference, my teacher told my mother, "The great thing about Clayton is he can wear a dress to school and not care what anyone thinks about him."

Why did I sign up for a 400-mile bike race? Because it's different.

* * *

Fifteen miles south of Parkdale, Oregon, Highway 35 takes an abrupt right turn and pitches up to an 8% grade. I shifted into a harder gear and got out of the saddle and started climbing. My legs felt good. The effortless, rhythmic hammering at the pedals told me I was in good shape and my training was paying off. I listened to the pace of my lungs and guessed my heart rate to be near 155, my lactate threshold. The road was empty that morning, so I dropped my head, kept my wheel near the white line and thought about all that had happened in the five years since I had last cycled up to Mt. Hood.

* * *

Katy and I had lived in Oregon five years earlier, during the summer of 2008. Katy had an internship with Intel, and I had promised to study for the MCAT, medical school's entrance exam. I should have kept my promise. After a summer of half-hearted studying, and a fall and winter of decent studying, I sat for the MCAT in the spring of 2009. Two passages into the Verbal Reasoning section of the exam, however, anxiety overran my ability to think clearly. I panicked. I skipped to the next passage and frantically began reading. I read all the questions, no idea. My heart pounded and sweat ran down my face, but this wasn't the sweat of cycling. This was the sweat of "Oh shit!" I weighed my options and made a quick decision. Ten minutes later, sitting outside on the grass, I called Katy and told her I had just walked out of the most important exam of my life. It wasn't the first time she asked herself, "Why did I marry this guy?" It also wouldn't be the last.

When Katy shared this unfortunate news with her parents, I can only assume that her father, Dave Clark, asked himself the same question, "Why did she marry this guy?" Before Dave gave me permission to marry his daughter, he asked me about my five-year plan. I said exactly what he wanted to hear – graduate from college and go to medical school – not just because I really wanted to marry his daughter, but also because, at the time, that was my five-year plan. What I didn't tell him was that I'm prone to make impulsive decisions, and I can't sit still and do the same thing for more than two years. If I had told him that after college I'd convince Katy to turn down a job from Intel and move to the Mississippi Delta to join Teach For America, and that halfway through medical school I'd press the pause button on life so Katy and I could go on the best trip of our lives, he might have asked for my ten or twenty year plan as well.

Katy is a lot like her father, in that she likes knowing what the future holds. But also like her father, she enjoys a nice challenge once in a while. The most important thing Dave has taught Katy can be summed up in a phrase he's told her a thousand times: "You can do hard things." And he's right; Katy can do hard things.

I suppose Katy's ability to do hard things attracted me to her in the first place. She has a knack for persisting through challenges and smiling in the midst of difficulty. Before we started dating, we spent part of a summer and fall training for the St. George Marathon. On one of our final training runs, Katy (foolishly) decided to break-in a new pair of running shoes. Large blisters started forming on the soles of her feet around mile five, but she still pushed through the 18-mile run. She had a hard time walking for the next few days, but recovered in time for the marathon. I, on the other hand, crashed my mountain bike the week before the race and a double layer of stitches over my knee prevented my participation. She ran without me.

The summer we finally started dating I asked Katy if she wanted to go on a hike.

"That sounds fun," she answered. "Where should we go?"

"I was thinking we could go up the Tram at Snowbird and then we could . ."

"Walk back down?" she stated, cutting me off.

"Not quite. We can follow the ridge west for an hour or so and then turn south. From there it's maybe 10 or 15 miles until we reach American Fork Canyon."

"I didn't know there is a trail between Little Cottonwood Canyon and American Fork Canyon," she exclaimed.

"I don't think there is."

Katy and I left a pick-up car at the mouth of American Fork Canyon, and Katy's mom, Jeanette, drove us up to Snowbird Ski Resort, about a two-hour drive away and on the other side of a legitimate mountain range – our obstacle for the day. Jeanette wished us luck and off we went. Seven hours into our hike, with a trail that was nowhere to be seen, and a bit afraid we might startle some moose sleeping in the dense brush, Katy and I sang songs – most likely *The Newsies* soundtrack – at the top of our lungs to warn any moose of our impending presence and knocked out our all-day hike. Not only did she keep up, she had as much fun as I did.

Later that fall our relationship started to heat up and I had the great idea of sleeping on a couch in the mountains above Rock Creek Canyon in Provo, Utah. We bought a cheap loveseat from the Salvation Army and I put it on my back and hauled it up the mountain. We slept that night up there on that purple, paisley couch and Katy woke up with a very red eye and a massively swollen face from an allergic reaction to midnight bug bites. She downplayed her discomfort (maybe because she didn't have a mirror) and didn't complain once. "You know what," I thought to myself the next morning, "I think I really like this girl."

* * *

Katy and I graduated from Brigham Young University in April 2009 and then moved to Lake Village, Arkansas to work with Teach For America. Teach For America sends recent college graduates to low-performing schools in some of our nation's most challenging school districts. After one year of teaching I retook the MCAT, this time with better luck. The only unsettling thing about the exam was the torrential rain and fierce winds that beat down on the hotel room the night before. As the storm intensified, a tornado warning sounded and I wondered if I'd survive to see the morning. Driving from Little Rock back to our home near the banks of the Mississippi River, I called Katy and jokingly told her I had again not completed the exam.

"It's okay, Clayton. I still love you. We can find something else for us to do," Katy reassured me.

"I know, but I really thought I'd go to medical school," I continued my joke. The phone was silent for a moment too long and I heard Katy holding back tears, so I gave in, "Just kidding, the test was fine."

"I hate you. Why do you always do that to me," she stormed. As her tears turned to anger I realized that I had crossed the line and ventured into the area of "jokes you really shouldn't play on your wife." I apologized.

I was accepted to the University of Michigan Medical School in Ann Arbor, Michigan in September 2011, but my class was overbooked and I accepted $80,000 to wait a year before matriculating. Every morning for an entire year, before Katy went off to work at Google and I would roll out of bed, I'd triumphantly announce: "Well, I made $219 today. Not a bad day, today. Not a bad day." I finally entered medical school in September 2012, only three years behind my five year plan.

* * *

First year medical students need to be able to answer one question, "What type of doctor do you want to be?" I didn't know. Unfortunately, "I don't know" wasn't sufficient to fend off friends, family, Katy's coworkers or other strangers. I decided I needed an answer, not just to appease these enquiring minds, but because I really did need an answer. What type of doctor did I want to be?

To solve this problem I asked myself three questions. First, do I want to work with kids or adults? That was easy, kids. I'd much rather care for the young and innocent than try to erase the ill effects of a lifetime of sedentary living and excess calorie, tobacco and alcohol consumption. Second, surgery or medicine? Surgery, of course. Nothing in medical school compares with going to the operating room and watching illness cured with a scalpel and some sutures. Third, what organ system? This was also easy, the heart. The heart is fascinating, and logical. The sequential arrangement of chambers and vessels makes it easier to understand than the gastrointestinal tract, kidneys or the infinitely complex nervous or endocrine system. I combined these three answers and came up with my specialty, Pediatric Cardiac Surgery.

I spent a significant amount of time during my first year learning more about this specialty. The pinnacle moment occurred one morning when I was shadowing Dr. Jennifer Romano. As she entered the operating room, friendly chit-chat ended and a serious tone swept through the room. It was go time. Dr. Romano made a vertical incision over the patient's chest, sliced through the sternum with a power saw, discarded the thymus, and three minutes later revealed a beating human heart – of an eight day old baby. It was awesome. The infant was placed on cardiopulmonary bypass, and for seven long hours Dr. Romano repaired congenital defects of this child's heart. *This is what I want to do.*

The first year of school came to a close and with no classes scheduled for June, July and August, a flurry of excitement swept across campus. Everyone was busy asking and answering the same question, "What are you doing this summer?" After that summer, one year would seamlessly transition into the next, school turning into residency, residency into fellowship and fellowship into a life-long career. The summer of 2013 would be the last three-month vacation most of us would ever have.

"What are you doing this summer?" Katy asked our group of friends as we sat down for sandwiches at Zingerman's Deli. I was half-way into the third bite of my D-Money Cuban Conundrum when Chelsea spoke up.

"We're going to Kenya," Chelsea answered. By "we" she meant herself and her husband, Matt. They're two of our best friends, and for obvious reasons: they are a bit older than traditional students, mature, out-of-state, married and they love doing all of the things that Katy and I enjoy. It's an easy friendship.

"That sounds great. What are you doing there?" Katy continued.

"Some sort of research. Michigan has a project over there and I'm not totally sure about all the specifics, but it should be a lot of fun," Matt answered, ever optimistic.

"And what about you guys?" Katy asked, looking towards Kenny and Amanda.

"Also going to Kenya," Kenny replied as he poured some baked beans over his Tarb's Tenacious Tenure.

"You guys are busy with school all year, and when you finally have some free time you leave the country. Just great," Katy protested.

"Don't worry, we'll be here in Ann Arbor," Tyler quickly added.

"That's right. Getting ready for the Tour, aren't we?" I asked Tyler, looking forward to another month of July bicycle racing.

"What are you doing again Clayton?" Amanda asked, unable to recall my plans for the summer.

"Also research. I'll be working with Dr. Romano," I responded.

"Oh fun, I've heard she's pretty intense," she answered.

Fun? Fun? I repeated the word in my mind. No, it didn't sound fun. The last free summer of my life and I'm doing research? *Sounds awful.*

There are two types of research - ree-search (accent on the ree) and ri-search (accent on the search). Ree-search is for aspiring hopefuls who commit large amounts of time to mundane tasks, just to add another line to their resume. Ri-search is for scientists and physicians who have built their career on a lifetime of scientific discovery and publications. I was going to be doing ree-search with little hope – or desire – of ever crossing over into ri-search. I signed up for a summer of research, not because I necessarily wanted to, but because all my classmates were doing it so I figured I should be doing it too.

The work that summer was tedious. I sat at a computer for a couple hundred hours, scouring electronic medical records in search of the minutest details about children's prior heart surgeries. The work was mundane, but in exchange for helping out on this project, I got to learn more about cardiac surgery, spent some time shadowing in the operating room and developed a relationship with a phenomenal surgeon and wonderful mentor, Dr. Romano.

During one of our weekly meetings, I asked Dr. Romano a personal question, "If you could start over, would you choose the same career?" Our conversation was not the warm and fuzzy discussion I was accustomed to; she really told me what she thought. "So many students show up at Michigan, get introduced to the wonderful surgeons here, and tell themselves, 'That's what I want to do.' But what you have a hard time understanding is that you have years of training ahead of you. Sure I knew I would have a seven-year general surgery residency, then two years of a cardiothoracic fellowship, and then another year to sub-subspecialize in pediatrics. And from the outset it seemed great, but when my friends started having children and families, it really made me think about the career I chose for myself. I'm not saying I don't like my job. When I'm in the operating room, I absolutely love what I am doing. It's my favorite thing in the world. But you need to decide what you absolutely love, and that includes what you love in medicine and what you love outside of medicine."

She gave me great advice. I consider myself fortunate to have a great mentor who helped me think about the difficult decisions that lie ahead . That conversation forced me to really think about what I love and what I wanted in my future.

* * *

I approached an intersection, and my mind was startled out of its daydream. Mt. Hood Meadows Ski Resort, Next Right, the sign read. As I passed the turn off and continued towards Timberline Lodge, a distinct feeling overwhelmed me. Sometimes answers come to us when we're looking for them; other times they come out of nowhere. At that moment a single feeling overwhelmed me: *this is what I love.* I had to think about it for a moment, because I wasn't expecting this sudden overwhelming feeling. With time it all became clear. I love cycling. I love being outside. I love the mountains. I love the freedom and flexibility to do things that truly make me happy.

These thoughts clashed with recent conversations from medical school and I realized something – I need to be honest with myself. I can only spend my time and energy pursuing what I truly enjoy. I'd rather have a week on my bike than an entire summer of research and publications. I didn't discard my intent to be a surgeon but I realized that whatever decision I might make, it had to be one I absolutely loved. It must also allow me to pursue the many other things I love in life. *Do what you love; it will all work out.*

I reached Timberline Lodge thoroughly exhausted and stopped just long enough to catch my breath before I turned around and descended the mountain. A huge smile stretched across my face. I had left that morning for a normal day's ride, but returned with slightly more purpose and direction in life. It wasn't until a month or so later, however, when the impact of *do what you love: it will all work out* would be fully realized. I was up late, long after Katy had fallen asleep, when an email via Warmshowers landed in my inbox and put me in a difficult spot between following my heart and listening to reason. Warmshowers is a website that provides reciprocal hospitality for touring cyclists. The email read:

> Hello Clayton!
>
> How are you? We are Valéryne and Luc from Lausanne, Switzerland. We left home in July 2011, and after 12'000 miles cycling through Europe and Asia, here is North America! From Vancouver to Denver. From where we took a train to Chicago, and arrived yesterday night. We'll leave July 17th and cycle to Detroit. We'll be in Ann Arbor on July 21st. Would you be OK to host us? We are easy going, don't like to disturb, love to share stories.
>
> Thanks in advance for your answer and hope to meet you!
>
> Bonne Route!
>
> Valéryne and Luc

The moment I read that email, large gears started turning inside my head. I had so many questions for these two cyclists. Where did you start? What is the strangest thing you've seen so far? What countries have you visited? What types of bikes are you riding? Are you tired? How much has your trip cost? What's your new favorite food? Any mechanical problems?

As my mind spun out an infinite number of questions, something strange happened. I realized I wouldn't be asking these questions out of curiosity about their trip. These questions were about my own trip. I knew that sometime, hopefully sooner than later, I would be riding my bike around the world.

KATY'S SMILE

August 2013. Ann Arbor, Michigan.

W hat are you going to get?" Katy asked, as we studied the menu at Haifa Falafel.

"A shawafel sandwich and . . . a side of hummus," I answered.

"What's shawafel?"

"I don't know, but hopefully some sort of shawarma-falafel fusion. What are you getting?"

"Do you want to split your sandwich and also get a salad? And are you getting a small hummus or a large one? I was thinking maybe I'd get a Fatoosh salad, does that sound good to you? Do you want to share some soup?"

Katy has serious menu indecision, especially at a new restaurant. She needs all the info before she can make a decision.

"I'm getting a shawafel sandwich and a small hummus. You can order whatever you want." I was trying to be patient; an argument now would spell disaster for the evening to come.

A Middle Eastern guy, about my age, stepped up to the register and asked what we'd like. I ordered and then the man turned to Katy.

"What is the best thing on the menu?" Katy asked.

"Well it depends on what you like," the man answered.

"Well, what is your favorite?" Katy persisted.

I knew it would be a while so I gave her my wallet, filled two Styrofoam cups with water and found a place to sit. A pit settled in my stomach. If Katy couldn't make up her mind about something as routine as ordering dinner, how would she ever decide to leave work at Google, further postpone having children, and spend thousands of dollars to ride a bicycle across Europe and Asia? I knew Katy would take some convincing and she'd have many questions that would need answers. For a week I had brainstormed her possible objections and crafted legitimate responses. Dinner at a new restaurant and an evening walk to Dairy Queen was a necessary prerequisite to put our relationship on the best of terms before I broke the news.

"What did you order?" I asked, when Katy finally sat down.

"Majaddara salad and lentil soup."

"What's majaddara?" I asked, trying to pronounce a word we were both unfamiliar with.

"I'm not sure, but the guy said I had to try it," Katy answered.

The uneasy feeling in my stomach diminished. Although she's indecisive, Katy is always willing to try something new; it's one of the things I love about her. It was the only reason I had any hope she might agree to join me on my immature and rudimentary plan.

"Katy, this is delicious," I sputtered, mimicking Bob Wiley's corn-on-the-cob feast.

"This majaddara is also great. You should try it."

We finished our meals, licked our plates clean (yes, the majaddara was great) and headed home in our Toyota Prius.

"DQ?" Katy asked.

"Of course. But do you want to go home first and walk over?"

"Walk over? What's gotten into you?"

Katy loves going on walks, but not me. I think walks are for old people. For me, going on a walk reminds me of bed-ridden hospitalized patients attempting to ambulate down the hallway so they can be cleared by Physical Therapy for discharge. I suggested we walk to Dairy Queen because a stroll through the neighborhood with a little bit of ice cream is music to her ears.

I ordered a small chocolate cone with chocolate sprinkles and Katy got a vanilla cone, no sprinkles. We meandered along Packard Road and enjoyed a warm summer night in Ann Arbor. To prevent my cone from melting and dripping onto the pavement, I carefully licked the ice cream in a circular manner, from the bottom up, creating a nice point at the top. When my ice cream gets down to the level of the cone, I scoop all the ice cream out of the bottom of the cone with my tongue before biting into the cone directly. Katy is the opposite; she takes a bite out of the cone with each lick of the vanilla ice cream, ensuring the ice cream and cone run out at the same time.

"Katy, can I ask you a question?"

"Sure what is it?" she replied, a bit concerned. I don't usually ask for permission to have a conversation with my wife.

"Are you ready?" I asked, stalling the moment to get her full attention.

"Yeah, what's the matter?"

"What do you think about cycling around the world?"

"What do you mean?" Katy answered, her face changing from concern to confusion.

"Cycling around the world. What do you think about it?"

"I don't understand. What are you talking about?"

"You and me. I take a year off medical school. You leave Google for a while. We cycle around the world."

"Are you being serious?"

"Sure, why not? We'll work for the rest of our lives. Let's do something else before life gets too busy."

She was silent. She realized I was serious and that the whole evening had built up to that moment. Little engines inside her complex mind instantly started processing hundreds of thoughts and simultaneously raised dozens of objections.

"What about Google?" she started.

I knew it would be the first words out of her mouth and I had an easy, but not too comforting, response, "It will be here when you get back."

A smile of disbelief emerged on her face. After college, Katy had turned down a job offer from Intel and joined Teach For America. We both spent two years teaching underperforming, raucous students in chaotic classrooms because I had convinced her that her quiet cubicle with triple the salary would still be there when she got back. She never went back.

"What about money, and our house? Will Michigan even let you leave? And what do you mean 'around the world'? Where are we even going to go? What about winter?"

"Anything else?" I asked.

"A whole year? I don't think I can sit on a bike seat for that long. What about starting a family? And what will our parents think?"

I was expecting Katy's landslide of questions. To have any chance of navigating her concerns, I'd have to break things down one by one. "Well, what do you want to talk about first?" I asked.

"Kids. I thought we were going to start a family," she began, curious how much thought I'd given to my plan. It was a legitimate concern; we were approaching six years of marriage without kids, and people, and especially Mormons, started to wonder whether we lacked faith or lacked sperm.

I shrugged my shoulders. "What's one more year?" I asked. Katy laughed and rolled her eyes. She couldn't believe she was having this conversation.

"What about money. How much will this cost?"

"Well that depends on how much money we have."

"Then you tell me," Katy countered. "How much do we have?" Katy knows that I am relatively oblivious to our finances and that she stood on higher ground in this category.

"That's where you come in," I responded as I put my arm around her. A week after our wedding, I had suggested we keep our savings in a large envelope underneath our mattress. She's been in charge of our paychecks ever since.

As a young girl, when other girls were playing Barbie or painting their nails, Katy learned about interest rates and the "time value of money". Her parents both got their MBAs after college. Her mom works in finance and both run their own businesses. Conversations at the Clark dinner table included lessons on business acumen and financial expertise (whereas dinner conversations with my family were geared towards Jim Carrey humor and "Is it going to snow at Alta tonight?").

"Do you even know where our money is?" Katy asked.

"We have a checking account and also an American Express Card. There's also a Roth IRA and Vanguard and an E-Trade something or other," I answered.

"Go on."

"You also have some CDs from your Grandma Bonnie and my Zion's Bank account might still have some money in it but I'm not sure." I stopped and hoped my answer was sufficient.

"Keep going."

I thought about it for a moment, before continuing, "There's also your Google Stock and our AmeriCorps money. And I've got about $800 in cash on the nightstand next to my bed from tutoring. And you have that other envelope with all the $5 bills in it in case the world comes to an end." This "diversification of our assets," as Katy likes to call it, is rather confusing and makes me wonder if the envelope under the mattress idea wasn't that bad of an idea after all.

"Okay. How much money is in each of these accounts?" she asked. She knew if she dug a little deeper I'd give in.

"I don't know."

"What if you wanted to check? How could you find out?"

"For the Key Bank account I could go down to State Street and ask Amy," I started. I went to the bank often and deposited stacks of $20 bills from my tutoring job with my friend Amy, the bank teller. I like the bank. I like the Dum Dum suckers. I like the idea that every time I came and went Amy had a growing suspicion that I was a drug dealer.

"Why not just look online?" Katy badgered me. "And what about Chase, Vanguard and E-Trade? How would you check those?"

I smiled and raised my eyebrows, admitting defeat. "Fine. I have no idea where our money is and I have no idea how much we have."

"You need me, don't you," she finished.

And she's right – I do need her. Katy is the practical and logical one; she always has been. I loved the idea of Teach For America but she figured out region matching, summer training logistics and housing. When I applied to medical school, she navigated the waters of job searching throughout the country. She got hired at Google, moved our stuff out of the Delta in three days (in fear of an impending levee break and a Mississippi River flood) and started putting money away in case of a "rainy day". Her beautiful mind sorts through all the possibilities and comes up with the most logical, efficient and financially viable option to get from point A to point B. If I am the artist that dreams of painting a masterpiece, she supplies the canvas, the paint, the brushes, and the easel and then finds a buyer for my work. And with my current dream of cycling the world, she had her work cut out for her.

After making some headway against the impracticalities of our possible departure, I helped her imagine the English countryside, the French bakeries, and the stories we'd be able to tell our grandkids when we got old and arthritic. Katy loves a good adventure just as much as I do, and I did my best to keep her focused on the big picture and not get bogged down in the minutiae of trip planning. When we came within sight of our house, I decided to wrap up our conversation with some simple steps to get the ball rolling.

"First of all, will you please find out how much money we have," I asked, with an emphasis on the please.

"Sure. But you need to find out how much this trip will cost."

"Deal."

"And then what?"

"If money is okay, then I'll talk to Michigan and see if I can leave school for a year."

"We also need someone to rent out the house while we're gone, and it can't just be anybody. I want someone clean, maybe we can find someone at church who needs a place," Katy added.

"And then if everything works out, will you talk to Google?" I asked.

"Yes, but only if everything else happens first."

"Oh, one last thing," I added as we entered our front door.

"What?"

"We can't tell anyone, at least not yet."

"What? I can't talk to my family?"

"Not yet."

"Well why not?"

"Because if this trip doesn't happen I don't want to be the guy who almost rode his bike around the world."

"Okay fine," Katy reluctantly agreed.

I let out a sigh of relief. The wheels of our trip were beginning to turn.

Over the following months, things started to fall into place. Projecting a budget for a bike ride across Europe and Asia was not easy. I anticipated roughly six months in Europe during the summer and fall, and then two months in India and three in Southeast Asia. Lonely Planet suggested a daily budget for each country, but I guessed our trip would be cheaper. We planned to travel exclusively by bike and assumed our travel expenses, apart from airfare, would be about zero. We also planned to use Warmshowers when possible, and wild camp where feasible. That would minimize hostel and hotel expenses. I decided on $50/person/day in Europe and $25/person/day in Asia as a frugal, but manageable budget. To estimate airfare, I entered some flights between Detroit, London, Delhi and Bangkok into skyscanner.net. The final factor to consider was the cost of new bikes, gear and other necessities. This amount was highly variable, ranging from $2,500 to $10,000 or more. I chose the conservative option, added up our costs and set a budget of $30,000. Sure it was expensive, but much less than a year of medical school.

Katy, meanwhile, tried to figure out how much money we had, and how much we might have in a year when we planned to leave. She told me that if we saved as much as we could, we just might have enough to go. Later, many people asked how we could afford this trip, which I suppose is a fair question. Most of our peers didn't have this much money lying around. We didn't have any kids, and Katy had worked for the past four years. Undergraduate tuition at Brigham Young University had been minimal and we both worked during college, so we weren't crushed with student loans. During medical school, I continued to work as a tutor and as an Airbnb host. We lived cheap, only splurging on the occasional tacos or falafel and Katy's childhood lessons on interest rates and savings accounts started to pay off – and pay for our trip.

At first, the thought of asking medical school for a leave of absence was daunting – a giant wall that blocked our escape.

"They aren't going to just let me leave," I insisted, as we revisited the subject for the umpteenth time. "And I think my scholarship was only valid for four consecutive years."

"If you don't ask we can't go," Katy reminded me.

"What am I going to say to them? Hi, I know you have students who take a year off to get dual degrees, to conduct research or to intern with the National Institutes of Health. Not me. I'd like to ride my bike for a year. What can you do for me?" I stated.

"What other option do you have?"

"I don't know. I could lie. Maybe I should tell them my grandparents are sick and I need to take care of them. Or I could tell them I'm having second thoughts about medical school and need a year to think about it."

"Do what you want, but I wouldn't lie," Katy cautioned.

I arranged a meeting with my class counselor and when the appointed day and time came I rode my bike up to campus, walked through the ever-confusing labyrinth of hospital stairways and hallways to my counselor's office, and sat down in a chair across from her desk.

"Hello Clayton, what can I do for you?" Amy asked, with her warm and friendly personality.

"I'd like to take a year off of school. If that's possible?" I was trying to be direct, but not demanding.

"Of course you can, for what reason?" she answered, concerned that something serious was bothering me.

I debated whether or not to tell the truth, as the great adventure of my life, of our life, hung in the balance. My mind weighed the two answers I had scripted and then my lips started moving, "I'm planning a bike trip around the world with my wife." I finished my sentence, sat back and took a deep breath. Peace and fear overwhelmed me. There, I said it. My future was no longer in my hands. If our trip didn't happen, it wouldn't be because I had wimped out. Milliseconds passed, but it seemed like an eternity because a simple, "I'm sorry, that's not possible" would have ruined our adventure forever.

"That sounds great," she finally answered. "So you'll be taking a personal leave? Is that right?"

"Yes," I said, my spirits lifting. "I'd like a one year personal leave." It sounded so simple, and I repeated Amy's words in my mind because I knew Katy would want all the details: *A personal leave. That sounds nice. When others ask why I'm leaving, I'll just tell them, "It's personal."*

"Okay, I just need you to fill out these forms and I'll take care of the rest. You'll also need to meet with financial aid and the registrar, but everything should be okay for you to take a year off, and your scholarship will resume when you return."

I entered her office full of despair, but exited triumphant. Four minutes later I was outside. The grass was green, the sky was blue and the bright sun lit up my ecstatic face. I jumped on my bike and raced off to tell Katy, who by now was just as excited about our trip as I was, the good news.

Katy's conversation with Google was more complex. After a couple weeks of deliberation, Katy finally got up enough courage to talk to her manager, Jon, about our plans.

"Hey Jon, I have something I need to talk to you about," Katy mentioned during a weekly one-on-one meeting.

"Sure, what is it?"

"Clayton and I have had this goal to bike around the world," Katy began, a bit nervous.

"Okay?"

"Let me put it this way. Do you ever feel like life is moving too fast? I mean, I love Google and I love my job, but time goes so fast. I love working here, but I also love traveling and seeing new places and I feel like if I don't do this now then I never will. I guess what I'm saying is that I really, really want to take a year off from Google to cycle around the world with my husband. Would it be possible to have my job back when I return?"

Over the next month Katy learned that Google could offer a six month leave, but not an entire year. They discussed other options, including working at Google offices in Ireland or India, but the work visas proved to be too complicated. With no solution in place, Katy met with Jon again and they made a decision.

"If this is something you really want to do, then you should do it," Jon encouraged her. "Send me an email when you're about home, and

I'll do my best to help you get rehired. Oh, and have fun."

* * *

In September, with two weeks to go until my 400-mile race, I was 70 miles into a twelve-hour training ride when I veered to the side of the road. In a fit of rage I cursed every foul word I could think of and then called Katy and asked her to pick me up. My right knee was throbbing. Weeks earlier the aches were minimal but that day my knee erupted into flames of pain. My race hopes were over. In the coming days my mood further plummeted as the energy of trip planning was dampened by long nights in the library. Each night, however, just as I was about to fall asleep, Katy would ask me the same question.

"Are you sure about this?"

"Sure about what?" I would mutter, mostly asleep.

"This trip. Are we crazy? We need to ask someone if this is a good idea or if we're terribly irresponsible."

After a week, I relented, "Okay, who do you want to ask?"

"How about your sister, Jessica?" Katy suggested. At first I resisted, but eventually decided that talking to Jessica might be a good idea. She had already graduated from law school, started a career, bought a home and could give us some perspective on how this trip might, or might not, fit into the next five years of our life.

In Croatia, ten months later, from an Airbnb rental overlooking the old city of Dubrovnik, Jessica wrote the following in our blog, The Touring Tandem:

> Last November my family spent Thanksgiving on Long Island with the Pratts. While we were at Hendricks Tavern waiting for dessert to come, Clayton and I moseyed around the restaurant and he said, "Hey Jessica, I have to tell you a secret and you can't tell anyone." He proceeded to tell me about his plans to take a year off from medical school and travel with Katy around the world ... by bicycle. My jaw dropped. Clayton said he was a little nervous to an-

nounce the news to some family members, for obvious reasons I suppose. I told him once he is done with school he can work for the rest of his life so his plan sounded awesome (and I was super envious).

On our flight home from Thanksgiving, Katy and I were bursting with energy. Our conversation with Jessica sealed the deal. In six short months, we'd be getting on a bike in London and heading east towards who knows where. It was so strange, but so exciting. Details still had to be worked out (who would live in our house, what bikes we would ride, which route to take) but we had checked off the big boxes and were free to leave.

"Are you sure you want to tell our families before we leave?" I asked. "It would be much cooler if we left without telling anyone." I love a good practical joke and was hoping not to pass up this once-in-a-lifetime opportunity.

"And what, you won't tell anyone else in your family?" Katy asked.

"Sure. In fact, for the first couple months of our trip we should communicate with our family as if nothing has changed. After we've been gone for a few months, when they ask how school and work are going we can send a postcard from Serbia." I suggested.

"What you do with your family is your decision, but I'm telling mine," Katy insisted.

* * *

"What are everyone's New Year's resolutions?" I asked, to no one in particular. It was New Year's Eve and my family was at Tsunami Restaurant and Sushi Bar in Salt Lake City.

"Eat more sushi," my youngest brother joked, as he piled his plate high and wide.

"Eli, I thought you were working on being less sarcastic?" my mother chided.

"But what will this world do without my humor?" Eli enquired, as he added some ginger and wasabi to his Fire Breathing Dragon roll.

The rest of my siblings took a moment to share their New Year's resolutions before Dylan interrupted, "New Year's resolutions are complete crap. It's just a bunch of lazy, fat people who blame their obesity on bad genes, and say they're going to eat better and exercise more. But you know they're not."

I nodded my approval, but didn't listen to what he said. My mind was busy rehearsing how I'd break the news to my family. Unfortunately, Dylan's less than optimistic thoughts on the New Year changed the conversation to skiing and Alta's weather forecast. When the sushi was gone, and my siblings' busy social lives began beeping their phones, I rescued the conversation.

"No one asked me what *my* New Year's resolutions are," I declared. Elizabeth projected a look of disinterest. Katy's eyes were glued on me, afraid of what might happen, but I refused to look at her. An odd look between us would ruin my surprise. Jessica also sat quietly, equally interested how the conversation would unfold.

"Okay Clayton, what are *your* New Year's resolutions? More school?" Eli asked.

"Thank you for asking. You know, this whole school thing has really got me down. I've been thinking I need a little time off." I cleared my throat. "I was thinking I'd buy a tandem bicycle and Katy and I will fly to London and we'll ride around England for a month. After that, maybe we'll go over to France and see the countryside."

I paused just long enough to let my words set in. A trip through Western Europe was feasible, but when one of them was about to ask a question I continued: "After France we might cross the Alps, make a stop in Germany . . . or Italy. Then continue through Eastern Europe to Turkey." As I shared more details, turned towards Katy. They knew that if they were going to get to the truth, it would have to come from her. "Then we'll head to India, see the sights, enjoy a Christmas in the sun, and end up somewhere in Southeast Asia. I hear Bali is beautiful in April."

Silence. Everyone's eyes were on Katy. It was quiet for longer than I imagined possible and I was impressed with Katy's restraint. I glanced over at her and saw a smile slowly blossom on her face. Our secret was out. Her radiant smile gave the answer to what they were all thinking, "Is he serious?" but more than anything, it reminded me that I had an awesome wife.

VICODIN

On a warm and sunny Friday afternoon in May 2014, I packed our brand new red, Co-Motion tandem and other touring equipment into the back of our Prius, picked up Katy from work, and headed north towards Petoskey, Michigan. The beginning of a trip is always exciting. The anticipation of new faces and new places must confront the anxiety that we might have left something important behind. I ran through my mental checklist one last time: Bike pump. Check. Katy's swim suit. Check. Four water bottles, sunglasses, wallet. Check, check, check. Turned off the lights. Turned down the thermostat. Cleaned the kitchen, so Katy will like me when we return. All checks. Alright, it's go time.

I sped down Packard Road with one eye on the road and the other on my iPod. Great road trips require great music, so I searched for the perfect song to start our drive. I pulled up to the corner of South Division and Washington, Katy jumped in the car, unloaded an armful of complimentary Google snacks and kissed me on the cheek.

The moment reminded me of my childhood, but I laughed at the different roles Katy and I played as compared to my parents. My mother was the one in charge of packing the car full of our camping equipment and coolers full of carefully planned breakfasts and dinners. When everything was in place and "the Tony" (our Toyota van) would start to back out of the driveway, my siblings and I knew it was time to run and jump in. My mother ran a tight ship, so being left behind was always a possibility. We would then drive downtown to the corner of 2nd South and Main Street to pick up my dad from work. He'd get in the driver seat, throw in a Grateful Dead tape and the family vacation would be underway.

Once we had left the rush hour traffic of Ann Arbor behind, Katy and I started talking about the weekend ahead.

"Here goes nothing!" Katy declared, her voice equal parts enthusiasm and anxiety.

"Let's just hope we don't screw it up," I joked, hoping to put her at ease.

Katy had good reason to be nervous. We were on our way to attempt what I guess you could call a bike touring dress rehearsal before our flight to London in five weeks. We thought it would be foolish to start a year-long bike trip without a little practice, so we mapped out a three-day, 150-mile loop in Northern Michigan to test our bike and other gear. We planned to cycle an average of 50 miles a day on our trip around the world, but instead of riding for just three days, we'd continue at that pace day after day through the summer, fall, winter and spring. If we couldn't manage three days, how could we possibly last a year? Katy had plenty of reason to be nervous.

"So, you really think this tandem is going to be a good idea?" Katy asked, bringing up a debate that had begun months earlier.

"I don't think it matters what we think anymore. We already bought the tandem," I stated. "Besides, I let you make the final decision."

Our tandem cost $6,000 (a bit expensive for a bike) and then a little more for the racks, fenders, water bottle cages, pedals, new cycling shoes and panniers. It was more expensive than two single bikes, but like all people who are good at spending money, we justified the purchase. We told each other that this bike would serve as our house for the year, and $6,000 divided by 12 months is only $500 per month, half of our current mortgage payment.

Deciding on a tandem was not easy. For weeks we debated the pros and cons of a tandem versus two single bikes. On our trip those debates became arguments. If I had to make the decision again, I don't know what I would do. Our tandem was the best of times, it was the worst of times; easily the best and worst decision we made before our trip started.

Most arguments in favor of a tandem are also arguments against one. Tandems allow for easy communication; great in theory. In the following months, however, Katy and I learned that the last thing we wanted after a heated argument was to be stuck to each other on our bicycle, with nowhere to go for five or six hours. Most days were full of lovely conversation; some were hours and hours of silence.

Another potential benefit is that the "stoker," or rider in the back of a tandem, doesn't have to worry about shifting gears, braking for cows, or steering a heavily loaded tandem (our total combined weight of ourselves and our gear was about 450 pounds) down a steep, winding mountain road in the Alps at 50 mph. After that particular descent, I believe Katy's exact words were, "Don't ever do that again! I thought I was going to die!" She was happy to not have to navigate the cattle-filled roads of India, but also had second thoughts about surrendering her independence for 10,000 kilometers.

I thought a tandem would simplify bike maintenance because I'd only have to keep one bike operational, instead of two. But, as we would find out, tandems have their fair share of problems.

As we rehashed this decision again and again one thought kept recurring in my mind. It was a thought I first had years before, as I cycled through British Columbia: *if you ever do this with Katy, make sure you're on a tandem.* The reason is simple, and stems from a basic character flaw of mine: I'm an impatient person. I couldn't bear the thought of having to wait for her to catch up on her own bike, hour after hour, day after day, week after week. I made my decision in favor of a tandem but gave Katy the final say. She eventually agreed. More than anything else, she didn't want to endure the daily reminder that she was going slow. She also hoped I would do more than half of the pedaling, which I did. If Katy had to make this decision again, however, she'd probably have to think long and hard about which phrase she likes less: "Hurry up, what's taking so long?" or "Are you pedaling back there?"

On our drive north I asked Katy if she wanted to play one of my favorite games. It's a simple game. I play a song and Katy guesses the title, then we switch. She hates this game. I insist we play, however, because it's essential to have a working knowledge of the jam bands of yesteryear to feel at ease during casual conversations or to join in on groups texts with the Pratt family.

A song title should be guessed within a second or two, but since Katy didn't grow up in my family, I can understand if it takes her five seconds to recognize the familiar cheer of an audience on a live track. For ten minutes we went back and forth guessing songs by Phish, the Dave Matthews Band, the Grateful Dead, Neil Young and the Beatles until, in a rather unexpected move, Katy unplugged my iPhone and replaced it with hers.

"I bet you can't guess this one," she asserted.

"Wait let me guess," I answered, before any music started playing. "It's Harry Potter, book five, chapter six. Am I right?"

"Aren't you funny," she retorted.

Then a song started and I knew the singer at once, Trey Anastasio, the lead singer of Phish. Prior to this moment, I prided myself on being a Phish expert, but I had no idea what song was playing.

> *Gonna take my bike out, gonna take my bike,*
> *Gonna ride it slowly, gonna ride just how I like.*

Katy let the song play for ten seconds but I had no idea what the name of the song was.

"Is this a cover?"

I didn't think it was possible Katy knew a Phish song I didn't, especially one about riding bikes.

"Nope, it's on one of their newer albums," she coolly responded.

"What, you've been listening to recent Phish albums?"

"A friend from work showed it to me," she boasted, aware this was the first time in ten years she knew a Phish song that I didn't.

"Well turn it back on," I demanded.

> *Gonna take my bike out, gonna take my bike, gonna ride it slowly,*

gonna ride just how I like.
Leave me way up here, up on the mountain,
Let me lie, uncovered on the floor,
Make me wonder when, you go away again,
If you're ever coming back here, anymore.
Gonna use my brakes, when I go downhill,
Gonna climb back on when I take a spill
Gonna peel my shirt off, gonna feel it burn,
Gonna keep my eyes closed, gonna miss my turn

This song became the theme song of our trip. Each day, we took our bike out, and rode it just how we like.

* * *

Petoskey is a charming little town on Lake Michigan's Little Traverse Bay. It's the type of wonderful small town I'd like to live in some day, because ever since our two years in rural Arkansas, Katy and I have been small town people.

"Taylor's parents are so nice to let us stay at their house," Katy commented, as our car crawled into the Swabash's driveway. Taylor is a friend from medical school and her parents had invited us to stay at their home before our weekend ride. We were about to knock when the door swung open.

"Welcome to Petoskey," Linda said, pronouncing the phrase identically to her daughter Taylor, with a thick northern Michigan accent. She invited us into the kitchen, opened the fridge, and insisted we must be hungry. I obliged. Linda's husband, Kirk, also a cyclist, came in from the back porch and drilled us on our route for the weekend.

"How are you getting out of town?" Kirk asked.

"I'm not really sure, but we have a map on our phone so I think we should be okay," I replied. I hadn't yet looked into the exact route, but couldn't imagine we'd get lost in Petoskey, a town of 5,000 people. Kirk wasn't convinced. He grabbed his iPad and spent the next hour giving us directions. When it was well past midnight, I excused myself to bed while Kirk continued to map out directions.

In the morning I put on my cycling clothes and stumbled down the hallway. I wasn't expecting Linda to make us breakfast, but I wasn't going to turn it down either. The kitchen table was covered in a delicious spread of orange juice, homemade bread, fresh fruit, oatmeal and dried Michigan cherries. "We should do this more often," I whispered to Katy when Linda left the room. "I haven't eaten like this in months."

After breakfast we packed up and I sat down on the front porch, under the warm sun, and put on my new Smartwool socks and cycling shoes. Nothing feels better than a new pair of Smartwool socks. We were just about on the road when Kirk ran out of the house, also dressed in a cycling outfit. "I'll just show you the way out of town," he announced. We followed Kirk until he was convinced it was entirely impossible for us to get lost, and then he let us continue by ourselves on our journey. It was a beautiful morning, quiet, peaceful and sunny.

"Will this happen everywhere we go?" Katy asked.

"What do you mean *this*?"

"A delicious dinner and an even better breakfast, recommendations for the next day, a free place to stay, a warm shower. We showed up as strangers and left as friends. Linda and Kirk were *so* nice."

"They are great, aren't they?"

"Yeah. Those cherries were so good."

"Here's the way I see it," I started. "If we were just riding across town we'd never be offered this type of hospitality. But when we tell people about our trip, they're intrigued. In some small way, I think, their kindness and goodness lets them feel like they're part of our trip. And you know what, I'm okay with that."

After an hour and a half, we arrived at Highway 119's Tunnel of Trees. The Tunnel of Trees is the perfect example of how amazing a bike ride can be. The country road dives deep into a thick forest and trees encroach right up to the edge of the pavement – you can barely see the sky. There were no cars on the road, so we sat upright, relaxed our pedaling efforts and I imitated giant slalom ski turns as we floated down the middle of the road. A cool breeze blew in our hair. It was complete freedom, and I could have ridden along that road forever.

"Are you sure taking a year off won't hurt your residency application?" Katy asked.

"You know those Emergency Medicine residents I emailed? Well I heard back from a couple of them." I responded.

"Oh yeah, what did they say?"

"You can open my email and read it if you want." One indisputable advantage of a tandem: Katy's hands are always free to get on our phone, look at directions, take pictures, read emails, prepare food or do any other task. As she read the email I heard her emphasize the important parts:

> I think cycling through Eurasia is frickin awesome . . . the vast majority of EM peeps would think this is awesome . . . help your application rather than hurt it . . . people take years off to do research and all kinds of other shit, in efforts to better their application. I say, if your heart is not in it, you're doing it for the wrong reason. If your heart says, take a year to go cycling and see the world - you should do it!

"Well that's good news."

Yeah, and guess what?"

"What?"

"I looked at the University of Utah's Emergency Medicine website and read their program director's bio. Guess what it said under her non-medical interests?

"What?"

"Tandem bike touring."

"Shut up!"

"And under the goals section it says, riding my bike around the world."

We stopped for lunch at Legs Inn, a Polish restaurant Kirk and Linda insisted we try. On the back patio, we enjoyed the sunshine on an unusually warm spring day in Northern Michigan. After I finished my golabki and kielbasa, and polished off the last of Katy's pierogis, we ordered dessert. I first saw the dessert from a distance. The Polish *szarlotka* is a crumble cake of apples, raspberries, strawberries, blackberries and blueberries that oozed out of a sugary crust and was buried underneath five or six generous scoops of vanilla ice cream. As the waitress walked in our direction, I offered a silent prayer that she would stop at our table. And when I looked up, the dessert was before me.

"Excuse me, I believe I ordered the large dessert. Hello!"

"Well you're in a good mood," Katy exclaimed. Katy isn't the biggest fan of movie lines from my childhood, but after a long winter and spring of Michigan weather and life inside, we were both happy to be outside, relaxing in the sun. It was a great moment. One we'll always remember.

"Of course, what's not to be happy about?"

I had thought a lot about happiness in the weeks leading up to our trip, mostly because just before we left I was asked to speak about it in church. Every good church talk begins with a little humor, and my talk had been no exception:

"On Saturday, I was at South U. Pizza getting some lunch," I had begun, standing at the pulpit. "As I stood in the small entryway, eating my Buffalo Chicken pizza, a kid walked in the door and just stared at me. He looked at me for much longer than usual, with particular interest in my ponytail, before he asked, "Are you a boy or a girl?" The audience erupted.

"In that moment I knew I had a decision to make. I could choose to be happy. Or I could choose to be unhappy."

I finished my talk by reciting a short story posted on the wall of Jimmy Johns, the freaky fast sandwich people. It's a story I've read many times since, and thought about often:

> An American investment banker was at the pier of a small coastal Mexican village when a small boat with just one fisherman docked. Inside the small boat were several large yellow fin tuna. The American complimented the Mexican on the quality of his fish and asked how long it took to catch them.
>
> The Mexican replied, "only a little while." The American then asked why he didn't stay out longer and catch more fish? The Mexican said he had enough to support his family's immediate needs. The American then asked, "but what do you

do with the rest of your time?"

The Mexican fisherman said, "I sleep late, fish a little, play with my children, take siestas with my wife, Maria, stroll into the village each evening where I sip wine, and play guitar with my amigos. I have a full and busy life."

The American scoffed, "I am a Harvard MBA, and I could help you. You should spend more time fishing and with the proceeds, buy a bigger boat. With the proceeds from the bigger boat, you could buy several boats, eventually you would have a fleet of fishing boats. Instead of selling your catch to a middleman you would sell directly to the processor, eventually opening your own cannery. You would control the product, processing, and distribution. You would need to leave this small coastal fishing village and move to Mexico City, then LA and eventually New York City, where you will run your expanding enterprise."

The Mexican fisherman asked, "But, how long will this all take?"

To which the American replied, "Fifteen or twenty years."

"But what then?" asked the Mexican.

The American laughed and said, "That's the best part. When the time is right you would announce an IPO and sell your company stock to the public and become very rich, you would make millions!"

"Millions – then what?"

The American said, "Then you would retire. Move to a small coastal fishing village where you would sleep late, fish a little, play with your kids, take siestas with your wife, stroll to the village in the evenings where you could sip wine and play guitar with your amigos."

I like this story. It resonates with me. After four years of college, and then four years of medical school, and an equally long residency, complete with late nights and on-call weekends, and then forty years of working, I just might be fortunate enough to retire. If I'm in decent enough shape and good enough health, I might be able to convince my wife to leave our kids and grandkids and cycle through Europe. An international cycling trip at that age would be a miraculous feat. Or, I could go now. This thought process convinced Katy and I that we were making a good decision, even a necessary decision. If we passed up this opportunity, we just might spend the rest of our life chasing what was right in front of us, and Katy agreed.

All good meals eventually come to an end, when you wish you were sitting down to the table instead of getting up to leave, and this one was no exception.

"You know what?" Katy mentioned, as we got back on our bike. "I think I could get used to this."

We had ridden 32 miles to get to Legs Inn, and were only 20 miles away from our campground. In my mind, cycling 20 miles shouldn't take much more than an hour, and I had planned for an easy afternoon ride. But that afternoon wasn't easy. It was sluggish. Our recent indulgence left our legs feeling like lead, and we barely crawled out of town.

"Are you pedaling back there?" I asked, when the slightest uphill dropped our speed to five or six miles per hour.

"Yeah. Are you?"

"Of course I am. How do you think our bike is moving?"

Every ten minutes or so we passed another mile marker, shocked that our hard work had only taken us a single mile. We finally arrived at Wilderness State Park and found a nice spot for the night. Katy grabbed the dry sack off our rear rack and started setting up our two-man tent, while I started boiling water with our mini camping stove and went in search of firewood. I don't remember what we had for dinner, but it was probably something dehydrated. The trick to camping equipment, and camping food, is space conservation. Smaller is better.

When it got dark we went to bed. We have matching his-and-hers REI Igneo and Joule sleeping bags, which conveniently zip together into one big bag. Our sleeping pads are ultra-lightweight, which is great for weight, but also means if there is as much as a twig underneath our tent I won't be able to sleep on my side all night. The larger obstacle to restful sleep, however, is the pillow situation. That night, I stuffed my corduroys into my sleeping bag stuff sack in an attempt to recreate a pillow consistency I am used to, but all night long I listened to my hair rustle on the nylon stuff sack.

In the morning we packed up our stuff, unlocked our bicycle from the picnic table, and cycled to the Mackinac Island ferry. We spent the afternoon cycling around the island before continuing on to Cheboygan to stay with Connie and Dale, a middle-aged couple, and our first of many Warmshowers hosts.

The idea behind Warmshowers is very simple. When we are out touring, other cyclists welcome us into their homes and give us a place to sleep, a warm shower, and more often than not, dinner and breakfast. Since these hosts are touring cyclists themselves, they understand one critical piece of information: we arrive hungry. A couple days on the road builds an unconquerable appetite, often requiring five or six meals, countless snacks and hearty desserts each day. Warmshowers hosts understand this and cook accordingly.

In most cases, we'd send an email to a host anywhere between the night before to one week in advance of our projected arrival, and ask to spend a night or two or three. They'd email us back and, hopefully, ask if we had any dietary preferences, which meant they were making dinner. When we are not on the road, we open our home – and refrigerator – to other touring cyclists, listen to their stories and work on repaying our karma. In the months since arriving home, we've hosted a five-person traveling theater group, three blokes from the UK and a Swiss gentleman. (We're still very much in debt.)

"So you're sure about this?" Katy asked. This was her first Warmshowers experience and she was a bit wary. Staying at the Swabashes was easy; they're the parents of a good friend. But staying with complete strangers, she argued, was different.

"But what if the beds are really dirty? Or they're weird? Or they attack us in the night?" Katy brought up concerns anyone unaccustomed to spending the night with strangers might raise.

"What if we leave their beds really dirty? Or what if we're weird?" I countered.

"We aren't weird and we'll offer to clean the sheets," Katy stated.

"But what if we attack them in the night?" I questioned.

"Well we won't."

"And neither will they. Sure they might be a bit odd, but don't worry. We'll be fine. Besides, when Connie emailed me back, she asked if we were vegetarians. That probably means she's got dinner waiting."

"Okay, we'll see," Katy muttered.

I crossed my fingers that our stay would go well. Katy's first impression of Warmshowers was important, especially so since our budget anticipated using WS hosts throughout Western Europe, where other accommodations are expensive.

Connie and Dale were as friendly as can be. After a cold lemonade and a hot shower, we sat down in their living room and started to talk. Katy covered the talking while I drifted to sleep – a very good sign that Katy was on board with the WS idea. Later that night, after a delicious non-vegetarian dinner of thick chili and cornbread, Katy and I went for a walk in the woods.

"Is your wrist okay?" Katy asked. "I noticed it bothered you on our ride and you held it kind of funny at dinner." Given my history of bumps and bruises, Katy is quick to notice when my body appears to be hurting.

"Actually, it hurts pretty bad, and I'm not really sure what's going on," I answered. "It's been aching all day."

Before going to bed I took 800mg of Ibuprofen, to go along with the 800mg I took before dinner and another 800mg I had at lunch. But my wrist ached all night. I couldn't even move in my sleep without noticeable pain. In the morning it wasn't any better. *How am I going to ride a bike for four hours today?* At breakfast I was forced to eat with my left hand.

After breakfast I went into the bathroom to brush my teeth (also with my left hand, which I'm not that good at) and I peeked into Connie and Dale's medicine cabinet, curious to see if I'd recognize any medicine from my recent pharmacology class. I saw a couple generic bottles that I skimmed over, but then I saw something that grabbed my attention. Vicodin. *That's just what I need*, I thought. As a fledgling medical student I was confident that if I went to a doctor, I would get a prescription for the same drug. Why waste the time of going to an emergency room, when the prescription is right in front of me? I listened carefully for anyone near the bathroom door, and when I deemed it safe, I quickly opened the bottle and shook two pills into my hand. I swallowed one of them and put the other in my pocket.

Our trip couldn't fail; it had to happen. And I felt responsible for making it happen. Without those painkillers, the agony in my wrist would have prevented me from cycling that day and would have left Katy wondering if we should call off our trip. That was not an option.

Fifteen minutes into our ride the opioid took effect and the pain diminished. Thirty miles later, we stopped at a gas station to refill water bottles and I took the other pill. For the rest of the ride my wrist felt fine and we eventually arrived back at the Swabashes around noon. We told Linda and Kirk about our great weekend, thanked them for everything and began the long drive back to Ann Arbor.

"Do you want to drive?" I asked. Driving in the late afternoon, especially after lunch, always puts me to sleep.

"Sure, I'll drive," Katy consented.

Katy turned on some Crash Test Dummies as I reclined the passenger seat and quickly fell asleep. Two hours later, I woke up and reached for the lever beside my seat to resume a sitting position. As I pulled on the lever, the pain in my wrist instantly returned, but worse than earlier. I shifted my body to try and reach the lever with my left hand, but as I twisted my body weight I felt a throbbing, excruciating ache deep inside my right knee. The painkillers had obviously worn off, and not only was my wrist pain worse than before, but I also had an aching knee unlike anything I had ever experienced.

In a few weeks Katy and I were supposed to ride a bike around the world, but after only a three-day practice ride, I had a wrist and a knee that I could barely move. *What's wrong with me?*

PART TWO

"Learn to ride a bicycle. You will not regret it if you live."

Mark Twain

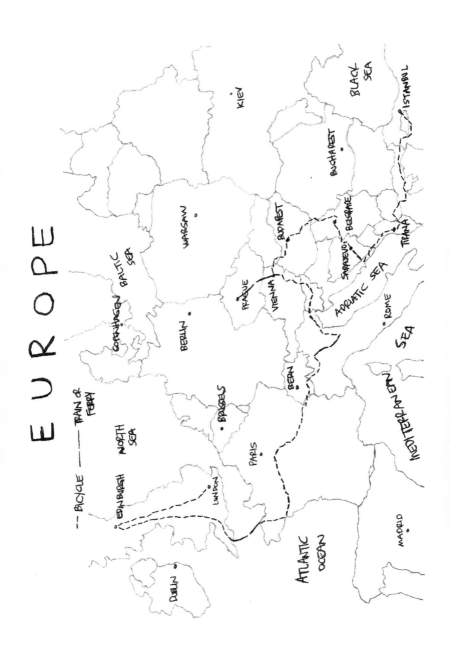

8 CHAPEL LANE

The night before our flight to London, we carefully disassembled, bubble wrapped and meticulously jammed our tandem into two cardboard boxes. We filled our bright yellow, waterproof Ortlieb panniers with four or five outfits, two sleeping bags, a tent, miscellaneous bicycle repair equipment and other odds and ends. Then, I checked myself into the Emergency Room.

I didn't go to the Emergency Room in search of a diagnosis. The month before our departure I had woken up every morning to Katy's enthusiasm, "Oh my gosh, I'm so excited for our trip to start!" followed by her demand, "You really should see a doctor about your wrist." I diagnosed a dorsal ganglion cyst on a previously fractured wrist caused by more-than-usual strain from the lower handlebars on our tandem compared to my other bikes. I had fixed the cause of this problem by getting a new stem, which raised the handlebars. But fixing the cause of the pain had not removed the symptoms; the pain remained.

My knee had hurt because my new cycling shoes and cleats were not in perfect alignment. Even the slightest misalignment can cause serious problems after hours of repetitive pedal strokes. Taking the Vicodin had made matters worse, because it had prevented me from noticing any pain while riding. I switched back to my old cycling shoes and within a couple weeks the pain went away. A month earlier, I had written off our practice ride as a complete failure. But it had done exactly what it was supposed to do – it exposed the flaws in our gear and equipment and gave us time to fix them.

"Hello Dr. Bassin," I laughed, as a familiar face entered the room. I had shadowed Dr. Bassin many times that year as my interest in Pediatric Cardiac Surgery had turned into an interest in Emergency Medicine. We knew each other well.

"What are you doing here?" he asked, his tone friendly but curious.

I explained my recent injury, my tentative diagnosis and informed him of my immediate departure from the country.

"I could remove the fluid from the cyst, but chances are it will just return," he began. "My suggestion would be to let it rest for a while. I realize that's going to be tough for you, but most of the time these things get better on their own." It wasn't exactly what I was hoping to hear; rest wasn't really an option. Before he left the room he added, "And have a great trip. It sounds awesome."

Eighteen hours later, on July 1st 2014, we boarded Virgin Atlantic Airways Flight 4 and shuffled down the aisle, looking for our seats on our overnight flight to Heathrow International Airport. Every ten seconds or so, Katy looked over at me and shrieked, "Aaahh!" She was glowing with excitement. Our long months of preparation were finally over.

"Are you an American?" a lady behind me asked, as I continued to shuffle down the aisle. She spoke English, but her words were drenched in such a thick accent that I imagined I was somewhere between the filming of Braveheart and Austin Powers. She heard our conversation, and our accents, so the answer to her question was obvious.

"Are you British?" I replied.

The British lady and I both laughed and exchanged smiles as we continued down the aisle past the First Class recliner beds.

"What, no beds?" I again joked, as we entered the Economy Cabin.

"You're in cattle class my friend. But it's better than sitting next to those whiny brats," the British lady cackled.

Deciding on a route across Europe was difficult. How do you draw a line between London and Istanbul and not miss anything? After a couple weeks of deliberation we decided on a tentative route to get our trip started, with a couple of firm deadlines and some general goals for the trip overall. We would ride from London to Edinburgh (the wrong direction, I know) and then southwest to Plymouth, England across the English Channel by ferry to Brittany, down to the Loire River Valley, then along it to Orleans, up to Paris, up to Copenhagen, over to Berlin, south to Dubrovnik and east to Istanbul, Turkey. To stay ahead of the cold weather, we planned to arrive in Istanbul in the beginning of November. After Istanbul we planned on two months in India and then three months in Southeast Asia, but our route in those countries was entirely undecided. We figured we'd plan that route once we got on the road.

A couple more specific goals were set for the beginning of our trip. That year, the Grand Depart of the Tour de France was in Leeds, England, just three days after our arrival, and only 240 miles northwest of Heathrow, making a quick trip north the first thing on our agenda. Ten days later, we had tickets for the ferry from Plymouth, England to Roscoff, France. Two weeks after that we hoped to be in Paris for the final stage of the Tour. We planned a moderately structured route, with deadlines to keep us moving, but also with enough flexibility to accommodate the unforeseen events and opportunities that would surely arise.

* * *

We landed at 6:50am, collected our cardboard boxes and panniers, and made our way to the parking lot. The ground floor parking lot was swarming with people, so we took the lift to Level 4 and began assembling our bike. That's right, assembling our bike, in the airport parking lot. We were going to start this journey off right.

Our tandem frame is "coupled," which means the frame splits into three pieces that can be packed in boxes and checked as normal airline baggage. A coupled tandem is great for international bike touring, otherwise most airlines slam you with $150 surcharges per flight per bike. Pathetic. If the 400-pound dude next to me doesn't pay extra for his ticket, neither should my bicycle.

The downside of a coupled frame is the necessary disassembly and reassembly every time we fly: front and rear cranks and pedals are removed; seats, fenders and racks taken off; tires deflated and wheels removed; and handlebars packed sideways. Small errors in assembling the bicycle would have drastic consequences on a long bike tour, and will occasionally cause me to scream and curse expletives in frustration.

"Oh, shit." I yelled, from the middle of the Level 4 car park.

"What? What is it?" Katy asked, as dread enveloped her body.

"You know how I got a new stem before we left, because my wrist was hurting and I wanted my hands up higher? Well this stem is the wrong size. I can't attach these damn handlebars to the frame," I shouted.

"How is it the wrong size, didn't you ride our bike to the shop before we packed it up?"

"Yes. But when we got to the shop, I got the new stem. I never reattached the handlebars to the bike to make sure it fit because we were in the process of packing it up. And I never even thought to check."

"Well, what should we do?" Katy asked, wondering if our trip would end before it began.

"What should we do?" I asked in an angry sarcastic tone. "We should send it back to Ann Arbor and tell our mechanic to give us a stem that's the right size."

"Well that's not an option. Why don't we just get in a taxi and go to a bike shop?" Katy calmly stated. Her logical suggestion would have made sense to anyone else.

"Taxi? That's not an option," I insisted. In my opinion, a bike tour starts and ends on a bike. "We're cycling out of here."

"And how are we going to do that?"

"When I was planning our route on Google Maps I think I saw a bike shop somewhere in the airport."

"Yeah, where is it?" Katy cut me off.

"I don't know, but can you go find it and get another stem while I put the rest of this thing together."

"Sure, anything else?"

"Nope, but hurry," I hollered, as she took off back towards the airport.

I was frustrated. Assembling a relatively new tandem in a hot parking garage is difficult enough; I didn't need the added complication of missing pieces. Twenty minutes later, having made very little progress assembling our bike, a short Indian man dressed as a security guard, and with a noticeable paunch hanging over his belt, appeared at the end of a row of parked cars. He saw my haphazard pile of belongings and slowly approached. As he walked towards me I hoped he'd just go away. I wasn't in the mood for a chat.

"What are you doing?" he asked as he looked at the empty suitcase, torn up cardboard boxes, a dozen strangely shaped bubble-wrapped items, and two bike tires strewn across multiple parking spaces. His accent was not British or American. In fact, he reminded me exactly of Apu, from The Simpsons, and it took all of my self-control to not laugh at his accent.

"I'm trying to assemble a bicycle," I answered, angry and irritated.

"You can't do that here," he muttered. Stranded in the Heathrow airport and sweating up a storm, with a bike that stopped working before it even started, the last thing I needed was someone telling me what I could and could not do in an empty parking space.

"Do what?" I replied.

He wasn't sure how to respond, because he couldn't think of a specific rule I was violating, so instead he asked me another question, "Where's your car?"

"I don't have one."

"How are you leaving the airport?"

"On my bike."

"Where are you going?"

"Istanbul." *There. How are you going to respond to that!*

The man was silent, and now he really didn't know what to say. I had won. "You'll need to move your stuff into one parking space. One person can only have one parking space." he exclaimed, before he turned around and disappeared behind another row of cars.

I dragged all our stuff into the confines of two white lines and continued the awkward balancing act of assembling a tandem with only one pair of hands and no bike stand; the process was almost impossible. I was just about to boil over when Katy finally returned.

"Any luck?" I asked.

"Is this what you were looking for?" Katy asked, with a smirk on her face.

"Well is it the right size?"

"It sure is."

"Thanks babe, you're a life saver. Let's hurry and get this thing put together. This Indian dude from the Simpsons keeps coming by and telling me we have to move."

Five hours after our plane landed, and only a little behind schedule, I took a two minute practice ride around the parking lot to make sure the shifters, derailleurs and brakes were working, without rubbing, and that our wheels were true and tires were holding air.

"I think she's ready," I announced.

"Can I get on?" Katy asked, wondering if our bike was in fact ready to go.

"You sure can."

I was optimistic our bike was good-as-new, and Katy was shocked the wrong stem only caused a minor setback. We attached our four Ortlieb panniers to our Tubus racks, and secured the Sea to Summit dry bag with bungee cords. Katy hopped on the bike and with a quick clip into our pedals – and a deep breath – we were off.

Leaving an airport on a bicycle, with no return flight and a world to see, is an incredibly liberating feeling. They say that a journey begins with a single step. In our case it was a single pedal, and what a journey it would be.

"Other side of the road. Go left. Go left," Katy yelled, as we left the parking lot and joined the busy traffic. The driver of the car I almost ran into stared at me like I was an idiot. It would have been similar, I suppose, to how a driver in New York would shake his head if a cyclist left JFK headed down the left side of the road into oncoming traffic. In theory, it's easy to ride on the left side of the road, but on that first day in England, every time we approached an intersection or a stop sign my instincts pulled me back to the right. And then Katy would yell, "Left. Go left!"

We exited the airport, turned left on the A4 and headed west towards Oxford. We immediately hit construction and traffic, so we detoured onto a sidewalk and through a couple of tunnels – not exactly the picturesque departure I had in mind. We continued along on a sidewalk for a few miles until we reached a gas station. We stopped and I bought a road atlas of the UK.

Before we left, Katy and I had never really decided how we'd solve a simple problem: "Which way do we go?" I preferred the old school method – paper maps. I like maps, just like my Grandpa Dick, and thought they'd be a nice souvenir when we returned home. They also don't require electricity or cell phone service. Katy disagreed. As a former Google employee, cycling across Europe without the guidance of Google Maps was heresy. Google Maps, however, required a SIM card that we hadn't yet purchased. The gas station's giant map worked okay for a while, but then we left the A4 and headed north to Oxford. It didn't take long before we ran into all sorts of problems.

England's smaller country roads rarely travel in a straight line. They change names and direction at roundabouts, and compared to the easy to follow country roads of the States, were terribly difficult to navigate. The atlas was also much less helpful than I had imagined, as many of the roads we traveled on that day were too small to be included on the map. We could have stuck to larger and busier roads, but they were full of traffic and lacked the countryside's scenic charm. The smaller roads were great for cycling, if you knew where to go.

To make matters worse, our rear derailleur started having problems. This infuriated me, as I had the derailleur adjusted just the day before. I spent half the day trying to look back at the rear derailleur to see what the problem was, only to hear Katy tell me to keep my eyes on the road. Then she'd inform me that we had missed our turn. Our first day of touring was supposed to be a delightful ride through the countryside. It wasn't. After missing multiple turns, riding into oncoming traffic (my fault), getting lost on a bike path, walking down a lovely dirt trail near a river, and a couple lucky guesses at directions (thank God!), we finally arrived at the Hoffmires in Oxford.

Day one was finished; we had conquered the world. Shelley

Hoffmire, our good friend's mother, cooked a delicious dinner and took us on a walking tour of the town and Oxford University. On our twenty minute drive home I think I fell asleep eight times. What I do remember from that evening is something Shelley said about life in England: "People don't have a lot here, their homes aren't large. But what they do have is nice." Small, quaint and very nice; that sums up Oxford.

"Are you sure you don't want a ride?" Shelley offered as we packed up our bike the next morning.

"You're so kind, but I think we'll be okay," Katy answered. Katy used the word *think* because she wasn't sure. We hadn't fixed our problems from yesterday: a somewhat useless map and a rear derailleur that was having issues.

"Take my phone number in case you change your mind," Shelley suggested. "Derby is 100 miles from here, that's a long ride for one day."

My wife is tough, tougher than most. But on that morning I can safely assume that she really wanted to accept Shelley's offer. She didn't know why we had skipped London, or why we would spend the next two days riding ten hours each day to arrive in Leeds just for the Tour de France. She declined the ride, however, because she knew I wouldn't accept it. Before our trip started I told Katy we must do our best to follow one simple rule: never use alternate modes of transportation when cycling is possible. On our year long adventure I expected we'd have long days, cold days, rainy days, scorching hot days, days with such bad roads it would be easier to walk, days with such steep roads it would be less painful to walk and days when we just flat out didn't want to be on the bike.

The difficulty and misery of our trip, I argued, and not just the wonderful moments, would make our journey memorable. Cycling around the world would be no fun if we got off our bike every time something didn't go as planned. Breaking this rule once in a while might be okay (and in retrospect, this may actually have been one of those times, but what can you do?), but accepting a ride – or "giving up" – on our first day would have set a terrible precedent. Katy agreed with my reasoning, but on that morning I knew she would have preferred to sleep in, go to brunch in Oxford and take a quick drive up north to Leeds.

Our day was exhausting. We left the Hoffmires at 8am and rode straight into town. First things first: a SIM card for Katy's phone and a rear derailleur adjustment. The mechanic adjusted our derailleur in about twenty seconds and I realized I had a lot to learn about keeping our bike up and running. We left Oxford around 9:30 and ate a delicious lunch at The Malt Shovel around noon. Two and a half hours of cycling is usually a day's ride, but we had just gotten started. Two o'clock came and went, then three o'clock, and then five. Getting closer. At six I wondered if we'd ever get there. We pushed on and finally reached our WS host in Derby at 7:30pm. We were spent.

Their home was a bit dirty, so instead of navigating the filthy kitchen, we ate dinner on a brick walkway in their garden. Exhausted, Katy and I then packed into their almost-comfortable pullout bed. Despite the less than ideal accommodations, we fell asleep the moment we crashed onto the couch. It is amazing how well you can sleep when every part of your body is tired.

The next day was similar; we got on the road at 8am and except for a quick lunch, we pedaled non-stop for eight hours until I pulled our bike to the side of the road.

"I don't think we're going the right way," I protested, my patience waning faster than my strength.

"Hold on, let me look at the map." Katy replied.

Over the past 48 hours I realized I was unable to steer the bike and simultaneously look at my paper maps, so I surrendered the task of navigation to Katy. She pulled out her phone and waited for Google Maps to load. Katy's new SIM card gave her phone Internet access, but slow access. Painfully slow. Slower than the rate at which we approached roundabouts, turns and intersections. Cycling back to back 100 mile days isn't easy. When you spend a considerable portion of the day going the wrong direction, however, it just makes things worse. The road was also incredibly hilly, which dropped our average speed to around 10mph, something we didn't foresee when we planned our route.

"What's the matter?" I asked, when I heard Katy holding back some tears.

"I'm tired. My legs hurt. You're mad because the derailleur is still having problems. You yell at me every time we miss a turn. We're going the wrong way. And we still have 40 miles left," Katy fumed.

"I'm sorry I yelled at you, but I'm just as tired as you are. I had no idea these first couple days would be so long and so hard and I want to get there just as much as you do. I know you're upset with your phone and directions, but I don't know how to fix that problem."

"You know how everyone says a tandem will make or break a marriage?" Katy interjected. "I think it's breaking ours. Maybe I should have just stayed at home and kept working at Google. I was good at that," Katy cried.

Her frustration with her phone, combined with her physical exhaustion broke her down.

"Stop crying. That's not going to help," I snapped. "And besides, you're tougher than this. We only have three more hours to go."

Of course, my rudeness didn't help. But my body hurt, my neck was sore and my toes were also tingling. I blamed Katy for leading us down the wrong road. Ideally, I would always respond to my wife with love and support, but sometimes my impatience gets the better of me. I was hard on her, and I felt bad about it.

We eventually got our bearings and pushed on towards Leeds. As we entered town, it started to rain so we stopped at a McDonald's for some much needed rest, free WiFi, hot chocolate and French fries. A hot beverage and salty fries never tasted so good, nor do I think they ever will. Katy double-checked our Warmshowers host's address, and eventually we summoned up the courage to go back into the rain and finish our nine-hour ride. Nine hours is a long time to be on a bike.

"I don't think anyone's here," I told Katy. We pounded one last time on the front door and waited a few more minutes. Still no answer. "And you tried calling them?"

"Yep, no answer."

"I can't stand in this rain forever. Will you please check the map again?" I asked, trying to be patient and polite.

"It says right here on the building, 8 Chapel Street."

"I know that's what the building says, I can read. But they said they'd be here all night and obviously no one is home."

"Okay, fine."

Katy rechecked her phone and realized their address was 8 Chapel Lane, not 8 Chapel Street. I hated the thought of getting back on our bike and placing my increasingly sore buttocks onto my seat and my tingling toes back into my pedals, but what could we do? We ventured back into the rain and rode across town to find Chapel Lane.

"Ah hell. Chapel Lane doesn't even have a number 8," I complained. Chapel Street wasn't the right address and now it appeared that Chapel Lane wasn't either. We were wet, cold, hungry and tired, and then Katy's phone died.

"You go over to that pub, charge your phone and try calling again. I'll ride around and see if I can find their house," I suggested, hoping a little time apart might calm things down. Fifteen minutes later I returned and saw Katy standing in the street, in the rain, her blonde hair dripping wet and her green Patagonia rain jacket a sharp contrast to the grey sky and dark cobblestone lane behind her. As soon as she saw me she walked into the middle of the road, threw her helmet at the ground and as it rolled into the overflowing gutter, she yelled, "I'm miserable. I hate this. I'm calling a taxi, getting an airplane ticket and going home."

I didn't say anything.

Seventy-two hours earlier Katy had radiated enthusiasm from her beaming smile as we boarded our transatlantic flight. But those emotions were long gone and seemed like a lifetime ago. Katy was defeated. Bad weather, physical exhaustion and feelings of helplessness on top of my impatience had broken her down. I couldn't solve her problem, so I said nothing. We sat down in the nearby pub and tried to sort things out.

"Now I call their phone number and it is disconnected. I don't think these people exist," Katy protested.

"Right. I'm sure someone creates fake profiles on Warmshowers just to email people and get them lost. That makes much more sense," I argued back.

"Well we can't get a hold of them. I'm finding somewhere else to stay," she responded.

"Katy, relax. Take a deep breath. We might be wet and cold and tired, but we're not dying. We're okay. I'm sure we'll get this all figured out."

I sat outside in the rain, hoping our problem would somehow resolve itself, and kept an eye on our bike while Katy stayed in the pub, found an outlet for her phone and tried to sort out our problem. She finally figured it out.

Our host's phone number in a recent email and the one on the Warmshowers website didn't match; they were off by a single digit. Katy called the other number and fifteen minutes later our host, Peter, showed up on his bike and apologized profusely about the mix-up. He escorted us through the downpour back to his apartment.

We parked our bike in the hallway of his building, grabbed the panniers, put a U-bolt lock around the frame and front tire, and headed up three flights of circular wooden stairs to their apartment. With each step our quads ached. It was the type of ache that workout programs desperately try to advertise, and a feeling that would become much too familiar. Halfway up the stairs we stopped to rest. We left our sopping wet shoes and socks in the entranceway and entered their apartment.

It was like we had come home. Delicious aromas filled the apartment and comforted our souls. Maya was busy in the kitchen making dinner. Their apartment was small, warm, spotless, and cozy. Clean sheets, blankets and towels were laid out on the side of their pullout couch. I collapsed onto the couch, and Peter poured me a glass of hot lemon tea while Katy went straight to the shower.

During those first few weeks in England, when we were riding too far and too fast, and we didn't have a decent map to get us there, Katy lived from one hot shower to the next. And I don't blame her. I ran our ship at a feverish pace – as evidenced by the back to back ten hour cycling days – and didn't take any time to stop for an afternoon of tea, scones and clotted cream. But for fifteen minutes each evening, while taking her warm shower, Katy was allowed to go slow and unwind. Each night, she recharged her optimism and mustered up the strength to continue for another twenty four hours, until her next warm shower. She dug down deep and was able to do hard things.

THE HILLS FROM HELL

The warm shower nourished my body as well, but also solidified some of my fears. Before hopping in the shower, I glanced at my sore buttocks in the mirror and noticed a red rash with raw skin in the shape of a bike seat on my white cheeks. My saddle sores hurt like crazy and didn't heal for a week or two. Under the hot water, the tingling in my fingers stopped, but the numbness in my big toes persisted. Over the next couple of months I'd occasionally scratch the inside of each big toe and wonder if I'd ever get normal feeling back. That numbness finally disappeared, somewhere in Bosnia if I'm not mistaken.

I liked our host Peter the moment I met him. His enthusiasm was palpable and it was obvious he longed to be out on the road. At dinner, he told us some stories of his most recent tour, from Leeds to Kolkata, India. His route had been similar to ours, except that after cycling across continental Europe to Turkey, he had continued overland through Iran and Pakistan before entering India. I was jealous. I wanted to ride a similar route, but Katy refused. The thought of wearing a hijab in Tehran or Tajikistan didn't appeal to her. I told her that a hijab would keep her warm during the winter, but she still declined.

"Peter, what was the most memorable part of your trip?" I asked.

"Definitely Iran. Iranians are the friendliest, most welcoming people I've ever met. It was hard to ride my 80 miles each day because so many people stopped me on the side of the road and invited me to their home. There were times when I had only ridden for an hour before I got stuck at someone's house with another cup of tea in my hands."

"But I thought a Yorkshireman like yourself enjoys a nice cup of tea?"

"Oh, I do. But one man can only drink so much tea. The most memorable moment occurred when a truck driver waved me down, hopped out of his lorry and gave me a giant melon. We're talking a *huge* melon. It was bloody warm that day so I sat down on the curb and ate the melon. The driver watched me eat the entire thing. After I finished the melon he gave me another. I couldn't possibly eat another, so I tried to tie it onto my bike."

"And the worst part?" I asked.

"Pakistan. The military picked me up at the border and escorted me across the entire country. It was a long time to sit in the back of a truck, and definitely not how I had hoped to see the country," he answered.

As he spoke, Katy made purposeful eye contact with me. It was clear she was becoming less and less keen on the idea of cycling past Turkey.

After dinner we stumbled down the street for a Reese's Peanut Butter Cup – our dessert – and then collapsed onto the pullout couch.

Sleep is an interesting thing. Prior to bike touring, sleep was just another part of the day. Whether needed or not, it's what people do to connect evening to morning. On our tour, however, sleep performed its much more important role: rejuvenation. Most nights we crashed into bed completely exhausted. Our bodies ached, our legs were sore, and our minds questioned our ability to keep going. But during those dark hours, sleep worked its magic and we woke up refreshed, whole and energized. The power of sleep is often underutilized when our routine tasks of driving to work, sitting at a desk, checking email, and watching Netflix at night doesn't push us to capacity. Each night our bodies had reached their limits, but in the mornings we woke up anew.

The next morning was the morning we'd been waiting for – The Grand Depart of the Tour de France. Leeds' population doubled as hundreds of thousands of cycling fans packed into town, jammed the narrow streets, and created absolute pedestrian gridlock. We got stuck in foot traffic and never saw the start of the race. *Damn.* Rather dissatisfied, we ran to the station and took the next available train to Harrogate for the finish of the stage. We arrived early and found a front row spot, about one kilometer from the finish line. We waited and waited, and then four and a half hours later the peloton whizzed by in five seconds. "Whoa! That was fast," I shouted.

"We skipped London, cycled all day long for three days, and got completely soaked in the pouring rain for that? Five seconds? I didn't even recognize anyone," Katy grumbled.

As soon as the peloton passed, we ran into a nearby house and watched the end of the stage on TV – and to find out who had won. Unfortunately, Mark Cavendish, Britain's hometown favorite, crashed 200 meters from the finish line and later withdrew from the race. Despite the frantic finish, I had managed to get a single photo with Cavendish, Sagan and Kittell, (the Tour's three greatest sprinters) all in the same frame. That picture alone was worth the three days of pain and suffering it took to get there.

The next morning we waved goodbye to 8 Chapel Lane and our new friends. Dressed in our cycling clothes, we headed to church. We decided it would be best to begin a yearlong adventure with God on our side, and we figured that if we went to part of church, and then rode like the dickens we could still get to Stage 2. At 9:00am, we entered Leeds' LDS chapel and found two empty seats in the back row. It was the first Sunday of the month, a day when members of the congregation are invited to testify of Christ and His Gospel. Katy and I sat back and admired the familiar Mormon phrases spoken in thick British accents.

Halfway through the meeting the Spirit fell upon me. *What? Share my testimony? Dressed like this?* I thought it inappropriate to speak in church wearing Lycra and carbon fiber shoes, but when the Spirit prompts, what choice do you have? I tiptoed to the front of the chapel, trying my best to prevent my cleats from clicking on the hardwood floor and stood at the pulpit.

"I don't usually wear spandex to church," I began. "But let me explain." I told them about our trip and the reason for my appearance, and then spoke about the trials we have in life and how we can learn from them. "I want to tell my wife that I love her," I concluded "and although the last 72 hours have been extremely difficult, we're going to get better at this and we're going to have a great trip. I'm so glad we're on this adventure together."

I walked back to my seat and as soon as the meeting ended we dashed out the back doors to our bike. Stage 2 had already started in the nearby town. We were almost out of the parking lot, when a large Polynesian man chased us down. *Oh no, did I offend someone?*

"Thanks for sharing your testimony," the man shouted. "If you ever get to New Zealand, please give my family a call and you'll have a place to stay." I entered his number in my phone, thanked him for the offer and we were off.

"See Katy, when people hear about our trip they're drawn to it. They want to help us out," I said, resuming a conversation we'd had before.

"Or maybe God is blessing us for going to church?" she countered.

"Or maybe people are tired of their boring, routine lives and would like to do some vicarious living?"

"Just keep telling yourself that." She rolled her eyes.

We cycled our legs off for ninety minutes in a desperate attempt to get to the small town of Oxenhope before the Tour arrived. We were on pace until we ran into a short 18% grade. I shifted into our easiest gear, but it wasn't easy enough. Our cadence dropped to an uncomfortably slow pace and we were barely able to keep the pedals turning. It was our first real test of climbing something steep, and although we made it to the top, it didn't go very well. We limped over that hill and eventually reached Oxenhope, joining thousands of riotous fans atop another steep, but short, green hill in the countryside.

On a typical day, I assume Oxenhope is rather quiet: a man and his sheep might be seen or heard underneath one of the tall oak trees on the side of the hill. But today was different. Dozens of kids in their polka dot King of the Mountain jerseys danced in the street. British flags blew in the gentle breeze. A shoeless fan, dressed in a Super Man costume, flew up and down the hill pouring more energy into the rowdy crowd.

We heard the distant rumble of helicopters, which meant the peloton was approaching. Moments later, the red Voiture Officielle vehicle, covered in Skoda advertising and a yellow LCL banner, blazed a trail through the thicket of fans, forcing them off the road to make way for the cyclists. The energy intensified and everything grew quiet. They were coming. Seven breakaway cyclists flew past, but I couldn't recognize any of them. Thirty seconds later, a wave of cheering from down in the town rolled up the hill while ecstatic, frenzied fans unleashed a horde of cameras and snapped hundreds of photos, hoping to get a picture of Froome, Nibali, Contador or another hero.

At thirty meters, individuals were unrecognizable, but the front of the pack was distinctly yellow. *Yellow means Tinkoff Saxo, Alberto Contador's team.* It was only a brief moment, but I saw him. The sight of his slender 5 foot 9 inch 137 pound frame sent chills down my spine. He is the greatest Grand Tour cyclist of the past decade. And then it was all a blur. The weightless cyclists danced up the hill without difficulty, and floated over a hill that had demoralized Katy and me. The last support cars and race vehicles finally passed and we sat down on a rock wall and watched the crowds get on their own bikes and slowly dissipate. An hour later, after everyone had left, I looked at Katy and asked, "Now what?"

"What do you mean?"

"I mean, for the past three months we've been on a hectic schedule. I studied for boards, you finished up at Google, we planned our trip, packed up our stuff and our house, flew to London, assembled our tandem and rode all day long for three days to get to the Tour. But that's all over now."

"Isn't it nice?"

A wonderful sense of freedom settled over us; we were free. No more deadlines. No more schedules. Just me, my wife and our bicycle.

* * *

The English countryside is stunning. Beautiful rock walls, stacked hundreds, or maybe thousands of years ago, crisscross endless hills colored in more shades of green than there are in any big box of Crayola crayons. Hills and fields are everywhere. The bleating of sheep and the ringing of cattle bells rolled over the fields and through the valleys. The bright blue sky with its large fluffy clouds put a magnificent smile on each of our faces. For the first time on our trip, we rode slowly and admired the beauty.

After a lazy 25 miles north and a shared plate of chicken tikka masala, we pitched our tent at a small campground in Malham, a village of 150 people. The campground sat at the end of a long, green valley, wedged between craggy cliffs that formed a natural shelter from Northern England's unpredictable weather, strong wind and sudden downpours. That night, however, the sky was clear and calm.

A group of high school students on a walking holiday, a national pastime in England, camped next to us. Dating back hundreds of years when common law first governed Britain, right of way walking trails stretch hundreds of miles across Britain. At some time in their lives, most Britons will spend a holiday or two walking one of these trails. Sixteen different walking paths, ranging from short day walks through the Cotswolds to the much longer 268-mile Penine Way, are maintained by The National Trails. It's a wonderful pace of life, which intertwines with British culture and is a fantastic contrast to the "faster is better" ideal of our increasingly busy world.

The host of Malham's campground was what they would call "a burly bloke," with a beard thick enough to keep out the winter. He marched around all day and night in knee-high rubber boots, with a metal cup full of ten pence coins at the bottom of his deep overall pockets and happily made change for anyone who wanted a hot shower. Katy jumped in the shower (housed inside an old rock outhouse of some sort) and I climbed the steep, rocky crag overlooking the campground and sat down next to a herd of sheep. Baa. Our trip had finally begun: camping in England with my wife, kind people everywhere we turned, a bike to go where we pleased and 39 more weeks to get there. It's why we decided to leave home.

In the morning we ventured into the ominous hills of Yorkshire Dales National Park. An early morning downpour sent us out of the hills and into Ye Olde Naked Man Café for a full English breakfast of sausage, bacon, poached eggs, grilled tomatoes, fried mushrooms, baked beans and toast with jam and butter. When that delicious plate arrived, I knew I wasn't at Denny's.

Eventually the sun peered its warm face through the somber clouds and we gathered our wet clothes, strewn throughout the café, and continued north into the Lake District. We checked into Ambleside Backpacker's Hostel (because as much as I like camping, I hate camping in the rain) and went into town for dinner. All the restaurants were too expensive so we bought sandwich supplies, a roll of Chocolate Digestives and a £1.10 giant berry pie at Spar. We missed out on the fine cuisine at Ambleside Tavern, but our picnic on the curb was equally enjoyable, and more memorable. After our last bite of pie, we tore off small pieces of a sandwich roll, soaked them in ridiculously spicy mustard and tossed them to the pigeons. The pigeons' heads spun around in circles as the intense flavor burned their mouths and noses. It was a simple meal for simple people, and we played with those pigeons for hours.

Katy saved the Chocolate Digestives for later. On our ride up to Leeds, Katy realized I can ride for five or six hours without eating, much longer than she can. For the rest of our trip, Katy carried a simple snack, typically that country's version of the Oreo, in our frame bag. When I noticed her pedaling slack off, as it occasionally would, and heard the munching of cookies I'd reach back with my right hand and say, "Hey, I want one!"

Ten miles north of Ambleside we crested the top of an 800-foot climb and pulled over at a rest area. An ice cream truck was parked in the dirt, next to a large sign pointing the way to Lake Thirlmere. Ice cream and cold lakes, two of my favorites. My love for swimming in freezing water began as a child at Cecret Lake in Albion Basin. My mother would pay me $20 to swim in the half-frozen lake and I never turned her down, as it was my only steady income in elementary school.

On the way down to the lake, another sign read, "Don't Swim. Too Cold." *Whatever.* Further down the trail we reached another sign: "Water is extremely cold, very deep in places, machinery in the water, strong undercurrents, dangerous blue green algae, people may become trapped in mud." That was almost enough to deter me. Almost. I dove into the calm reflective water and gasped for air as the cold water stole each breath from my lungs. As I swam, Katy polished off her ice cream but I returned to the shore in time to help her finish a bag of Haribo Tangfastics gummy candies. The swimming, and the gummies, were fantastic.

The next morning we explored the 900-year-old Carlisle Castle and that afternoon cycled past Hadrian's Wall: the northernmost border of the Roman Empire, built to keep out the barbarians from the North, and the inspiration for The Wall in the Game of Thrones. The rich history of prior civilizations throughout England and the rest of Europe make Utah's 250-year history feel like events that happened yesterday.

"I can't believe it," Katy exclaimed.

"What? What can't you believe?"

Katy has a tendency to begin a conversation right where her internal thoughts leave off and I'm supposed to guess what she's thinking.

"We're leaving England today. And we'll be in Scotland tonight."

A single day on a bike never took us far, but after a week we had covered 387 miles and were at the doorstep of our second country, I think. (I never did figure out if Scotland is its own country.) I plugged my iPhone into our Goal Zero portable speaker and blasted some Neil Young for all the sheep to hear. We cruised up and over the hills, and after a sharp turn a bridge took us over the Liddel Water River, we saw a simple sign on the side of the road: Welcome to Scottish Borders. Katy paused the music and we hopped off our bike to celebrate. Then, a real Scottish looking fellow stumbled out of his camper.

"Whaur urr ye ridin' from?" the middle aged, scruffy red headed man asked in a bizarre accent. Accents don't change quickly as you travel across the States, but compared to the English spoken that morning, this guy was unintelligible.

"We came up from London." I answered, my own accent slow and clunky.

"Weel 'at's bloody brilliant. Whaur urr ya heed'd?"

"To Edinburgh tomorrow, but then down to continental Europe and over to Istanbul." Katy answered.

"Hoo lang dae ye hae fur yer holiday?"

"Ten more months."

"Weel ye jammy-buggers," the Scot bellowed.

Jammy-buggers? Jammy-buggers? I had no idea what he meant, I still don't, but we decided to take it as a compliment and considered it our official welcome to Scotland – the home of haggis, golf and William Wallace.

Around dinnertime we rolled into Melrose, another small town with just a handful of one-way streets adjacent to the River Tweed. Double yellow lines painted on Buccleuch Street in front of The Co-Operative and Spar meant no parking. In the United States, where mothers in Suburbans fill large shopping carts with processed foods from Walmart and Costco and then pack their double door Sub Zero refrigerators to capacity, no-parking would pose a serious problem. But not here. These villagers arrived on foot or by bike and bought just a basket full of fresh produce and local food before returning to their simple apartments, or their quaint homes in the countryside. Life was simple.

Across the street was The King's Arms pub, with fresh flowers in the windowsill and lunch and dinner specials written on chalkboards near the entrance. Next to the pub was George and Abbotsfords Hotel, and at the bottom of the hill near the river was the Melrose Rugby Club, with its manicured lawn and yet another shade of green. It was a delightful town, as they all were for those few days between Leeds and Edinburgh. A town where people knew their baker by name, waved to the postman and caught up with their neighbors on the street corner during their evening walk.

After circling around town, and answering Katy's repeated question of, "Could you live in a town like this?" we stopped at the River Tweed for a swim, a bath (which is really just swimming with a bar of soap) and to search for a place to lay our sleeping bags. The sun was still high in the sky, and the cool water was refreshing. I emerged from the river clean and ready for an evening in town, so I hid behind a tall pine tree and threw on my Gramicci shorts and yellow Michigan t-shirt. That far north during the summer the sun doesn't set until late and it isn't dark until after midnight.

Scotland has a "camp anywhere" policy that permits just that, camping anywhere. We were hesitant at first, but after locating a spot to sleep in the corner of a large field we stashed our gear in the trees and ventured back into town.

Dinner was again from the Co-Op, and again eaten on the curb, although without the pigeons. This time, however, we were only half-way through our dinner when we started brainstorming our next meal. After a week of cycling, our appetites had caught up with our exercise and a single dinner would no longer suffice.

Our second dinner that evening was a giant plate of nachos at The King's Arms pub, not only for the cheesy, spicy nachos but also because they had free Wi-Fi and a public telly so we could catch up on the Tour and The World Cup. Germany 7, Brazil 1. Froome crashed out of the Tour. Andy Schleck needs to have surgery. It was a crazy day for sports. Our energy eventually failed us and we left the pub, crossed the footbridge over the river and surrendered to our sleeping bags. The sky was clear, and although it was still daylight, we fell effortlessly to sleep.

We slept peacefully until the early morning when the frenzied barking of a dog racing through the field instantly woke us up. Our immediate reflex was to fight or flee, but we were prepared to do neither. We crawled out of our sleeping bags and wondered if we'd be in trouble for camping in someone's field. A slender and stern looking gentleman, clothed in clean trousers and a plaid shirt, chased behind his dog and after a quick look at our scattered belongings asked, "Not much of a bike trail. Are you camping here?"

The answer was obvious. "Yeah, we did," I replied, half apologetic and hoping for the best. I hoped he'd notice my foreign accent and go easy on us, maybe even let us off the hook.

"It must have been a great night for camping," he replied. "I'm just out for my morning walk with Buzz. He likes chasing the rabbits, but he never catches them. Good day." And on he went.

"Wow, that was so different than back home," Katy mentioned as we meandered back to the river for our morning bath.

"It sure was. It feels good to mingle with these laid-back country folks. I like it a lot."

On our way out of town we stopped at the ruins of Melrose Abbey, and then at The Bakehouse. The 850-year-old Abbey, and supposed resting place of the heart of Robert the Bruce, was very interesting. But the pastry display case at The Bakehouse, stocked full of Scotch Pies, Haggis and Cheese, Cornish Pasties and Yum Yums is what captured my attention that morning. Since we had camped the night before, and had a WS host lined up for that night, we had our full budget of $50/person/day to spend on food. That's my type of traveling. We shared one of each Scottish pastry, and told ourselves that we weren't overeating because our bodies required the calories for our day's ride. Which was true. During the first two weeks of our trip, we ate four or five meals a day, along with multiple snacks and second desserts, but I still managed to lose ten pounds. Eat, sleep, cycle. Eat, sleep, cycle. We were only in Melrose for eight waking hours, but managed four hearty meals and fell in love with that little town.

On a hill overlooking Edinburgh, we stopped for a quick rest before our final descent into the Scottish capital. Navigating narrow roads and city traffic is tough work on a tandem, and it's best done on our "A" game. As we munched on Katy's Chocolate Digestives, I noticed an elderly man with two grandkids a couple meters away fiddling around with some squawking cages in the back of his truck. I watched for a moment, when, without warning, the man opened the cages and a dozen or so pigeons burst into the air, circled overhead twice to orient themselves and, barely avoiding the lorrys barreling down the highway, took off towards Edinburgh. Amazed at what we'd seen, we struck up a conversation.

"Where are the pigeons going?" I asked.

"Thayur headin' haem," he replied, his Scottish accent thicker than the burly bloke at Malham's campground.

"How do they know where home is?"

"Nae a body knows, but thay dae nae aye mak' it."

"Don't always make it? Why not?"

"Weel ah race thaim noo 'n' again. Mah lest race wis fae Ypres, Belgium back haem tae Auld Reekie, about 530 miles. Nae a' o' thaim made it. Tae many peregrine falcons, and the hail is stonner thaim."

"Did you say race them?" I responded, again embarrassed by my lackluster and uninteresting accent but also entirely confused as to what he had just said.

"Aye laddy, a'm a pigeon racer."

Whenever I think of Scotland, before I think of haggis or William Wallace or Neeps and Tatties, I'll always think of the pigeon racer on the hill overlooking the city of Edinburgh. *Aye laddy, a'm a pigeon racer.*

In Edinburgh we stayed with Andy and Olivia. Andy is also an avid touring cyclist, who had recently completed a tour through South America.

"How's your trip been so far?" Andy asked, after we settled into their apartment.

I was about to say it had been going great, but Katy jumped in and recalled our difficult evening in the pouring rain and inability to find 8 Chapel Lane in Leeds. As Katy spoke, it was obvious her emotions were still firmly attached to the recent incident, and I could tell Andy was a bit amused, but he listened patiently.

"And what was the hardest part of your trip?" Katy asked, after thoroughly rehashing the last few days, but also feeling like maybe she was talking too much.

"Well, because you asked, I was riding down a steep road outside Quito, Ecuador doing about 40mph when my front rack fell off my frame, my panniers destroyed my front wheel and I went flying over my handlebars. I broke my collarbone in a couple places and spent the next three months sitting in a hammock on the beach under an avocado tree. It wasn't the worst way to spend three months, but definitely not what I had planned. And it hurt like hell," Andy answered, in a very matter-of-fact tone.

"I'm so sorry. That must have been terrible," Katy responded, feeling a bit embarrassed about our comparatively minor difficulties.

"Don't apologize. You didn't do anything wrong. And besides, it was awful when it happened, but I'm fine now. In fact, sitting in that hammock was a time of my life I'll never forget."

The next day was a rest day. We visited Edinburgh, the castle and H.M.Y. the Royal Britannica. More importantly, Katy learned a valuable lesson that day and I made an unfortunate error. Listening to Andy's story, Katy realized that things don't always go as planned. But regardless of what happens, things usually turn out okay (and, in retrospect, people often joke about the most difficult times). Learning that lesson, and implementing it when difficulties arise, however, are two very different things.

My mistake was deciding to turn around in Edinburgh and head south, intent on sticking to our schedule and getting to our ferry on time. If I could change one thing about our time in Europe, I would have kept riding north, past Edinburgh and up to Falkirk, Stirling, Loch Ness – to see the Monster of course – and through the Scottish Highlands to John o' Groats. I prefer the rugged, untamed mountains to the manicured countryside. We should have gone north. Katy learned her lesson that day in Edinburgh, but I wouldn't learn to slow down for a couple more weeks.

Andy left a note and a treat on the counter for us: "Katy and Clayton, Bon Voyage! Come back sometime and explore Scotland properly. Not as good as haggis, but cheese and oatcakes are good touring food too." The oatcakes were delicious. I look forward to the day when we'll take him up on his offer and see the Scottish Highlands.

We packed all our stuff into a rental car (this might need explaining: our original plan was to turn around after Leeds and Stage 2 of the Tour, but we decided to continue north to Edinburgh, fully aware that to get back on our original schedule and reach our ferry on time we'd have to rent a car and drive south.) We had a delicious, but expensive, dinner of Haggis with Neeps and Tatties at Dubh Prais, and began the eight hour drive south. On our drive we saw as much of Britain as possible. We explored Hadrian's Wall by moonlight, peeked into Strawberry Fields, strolled down Penny Lane, made a quick diversion through the Cotswolds and arrived in Bath just minutes before the rental car office closed. Phew. What a day.

Before our trip began, I allotted two days to ride the 121 miles from Bath to Plymouth, England where we'd catch the ferry to Brittany, France. However, those 121 miles were calculated on Google Maps and assumed we would cycle in a straight line between towns, on busy roads. Cycling on scenic back roads, as we now preferred, lengthened the ride considerably. To make matters worse, these smaller roads travel straight up and over and down all the hills, and never go around them. Ever. I assumed this 121 miles would entail two easy days of cycling to get to our ferry, but I was wrong.

The road through the southwest of England was relentless. Our granny gear wasn't nearly easy enough for the 15% to 18% grades. We barely pushed the pedals around in circles and our quads exploded in pain. Up and down and up and down. After a while we didn't know which was worse, the physical exhaustion of going up a hill, or the fury and rage of going right back down the other side, because in Devon, what goes down must come right back up. Towards the end of the day, our exhaustion turned into anger, but at least not anger towards each other.

We uttered prayers each time we reached the top of a hill, "Please don't go down, please don't go down, please don't go down" and then violently cursed when the road would do just that, "Oh holy shit, mother of all that is holy! Damn you, damn you, you damn road. Why can't these damn roads stay flat for longer than thirty god damn, mother fucking feet?"

Our loaded tandem flew down the steep, windy roads and I clenched the brakes with all my strength just to keep our bike on the road. Our first day out of Bath turned into an 80-mile ride, with so many hills that a year later, the very thought of that day evokes PTSD.

We reached the small village of Feniton, utterly exhausted, and called our host, as requested. Moments later a bubbly, middle-aged, very English lady appeared on her bike and escorted us down a lovely, but always hilly, single track road with ten-foot-tall hedges to her charming home in the countryside.

"Where did you come from today?" Stephanie asked as the narrow lane got steep and we disappeared behind her.

"Bath," Katy responded, out of breath.

"Are you mad?" Stephanie replied, in a brilliant English accent.

"Yes, I think so. We have mountains back home, but nothing compares to these hills."

"You didn't come through Crewkerne did you?"

"Uhh, I think we did actually."

"Well that's bloody brilliant, the ride you've just done. A couple weeks ago a Swiss couple attempted that same route. When they got to Crewkerne they called and asked for a ride."

I looked back at Katy and smiled. She just shook her head in disgust and wondered *why oh why does my husband insist on making this trip so much harder than it has to be?*

At Stephanie's quaint home, we set our bike against the old shed in the garden and were treated to tea and cookies by Freya, Stephanie's daughter. I've mentioned it before, but it's not possible to overstate the gracious hospitality offered to us within minutes of arrival. Each day, complete strangers rescued us from the storm of exhaustion and defeat. Dinner was served in the garden: homemade vegetarian chili smothered a baked potato which was dripping in butter, accompanied by a green salad and mango juice. Dessert was cheesecake with blueberries. When the meal was finished Stephanie, Freya and Katy talked about all things Harry Potter (J.K. Rowling attended college in the nearby town), while I politely excused myself to watch the World Cup Finals and eat chocolate truffles.

The first turn of the pedals the next morning was painful. Our torn muscle fibers screamed and refused another day of pedaling. We'd ridden too many miles, up too many hills, and our bodies let us know. Without sufficient rest, our legs were weaker and skinnier now than when we arrived in Oxford. The day started out uneventful until an old lady drove up next to us and I put my hand out on her car to brace us. We balanced for a moment, but as the car passed us I lost our balance and we crashed. We weren't going fast and no major harm was done, just a couple of bumps and bruises to add to our aches and pains. Out of nowhere, however, a very friendly old man came running down the road.

"I just saw what happened, would you like to come in for tea?" he asked.

"Tea?" Katy repeated, getting up off the ground and brushing herself off.

"Yes. You must come in and have some tea."

"No, but thank you. I don't think we need any tea," Katy answered, a bit confused.

"Are you sure? Don't you need to sit down and have a cup of tea?"

I interjected. "No, but thank you. We better keep going. We

need to get to Plymouth before evening to catch the ferry to France."

"Well are you okay?"

"I think so, just a scrape or two," Katy answered.

Only a true Englishman would offer tea to complete strangers involved in a cycling accident, before asking if they were okay. We insisted we were okay, and we were, but not taking him up on his offer was a huge mistake. Not because we needed a tiny cup of burning hot liquid; tea is all about connecting with people. Passing up an opportunity to accept a generous gentleman's offer to sit in his home and share a cup of tea was a mistake. A mistake, we decided, we wouldn't make again. From then on, we decided that we would never decline an offer to connect with a stranger. Cycling is just cycling. Sharing tea and talking about life in the English countryside, however, makes bike touring great.

Dartmoor National Park was our final barrier. A serene monster. The difficult terrain of yesterday returned and punished our already weak bodies. Sweat poured down our faces and our legs screamed. Halfway through the park a steady 30mph headwind picked up, to pile extra difficulty onto the 12% grade. We crawled up to a rest area below the highest hill in the park, and collapsed on the grass for lunch.

"Which of our friends do you think would have turned around by now?" Katy asked, staring out over the vast green landscape.

I opened my eyes and stared up into the dark sky, "I don't know why anyone would put up with what we've done the last two days," I answered.

"Then why are you still here?"

I thought about it for a while, but gave a simple answer, "Because I'm stubborn. I don't know if it's a good trait, or a bad one. But I'm too stubborn to give up."

"If you're still here because you're stubborn, then why am I here?"

The question wasn't directed at me. She was asking herself, not for the first time, or the last, why she was on this trip. Without an answer to her question we finished lunch and resumed our slow crawl up the hill and into the wind. People at the rest area laughed out loud – we literally heard them laughing – when they saw our sluggish pace. We would have celebrated when we reached the top of the hill, but we didn't want to risk getting blown over, or blown backwards, so we continued. Cycling downhill into the wind wasn't much faster than uphill.

At a small intersection 15 miles before Plymouth, we stopped to consult the map and speculate which route into town might have the fewest hills. Just as we made our decision, a tourist bus going our same direction came barreling down the road. The bright beaming smile on the driver and tour guide were a great contrast to our defeated spirits. I stuck out my thumb, mostly as a joke, but also very willing to accept a ride into town at this point. The tour guide smiled and I read the look on his face, "I've been on this road a thousand times. I know what you're up against. But keep going, you're almost there."

"Maybe we should just set up camp here," Katy suggested as the bus passed.

"Or we could throw our bike away and start walking," I added.

"Do you think one of those donkeys back there could carry us? Could we tie our bike onto two donkeys?"

"Maybe we could just break some law and the police would have to take us to Plymouth."

"Good idea. What law?"

"I don't know, but I'd do anything to avoid one more pedal on this awful bike and these damn hills."

We laughed and laughed about our self-inflicted difficulty (and how our family and friends back home thought we were off having a lazy ride through the country) and then we toughened up and got back on our bike. Only fifteen more miles. One more hour. We can do this. Those sixty minutes were some of the longest of my life.

* * *

That night on the ferry, after our bodies collapsed into the corner of the most deserved showers of our lives, and after we used our last bit of energy to chew our dinner, we retired to our bunk beds on Deck 8 Room 8009 of the Armorique. We were spent. Katy flicked off the switch and thoughts of the last 48 hours raced through my mind. I was mostly asleep when Katy's whisper startled me, "It's happening."

"What's happening?" I muttered.

"This trip. I used to wake up every morning and tell you I couldn't believe we were going on this trip."

"And?"

"And now we're here. England is already over."

Katy was right. The wrong stem at the airport, the frantic two days to see the Tour, the beautiful English countryside, lots of rain, lots of sun, camping in Melrose, swimming in Lake Thirlmere, a day in Edinburgh, and the hills from hell. Those two weeks were all a memory now. Our trip was happening.

"Oh and you know what?" I whispered. "You thought Scottish was hard to understand. The French on this ship sounds like a different language entirely."

PAIN AU CHOCOLAT,
S'IL VOUS PLAIT

"Are you going in there or not?" Katy again asked, pointing to the boulangerie down the street. We were huddled under the awning of Les Trois Crevettes on Rue Jeanne d'Arc, hiding from the drizzle that covered Brittany on that grey, overcast morning.

"Hold your horses," I replied. "Unless you want to try?"

At 8:57am, an hour after we got off the ferry, the street was empty. But at 9:00am, a dozen men and women simultaneously appeared, with umbrellas or the morning newspaper held over their heads to block the falling rain, and quickly disappeared into Boulangerie Guillou. It was a routine they knew well, but one that frightened me. The French visit the boulangerie every day, often twice in a day, because the French love their bread almost as much as they love their cheese. In a country with 400 different types of cheese, that's a lot of love. I repeated a few French phrases in my mind, and walked into the shop.

"Bonjour Madame," I uttered, after the last customer left the shop and the chances of embarrassing myself as the uncultured American diminished.

"Bonjour Monsieur," the lady behind the counter responded.

"Je voudrais deux pains au chocolat, s'il vous plait," I asked, the word 'pain' with my best nasal sound.

"Oui."

"Et une framboisier et une baguette. S'il vous plait."

I breathed a sigh of relief as she selected the first three items, placed them in small paper box and then turned to the back wall for my baguette. I congratulated myself on a successful first attempt at what would surely be many foreign languages, but then the lady turned and looked at me. Her face asked a question, but I had no answer. I looked over my shoulder, hoping another customer had caught her attention, but I was alone. An awkward silence lasted for a moment but then it was obvious; three shelves covered the back wall of the bakery, each holding four or five baskets, and each basket overflowing with a different type of bread, all of them resembling baguettes. I realized that asking for a baguette in a boulangerie was like asking for equipment at REI. She pointed to the nearest basket, so I just nodded in approval.

"Quat quarante," she muttered, as she looked up from the cash register and made eye contact with me. I was speechless. The problem with speaking just enough French to sound intelligent means others respond in French. They didn't teach me how to *hear* French in my Junior High French class, sixteen years earlier.

"Quat quarante, s'il vous plait."

Unsure of exactly how much I owed, but assuming she was asking for money, I took €20 from my wallet and handed it over the counter.

"Merci," she exclaimed, as she made change and I left the store.

"Merci."

I ripped open the box and selected a chocolate croissant, careful not to smear the raspberry frosting from the framboisier. The first bite was heavenly: soft, warm, and chocolaty on the inside with just enough crunch on the outside. I finished my chocolate croissant before I reached Katy.

"Thanks for saving me some," Katy exclaimed, noticing the chocolate at the corners of my mouth.

"Don't worry, I got two."

I handed Katy her pastry, and started on the framboisier. We had intended to save the baguette for lunch (I don't typically eat plain bread for breakfast) but arriving in France was a celebration. The baguette was perfect, on such a different level than any bread I had ever eaten that it seems silly to attempt a comparison. To be perfectly honest, calling it bread seems inappropriate.

"I know we just got here, but it's going to be tough to leave this country," Katy commented.

When we finished the baguette, I returned to the boulangerie and repeated my order, this time pointing to the specific baguette I wanted. The lady in the boulangerie smiled, happy that I'd taken a liking to her baked goods and commended me for quickly learning my way around a boulangerie (at least that's what I think she said).

England had been hilly and hard. Too hard. During those first eleven days, we had climbed 27,000 vertical feet, just shy of a trip up Mt. Everest. When our ferry landed and our Schwalbe Marathon tires rolled onto Continental Europe, we promised each other to do two things: cycle less and eat more.

"I wonder if most people bike tour this way?" Katy asked later that evening, after her shower.

"What way?" I questioned.

"Today we ate at two bakeries, rode an easy 18 miles in a little over an hour, arrived at our WS host's home before noon, walked around town, and took a nap."

"It is pretty nice."

"And now Benoit is downstairs cooking us dinner. Let's go. It smells delicious."

Katy and I made our way down the old, wooden staircase and sat at a large, square table adjacent to the kitchen. Benoit and Clothilde are not members of WS, but were referred to us by their friend, who is a WS host and who felt terrible he couldn't host us. Benoit and Clothilde, and their two children, Juliette and Yann, live in a home that sits on a small cobbled walkway on the side of a hill overlooking the main square of Morlaix. It was only a short afternoon walk from the Riviere de Morlaix and its rustic sailboats. I quizzed Juliette on her English numbers and colors until 7:30pm, when Clothilde came through the door, dropped fresh baguettes on the dinner table and exchanged the customary kisses – faire la bise – on each of our cheeks.

Then dinner began.

"Bon appetit," five-year-old Yann shouted as he grabbed a few pieces of baguette and smeared a large swath of pork spread and butter on his plate, officially beginning our meal. He wasn't reprimanded for his abruptness, so we followed. After eating more bread than we should have, Clothilde filled my plate with roasted tomatoes, zucchini, eggplant and balls of mozzarella. I savored each bite. After one plate I was still hungry, but wasn't sure if I should have a second serving. How many courses were left? *Should I eat up? Should I slow down?* Eating dinner with the French, in courses, was an interesting difficulty. Katy and I grappled with it each night, never sure how many courses remained, and feeling rude to ask, we battled with the dilemma of not knowing whether we should have another serving because the meal was almost over, or to slow down because there was a lot more coming. Following the vegetable platter, fresh eggs that Yann had collected from his own chickens were served English style. After Juliette soaked up her last piece of runny yolk, she took off to the kitchen and returned with a plate of four cheeses.

"The French love cheese," Clothilde began, making a sweeping, but likely true, generalization. "You must know Camembert, it's from Normandy."

She cut a giant triangle from a white cheese in a round and placed it on her plate. Based on her serving size, I thought she was just having that cheese, similar to the way health conscious individuals often select a single dessert from an assortment.

"Comte is a bit tougher. We love Comte," she continued, cutting an equally large slice from a pale yellow cheese with a tougher rind.

She then carefully unwrapped a dirty, bluish cheese from a plastic wrapping, cut off a smaller portion, and quickly rewrapped it. "Roquefort is a blue cheese. It comes from sheep milk."

"And this one is chevre," she concluded, with another slice from the fourth cheese, as large as the first.

"Do you eat them a special way?" Katy asked, excited that the stories of the French and their cheese were unfolding before us.

"Of course," Benoit chimed in. "You must eat the strongest one last, the Roquefort."

"Do you ever eat cheese with crackers?" Katy asked.

"Non, avec pain." Clothilde boasted. For her, the thought of cheese with crackers was utterly preposterous.

When each person had cut a portion of each cheese and we were just about to begin eating, I thought I'd share some of my knowledge about cheese.

"In America, we also have cheese," I commented.

"Oui?" Clothilde answered. The intonation in her voice suggested she was unaware that cheese existed outside of France.

"It comes in a resealable plastic bag, with a flavor Ziploc seal. It's dusted with some sort of preservative and it says Kraft Foods across the front."

"This is not cheese," Clothilde laughed, as she threw her head back in disgust. "In France this is not possible."

The cheese was divine. Smooth and creamy, firm but subtle, pungent and wonderful; I never knew that cheese could have so many flavors. A sweet, but light, dessert of red and black currant berries capped off this wonderful meal. It was now 10:30pm, we'd been eating for three hours, and Juliette and Yan, who were polite and quiet throughout the meal, excused themselves for bed.

"That was the best meal I've ever had," Katy whispered as we fell asleep and our first day in France came to a close. "And these were the best behaved children I've ever met," I added.

After breakfast, we carried our bike and panniers up the narrow, cobblestone walkway to the main road and began our ride south to La Baule, where the Loire River empties into the Atlantic Ocean. From there, we would follow the Loire east to Orléans, before turning north for Paris, which we would reach in about a week.

A couple of kilometers south of Morlaix, we got on the Voie Verte, an old railroad track converted to a bike path after the Second World War, and cycled through the Parc Naturel Régional d'Armorique. It was nice being on the dirt pack, rolling through dense trees, between pastures of black and white Holstein cattle grazing in the sun, and away from highway traffic, where each car that raced by left me feeling that we ought to be going faster. We arrived at a campsite in Mur de Bretagne after a leisurely five hours, and 100 kilometers, on the bike. As opposed to our hectic schedule in England, this was the type of day I had anticipated before our trip began.

After a swim in the lake, we plopped down on a cement path near the campground shop. With WiFi access, we began the daily task of route planning, finding WS hosts, and updating our blog. As I waited for the sluggish WiFi, an enormous gentleman ambled down the trail, wearing a blue NY Yankees baseball hat, an untucked dress shirt, dark khakis and blue crocs. I imagine his belt was taller than he was, but he wore a smile, presumably spoke some English and he had a skip to his step that intrigued me.

"How you doing there ma'am?" he asked Katy in an unfamiliar accent.

"Doing well," Katy answered, happy to converse in English.

"Where are you from?" the enormous man asked.

"Well I'm a Yankee, just like your hat," I answered.

"Well damn me." He slapped his hand on his knee and used his belly to generate a deep rumble of a laugh. "I'm not a Yankee. I'm from Ireland. The best country in the world."

"Oh really?" Katy questioned him.

"Actually, I believe Italy is the best country in the world, but nobody's better than the Irish. How are you liking France?"

"We love it here," Katy answered.

"Not me, the French are too ignorant. I'm just on my way home from a Catholic Pilgrimage in Italy. Where are you headed?"

"We're riding that bike to Turkey," I answered.

"Between you and me brother, I'd never go across Europe on a bike." He pointed again at his belly and laughed, "I could never make it up those hills. Do your mom and dad know you're out here?"

"They do."

"And they're okay with it? If I were your dad I'd be lighting candles, sprinkling holy water and looking for the best priest I know."

"Well I'm not sure our parents are doing the same."

"I'm going to the pub later, can I buy you a Guinness?"

"I'd love to come to the pub, but I don't drink Guinness."

"Guinness did this to me, 15 or 20 pints a day for too many years," he exclaimed, doing half a dance. "And do you like to sing? Irish people love singing when they're drunk."

In the morning we attempted an early departure, but Patrick, our Irish friend, invited us into his camper for eggs, toast and "good ole Irish tea." Despite already having enjoyed a breakfast of baguettes and pain au chocolat delivered fresh to the campground that morning, we sat down for more conversation. Patrick shared his opinion on every country on our itinerary while his wife made Katy and I tea and breakfast. "In Turkey, they will kill a man for nothing," and "India has the worst roads in the world, five or six accidents on each road every day." It was the best Irish tea, with the best Irish man I've ever met.

Two days later, after 150 kilometers on rolling hills under sunny skies, we arrived at the home of Sandrine and Pascal in the small town of La Baule. When I was five, Sandrine lived with my family as an au pair before beginning her university studies. Katy and I spent two nights in La Baule – taking our third rest day in two and a half weeks – and Katy got the mini vacation she was hoping for. We enjoyed a day on the beach, a delicious seafood barbeque dinner (although without any cheese, which Sandrine said was okay, because she was born in Morocco and isn't 100% French) and a race around narrow, winding streets in Pascal's Porsche, while Sandrine clenched her fists, closed her eyes, and in her French accent yelled, "Oh shit! Oh shit! Oh shit!"

"Would you like a glass of wine?" Pascal asked as he loaded our plates with sardines from the barbeque. We bought the sardines fresh at the outdoor seafood market that morning, and not only were they delicious, I was surprised to learn that sardines don't always come in a can.

"No, thank you. Water is fine," Katy answered. It was a knee jerk response. As members of the Church of Jesus Christ of Latter-day Saints, we don't drink alcohol and Katy passed up the beverage without much thought.

"Why not? You're in France. You must have some wine."

Katy attempted to explain our religious reasons for not drinking alcohol, but Pascal wasn't convinced, "If you are in my house, as my guest, you must have a glass of wine."

Pascal poured us each a glass of red wine and instructed us on the proper way to drink. Katy and I turned to each other and, after a quick swirl of the glass, said, "When in France?" It was my first ever glass of wine (a botched order of virgin daiquiris years earlier in Mazatlan, Mexico was my only prior drink), and to be honest, was a bit pungent; it reminded me of cough syrup. I looked around, and noticing that the wrath of God wasn't descending out of the clouds, I took another sip.

On Sunday morning, we said goodbye to Sandrine, and Pascal emerged from the basement to stop working on his motorcycle, so he could wave us goodbye. The ride out of La Baule was very quiet, since most of France closes around noon on Sundays. We followed the Boulevard de l'Ocean along the beach, until we arrived in the industrial port city of Saint Nazaire. A little further east, a tailwind picked up and sent us flying – in our large chain ring – toward Nantes. We rode fast, trying to stay ahead of a chasing storm, but eventually got hit with the downpour, and went for cover under an overpass a few kilometers short of our destination. To lighten the mood, I turned on the Beatles *Why Don't We Do It In The Road?* and we polished off half a jar of peanut butter. I love eating peanut butter with my fingers.

The next day was similar. A couple of hours into our ride, Katy informed me it was time for lunch, so we stopped at a Carrefour and I went in for lunch supplies.

Before leaving Ann Arbor, we had packed our panniers to capacity, without much space to carry food. This became a problem, so we bought a school lunch box and bungeed it to the top of our rear rack. Unfortunately, this lunch box only carried a lunch's worth of food, so trips to Carrefour, Aldi, Hofer or Spar were a daily occurrence. I exited the store with an armful of baguettes, sausages, Camembert, tomatoes, Dijon mustard, peaches and a large Schweppes Bitter Lemon (the best!) and we sat down on the sidewalk for lunch.

"Bon appetit," a lady sang as she walked past.

"Merci."

"Bon appetit," the next passerby repeated the phrase.

"Merci."

A few minutes later, a mother walked past with two children. "Bon appetit. Bon appetit. Bon appetit."

"Merci. Merci. Merci."

Out in public, the French rarely engaged in conversation and often resisted speaking any English they might know. Others often interpret this behavior as arrogance, as our Irish friend, Patrick, was quick to acknowledge. But when food enters the equation, things change entirely. Wherever Katy and I sat down for lunch, we were always greeted with multiple "bon appetites." At every dinner in a French home, the French changed from quiet and reserved to some of the most gregarious people in Europe.

We arrived in Angers that evening around 5pm, and went for a quick swim in the Lac de Maine. We couldn't find a way to lock our bike up to anything with our small U-lock, so we draped a week's worth of dirty clothes over the handlebars and panniers in an attempt to deter theft while we swam. Our bike wasn't stolen, so maybe it worked.

After drying off, Katy and I resumed arguing about who was responsible for the directions to the home of our next host, Michel, when Katy noticed something that changed everything. Despite not having an Internet connection, our Google Maps app had retained the loaded map from that morning's WiFi *and* the GPS still worked. It was a navigational breakthrough. For the rest of our trip, directions became much easier. As long as we had WiFi every other day or so, and battery power, we could load maps into Google Maps stored data and use GPS to direct us to our destinations. Thus, our debates switched from not knowing where our hosts lived, to pointing blame when maps weren't loaded.

Michel, more than anyone else we met, loves bike touring. We entered his apartment and were blown away by the cycling paraphernalia – metal bike signs from the roadways of various countries, photos from his many tours, and piles of maps – that covered his home. Maps are the visible mark of a person who loves exploring new places and recording the minutest details of how they got there. During dinner, Michel told us the story of his first bike tour. In 1986, on a steel frame 10-speed, he set off on a 17-month ride from Brest, France to Hong Kong and dealt with the 5,000 meter passes of Tibet and a subsequent illness where he lost 35 pounds. "This is the best thing I have ever done," he finished his story just as dessert was being served. He cooked us his mother's recipe of Patés de Prunes, a local Brittany dessert typically reserved for winter, but he said our visit justified a celebration. As dinner came to a close, I noticed Katy's head bobbing as she dozed off to sleep so I excused her to bed while Michel and I stayed up late and looked at his old cycling photos. After sharing our proposed route, Michel told me his next trip would begin in Boston. He would ride west to Vancouver, Canada before riding literally around the perimeter of North and South America, down to Patagonia along the west, and then back up to Boston in the east.

"That's a long trip you have planned," I remarked.

"But why not?" he answered.

Why not? It was the same answer I'd given a year before when discussing my plans for a 400-mile bike race in Oregon. Yeah, why not?

In the morning Michel took us on a three-hour cycling tour of Angers. Around noon, after visiting the main cathedral and castle, we followed Michel through an old quarry, where we crossed a small river on a little pull boat before arriving at Eurovelo 6. The Eurovelo Network is a group of 14 cycling routes that follow small roads and designated bike trails across Europe. Eurovelo 6 runs from Nantes, France in the west along the Loire, Rhine and Danube Rivers to Bulgaria's border on the Black Sea, 4,448 kilometers to the east. On that afternoon, the EV 6 bike path was crowded with other touring cyclists, families out for a ride, dog walkers, and a host of others enjoying the summer sun.

"How's our trip going so far?" I asked Katy, as we weaved through runners on the busy trail. Although we were on the same bike, met the same people, and ate the same food, it had quickly become apparent that we responded differently to these situations and an occasional "how are things going?" was helpful to keep things rolling smoothly.

"Good, what do you think?"

"It's good and all, but we need an adventure."

"What do you mean 'an adventure'?" Katy responded, afraid of what might be bouncing around in my head.

"In the past eight days, we've stayed with hosts seven times. Which has been great, don't get me wrong."

"But?"

"But I don't think I can sit down to another three-hour dinner. I need some space. I want to sleep in the woods and do our own thing for a couple days." Katy was quiet so I added to my case, "Besides, you were the one falling asleep at dinner last night."

"So what do you want to do?" Katy asked.

"We should start wild camping."

"Wild camping?" Katy questioned.

Wild camping is just as it sounds, camping in the wild. It exists for two reasons: it's easy and it's free. The daily tasks of sending emails to WS hosts, looking online for a place to stay, and then finding directions to that place require a lot of time and Internet access. Accommodations throughout Western Europe are also very expensive. On the other hand, wild camping is free and requires almost no planning. You cycle until you're tired and then look for a spot to pitch a tent.

"Okay. If you find a place that I agree to, we can do it."

"Oh, and one other thing."

"What is it?" Katy asked, not wanting to concede any more of her traveling comforts.

"These flat roads are boring. The hills in England were tough, but I miss them."

Katy didn't say anything. The thought of intentionally looking for more hills aroused painful memories and opened wounds that were only a week old.

"You want to go out of your way to make our trip more difficult?" she asked.

"Yeah. I say we change our route and head towards the Alps." The monotony of five days on flat roads lacked the challenge and excitement of climbing hills and soaring down the other side. Our planned route through the flat countries of Belgium, Amsterdam and Denmark wasn't appealing to me. In England I had longed for the flats, but, once in the flats, I wanted to climb mountains. I suppose it's only human nature to want what you don't have.

"Let's try wild camping first. Then we can talk about the Alps," Katy suggested.

Our first attempt to pitch a tent in relative seclusion didn't go as smoothly as I planned. Our search for a good spot was doubly complicated by our fear of trespassing and an overnight forecast for rain. I love camping, but I hate camping in the rain. Growing up in the desert of Utah, camping trips never included rain, or the awful surprise that greeted us in the morning – dew. Morning dew. Utah doesn't have dew.

Eventually we found a small, somewhat traffic-free bridge over the Loire River near Langeais. We set up camp underneath the bridge to shelter us from forecasted storms, and had a swim in the Loire before dinner and bed. We slept terribly. We tossed and turned all night. Just as we were about to fall asleep a car would come along, and its tires would thud at the interchange between the pavement and metal bridge, jarring us with a clanking metallic echo thirty feet below. These disruptions were accompanied by a symphony of frogs and a host of bugs and birds that were either singing or dying, I'm not sure which. We saved $22, and had a lousy, but memorable, night's sleep.

In the morning, despite the rough night, or maybe because of it, we felt we were finally figuring out the rhythm of the road. We'd been on the road for twenty-one days, had slept in almost as many different places, experienced rain and sun, hills and flats, comfy beds and the cacophony of amphibians, and were halfway through our third country (if Scotland is a country). At 8am, we arrived at the Château de Villandry and spent a few hours exploring the castle and its impressive gardens. I suppose many books have been written about these gardens, but as I am not a horticulturist, all I can say is that it is the most elaborate and geometric arranged display of plants, flowers and shrubs I have ever seen. After Katy reminded me of the gorgeousness of the place, for the fifth time, we got back on the road.

"You're sure you want to cycle through the Alps?" Katy asked, as we passed multiple tour buses filled with gawking tourists, just beyond the castle gate.

"I think so. The Netherlands and Denmark are just going to be too flat for too long."

"Maybe, but don't you think the Alps will be too steep for too long?" Katy responded.

"Maybe. But at least it will be a challenge."

"Cycling around the world isn't enough of a challenge?"

"Not if we just stick to this flat road."

"Well I don't want to go if you're just going to tell me I'm not pedaling enough. And have you made a decision about getting an easier gear?" Katy asked.

Both her question and her concern were valid. Most touring bikes are geared similar to mountain bikes, with very easy gears which make climbing steep roads relatively easy. Our tandem, for better or worse, is geared more like a road bike. It lacked the very easy gears that would come in handy on steep gradients. The difficulty of dragging our loaded tandem over the hills of England, and the screaming quads that accompanied it, had largely resulted from this problem – our bike lacked the gearing of a traditional touring bike.

Katy's concern of pedaling inequality was not specific to us and our tandem, but something common to all tandem cyclists. Captains (rider in front) and stokers (rider in back) debate incessantly about cadence, pace and whether or not each cyclist is pulling a fair share of the weight. Katy and I were no exception. It goes something like this:

"Are you pedaling back there?" I'd ask, when I felt our pace slowing.

"Yes. Are you?" Katy would answer.

"If I wasn't pedaling, how would we be moving?"

"Well why don't you think I'm pedaling?"

"Cause I've been pedaling the same amount all day, and all of a sudden we're barely moving."

We had this argument almost every day. It's just what we did. Sometimes the argument was lighthearted and joking, other times it was fueled by mistrust and anger.

In the beginning of our trip, I went to such great lengths to prove I was in fact doing more than my fair share of the pedaling that when we arrived in Morlaix, France I had both of us get on a scale and weigh ourselves. I had lost ten pounds and she had only lost five.

"See, I must be pedaling more than you," I declared. Katy's frustration was only compounded when strangers, upon hearing that Katy sat in the back, would always tell her how nice it must be to just sit back, kick up your legs, and relax and let me do all the work.

After dinner that night in Blois, we walked along the Loire and shared a couple of gigantic Mr. Freeze stickless popsicles from Epicerie de Vienne. I took Katy's hand and she took mine. The Loire was beautiful, and after the sun had set we stared at the reflection of the full moon in the giant river. I loved that moment. I loved that my crazy idea had somehow become reality and Katy and I were in central France making our dreams come true. But most of all, sitting between the moon and the river, I loved my wife. Only someone as incredible as her would join me on this adventure, and keep a smile on her face while juggling the difficulties of the road. We made the long walk back to the Val de Blois Campground and crawled into our tent for the night.

The next day began with fresh baguettes and pains au chocolat. Only in France do public campgrounds have a sign up sheet for ordering bread and pastries, to be delivered fresh the next morning. That afternoon we stopped at Chateau de Chambord, the castle of all castles. Commissioned in the mid 16th century by the 26-year-old King Francis I, who wanted a hunting retreat from which he could escape his busy life in Paris, the castle features 440 rooms, 282 fireplaces, and 84 staircases and has a double helical twisting staircase designed by Leonardo da Vinci, which allows two people to ascend the stairway simultaneously, and maintain eye contact but never cross paths. It's quite the hunting retreat.

Construction required 1,800 workers and cost roughly half a million French livres, which I can only assume was a lot of money back then. It was supposed to be castle living at its finest, but the building was impossible to heat in the winter because of its giant vaulted ceilings and difficult to stock with food due to its remote location. Francis died of a heart attack only a year or so after it's completion, and only spent a total of seven weeks there. The castle was then left vacant for over a century until King Louis XIV restored the castle and added a 1,200 horse stable.

After thoroughly exploring the castle, we meandered through the ever flat French countryside to Orleans. Our hosts, Gregory and Muriel, had a newborn baby and some family in town, but let us pitch our tent in their garden. Half an hour after we arrived, while Katy was in the shower, a storm crept in and someone unzipped those large dark clouds and large buckets of rain sent me scrambling with all our stuff into their garage. I grabbed a broom and swept up some sawdust and cobwebs, hoping to make our "room" look presentable. We'd never slept on a dirty cement floor together and I wasn't sure how Katy would take the news.

"I hope this is okay. I tried to clean up a bit," I announced as Katy returned from her shower. I was a bit nervous that sleeping on a cold cement floor in someone's garage would be unacceptable.

"It's great. Just nice to be out of the rain."

Phew. Katy was learning to roll with the punches. I suppose a few days of camping began to redefine Katy's notion of "acceptable sleeping conditions."

After dinner, Muriel asked Gregory to get the chocolate dessert from the kitchen. Katy and I exchanged smiles. Would the presence of Gregory's parents call for a special dessert? Gregory brought out a single bar of dark chocolate. The bar was passed around the table and the six of us broke off a single square of chocolate and set it on our plates. I don't usually need a plate to eat a single piece of chocolate, but I tried to be polite and follow the custom. After too much talking, Gregory picked up his chocolate. I took this as a sign we could begin so I quickly ate my piece, assuming that if I finished first I'd get another piece. I grew up in a family of five hungry kids, and this sort of logic had governed most of our family dinners. My hasty eating was a bit premature, however, as our hosts only took a small bite and placed the rest of the square on their plate. *What is going on?*

For ten slow minutes, as I sat without chocolate, and too shy to ask for another piece, everyone slowly nibbled away at their smaller and smaller piece. When each person finished, I thought I'd finally get another piece, or maybe another dessert. But it wasn't to be. The rest of the bar was wrapped up and saved for another day. *Come on! In America each person gets their own bar, not their own square. What is this?*

That night, as the rain beat upon the rooftop, and as I lay quietly on my camping pad on their garage's cement floor, I thought about that piece of chocolate. Why was it so hard for me to see that half-eaten bar of chocolate wrapped up and returned to the kitchen? I thought about it all night, and maybe came up with an answer. In America, the purpose of dessert, is dessert. We eat because we like food. But in France, the purpose of dessert is people. They eat because they love to spend time with others. That's why their meals are served in multiple courses and that's why they saved half of the bar of chocolate for later. Because tomorrow night they can open up the rest of that chocolate bar and pick up their conversation right where they left off.

"So, what way are we going?" Katy asked in the morning. I heard her question, but it didn't register. I was concentrating on adjusting the cable tension on our rear derailleur.

"Did you hear me?" Katy asked.

"What?"

"Which way are we going?"

"Oh. I vote for the mountains, but you can choose."

"I knew it," Katy answered. "You're always looking for the difficult way to get somewhere."

We loaded up our bike and were off. Almost off. While I adjusted the rear derailleur Katy took charge of directions, but her directions required carrying our bike down some stairs, walking across a dirt trail and heaving our bike over a guardrail to get on the correct road out of town. Let's just say our day didn't start well. In Ann Arbor, a morning argument ends when Katy gets on the bus for work and I leave for school on my bike. On a tandem, however, the argument just continues. Frustration and silence lasted the better part of 86 kilometers, until we arrived at the apartment of Sandrine and Ronan in Nevers. Desperate to have someone else to talk to, we barged into their apartment. I practiced my French with their kids Edouan and Yann while Katy talked to Sandrine, who had just finished a 14-month bike tour with her husband, Ronan, and their four- and two-year-old kids.

"Did you guys ever argue on your trip?" Katy asked over dinner.

Sandrine and Ronan looked at each other and just started laughing.

"When we were on our tour we argued more than we ever have," Sandrine answered, Ronan nodding in affirmation. A weight lifted off Katy's shoulders.

"I can't tell you how happy I am to hear that," Katy sighed. "What did you guys argue about?"

Sandrine gave the long answer, which included the difficulty of sticking to a breastfeeding schedule and dealing with two kids who would start fighting in the bike trailer, which would cause Ronan's bike to weave down the road.

"What do you argue about?" Sandrine returned the question.

"What don't we argue about?" Katy responded. "Who is in charge of directions, spending money on food, where we will camp, mechanical problems, basically everything."

"Don't worry about it," Ronan encouraged. "We were the same way. With time, you'll start to figure things out."

"Oh, and Clayton loves telling me I'm not pedaling hard enough," Katy added.

"Based on the route you've shown us, I think you guys need to slow down," Ronan added. "It took us a while to learn this. When we started our trip, we were trying to ride 80-100 kilometers a day. We assumed covering a lot of ground was necessary for a successful tour. But what worked for us was going slow. You'll see more if you go slow."

These were difficult words for me to hear, but they immediately resonated with Katy. I did feel like we were trying to do too much, too fast, but slowing down went against my well-engrained road cycling mentality of faster and longer.

The next day we had arranged to stay with a host 115 kilometers and 1,000 meters of climbing away. It wouldn't be our hardest day, but it wasn't the day to try our new plan of going slow and seeing more. Our morning, however, was full of optimistic energy, feeling better about our imperfect relationship and looking forward to leaving the Loire River Valley and heading into some rolling hills. The day was magnificent. As we approached the first of many hills, our enthusiasm hammered away at the pedals and we soared over the hill and coasted down the other side. Our legs had recovered during our flat days on the Loire and we felt very strong.

Halfway up our largest climb of the day, and four hours into our ride, Katy demanded a lunch break. Her roll of Oreos had run out.

We sat down on the side of the road and unloaded our lunch: two salami, brie and tomato baguette sandwiches, a pain au chocolat, a bowl of yogurt with granola, two peaches, and a liter of Scwheppes Agum. Passengers in passing cars shouted bon appetite and we raised our sandwiches in approval. After a quick power nap we finished a bar of chocolate (a whole bar) and continued our climb. At the top, we stopped at a crêperie to celebrate.

As we approached Marmagne, I quizzed Katy on basic French because our WS hosts for that night had warned us they spoke no English. They were on the WS website, not because of any bike tours of their own, but to reciprocate the hospitality their son was receiving during a current tour of his own. (Fun fact: we would catch up to their son Edouard six months later, in Northern Thailand.) A kilometer or two north of Marmagne, and atop a formidable hill, we rode down a narrow lane to a large farmhouse marked "Les Sauvageots."

"Bonjour," I shouted from behind a large metal gate.

A large black lab came barking through the yard and chickens went flying.

"Bonjour. Bonjour." Pierre and Jacqueline followed behind and exchanged customary French kisses on cheeks, while I recalled my prepared introduction. My French had improved considerably in the prior week, and I was optimistic our evening would be manageable.

"Bonjour Madame et Monsieur, comment allez vous? I asked.

"Je vais bien. Comment était ta journée? Pierre responded.

"Tres bon, c'est tres beau ici."

"Merci, merci."

"Et merci pour la maison pour dormir cet soir." I responded. It wasn't a grammatically correct sentence, but I strung the words thank you, house, sleep and this evening together, hoping it would get the idea across.

Pierre and Jacqueline's stone farmhouse, built in 1712, overlooks the village of Marmagne and is surrounded by green fields with cattle and goats, a barn, and a field full of pigs, chickens and rabbits. Tall trees stand alongside a stream that winds through the yard, a table and chairs sit in the nearby garden, and other homes and farms dot the hillside.

Dinner began in the garden just as the sun was falling, and in simple French I asked about their family, cycling and life on the farm. Jacqueline eventually opened up and spoke a tiny amount of English, and Pierre, not wanting to be left out, but without speaking any English, employed an astonishing amount of hand gestures and facial expressions to be a part of the conversation. The conversation was a 10/10 for enjoyment and amusement, but likely a 1/10 for quantity of information communicated.

For a brief moment, I thought about home. If non-English speaking cyclists came to my home, would I engage them with the same energy and hospitality? Or would I leave a meal on the table and blow them off, citing the language barrier as an excuse for my abruptness?

The dinner was great, but the dessert was legendary. When we had finished our bread and cheese and Pierre had cleared the table, Jacqueline brought out a plum crumble dessert in a circular pie dish. To be polite, we began with small slices. The first bite was sweet, crunchy and had an irresistible tartness.

"J'adore le gateau. C'est tres bon, Madame," I blurted out as my fork went in for another bite.

"Oui, les prunes sont tres acidique."

We quickly finished our first piece and Pierre insisted we cut another, larger slice. I was halfway through the second serving when my taste buds took hold of my body and I shouted, "Faye, this is delicious!" That gesture is, in my opinion, the best way to compliment a delicious meal. That evening became the gold standard by which we will measure all future meals and dessert. The perfect weather. The beautiful countryside. Fascinating hosts. And a delicious plum crumble that was tres acidique.

Breakfast was more of the plum crumble, and when we couldn't eat anymore, Pierre packed up the leftovers for us and hurried off to work. But we stayed inside. It was pouring rain that morning, and the forecast predicted it wouldn't let up anytime soon. In fact, the forecast for the next three or four days was solid rain.

I don't like getting wet. I don't necessarily mind *being* wet, but I hate *getting* wet. On prior days, rain would creep up on us during a ride and there wasn't much to do about it. Voluntarily walking out into the rain, however, and getting soaked before we had even begun our five-hour ride for the day was a different story entirely.

After an hour of futile waiting, we mustered up a little courage, wrapped plastic bags around our Brooks saddles and got on our bike. We were soaked before the first turn of the pedals, drenched a moment later, and had the squishy, spongy sound between our toes before we got out of town. We resisted getting wet and lamented our awful situation. But then something changed.

Once we were totally soaked, and couldn't get any wetter, our spirits lifted. I had dreaded getting wet all morning, but once it had happened, once we *were* soaked, once my socks were dripping and my toes had become pruney, there was no longer anything to worry about. The dread lifted; the situation immediately improved. And on top of that, being wet wasn't really that bad. In fact, it was fun. We were kids playing in the rain, without a care in the world, comforted by the fact that a warm shower and a clothesline were just a couple hours away. We resisted getting wet, but being wet was rather enjoyable.

Around 2pm, we spotted a boulangerie and ducked under an archway, and out of the rain, for lunch. I'm okay with being soaking wet myself, but soaking wet baguettes? – that's not okay. We had two baguettes, a nine-inch stick of salami, an entire round of Boursault cheese, two pain au chocolats, two raspberry framboisiers, a tupperware full of leftover plum crumble dessert, a peach, some yogurt, a bar of chocolate and a bottle of Schweppes. Our appetites were in full swing, and we had adjusted to the Hobbits' eating schedule: breakfast, second breakfast, elevensies, luncheon, afternoon tea, dinner, and supper.

"This is getting out of control," Katy proposed, smearing a large portion of Boursault, a triple cream cheese that is more dessert than cheese, onto a piece of baguette.

"But it sure is good," I laughed.

"Maybe we should call someone back home and ask them how much they eat for lunch, because I have no idea what a normal meal looks like."

Katy was right; our sense of portion control was long gone. In twenty minutes we each consumed about 3,000 calories and an hour later were left wondering if we had anything else to munch on. Each night, just before bed, we shared a chocolate bar. If Katy fell asleep early, I ate it all by myself. Katy's biggest flaw as a wife, prior to entering France, was her claim that she "doesn't like chocolate." It didn't take her long to see the light.

The afternoon ride was more rain. We arrived in Cluny that evening and emphatically wrung out our socks in a sign of victory, shaking the last drop of rain from us. The following two days took us 165 kilometers to Poncin. The weather each day was the same, raining when we got on the bike and raining when we got off. Each night, we stayed with gracious WS hosts who apologized profusely about the unusually wet weather.

We left Poncin under cloudy, but dry skies and headed towards Geneva, Switzerland – country #4. It wouldn't, however, be our last day in France. We planned to skip over to Chamonix after Geneva before leaving France for good.

The ride to Geneva started on rolling roads, through fields of sunflowers. The road gradually started to pitch up and eventually we hit a nice little climb that stretched up into the clouds. Our legs felt great and the gradient was much more manageable than the hills of England, which reassured Katy and I that climbing the Alps might be enjoyable, instead of just painful. We stopped at an Aldi before hitting the Swiss border (and Swiss prices) and stocked up on five or six bars of chocolate and the same amount of cheese.

"Thank you so much for coming," Ale exclaimed when we arrived at his apartment in Geneva. His words surprised me. Never before had we been thanked for coming to a host's home.

"No," I responded. "Thank you."

Ale (pronounced uh-lay) was good friends with Michel, our host from Orleans. Their apartments were identical: maps on the walls, an old steel frame hanging in the entranceway, and bike paraphernalia everywhere. We dropped our stuff and Ale took us on a tour of Geneva to see the headquarters of the United Nations and the Red Cross, and Lac Leman. We eventually stopped on a bike path on the banks of the Rhone. The sun was out and it was a hot afternoon. The river looked delightful.

"Follow me," Ale shouted.

We locked up our bikes and followed him past a hundred sun-worshippers lounging under the blue sky. Every time Katy noticed a girl's body getting too much sun in too many places she'd whisper, "Don't look over there." After a ten-minute walk up the Rhone, Ale jumped into the river and was quickly swept downstream. We followed. The strong current carried us down the river, where we swam to the side of the river, grabbed hold of a ladder and pulled ourselves out near our parked bikes. Ale had warned us not to miss the ladder or it would be 15 kilometers until the next pull out spot. We basked in the sun all day, and when we got too hot, we walked upriver and jumped in, each time venturing further into the middle of the river before frantically swimming back to the pullout ladder. It was just what we needed after three days of solid rain.

The next day was August 1st, the Swiss National Day, and Katy and I spent the day celebrating their holiday, and one month of being on the road. Four countries and 2,275 kilometers down, many more to go. When the midnight celebration was over, we met Ale in town and began the walk back to his apartment.

"Ale, I have a question for you," I stated.

"Sure, what is it?"

"When we got to your apartment, you thanked us for coming. You're the only person who has done that. How come?"

"Back in 1991, I was cycling through Turkey and so many people I didn't know approached me on the streets and invited me into their homes to stay for the night and have a meal. It was the first time I met such friendly people. The cycling part of that trip ended a long time ago, but the real trip is still not over. When others come to stay with me, I am able to repay the hospitality others showed me twenty years ago. 1991 was a long time ago, but I hope when you get to Turkey you'll find that people there are just the same."

BUON APPETITO

At 4:55am, I was fast asleep on the top bunk of my bed at the Gite Le Vagabond hostel in Chamonix. Two days earlier we had left Geneva, climbed a steep back road to Les Houches, foraged for wild berries, and enjoyed a late-night meal at Midnight Burger in Chamonix. The next day was overcast; Mont Blanc, Western Europe's tallest mountain, hid her white face behind the grey clouds.

Five minutes later, at five o'clock on the dot, David Bowie woke me from my slumber and I frantically searched for my iPhone in the dark, hoping not to wake Katy or the British gentleman on the bunk bed next to ours. I hopped off my bunk, fiddled with the squeaky lock on the old wooden door, and looked out the hallway window. Clouds. *Damn.*

"Clayton, did you check?" Katy whispered, an hour later.

"Yeah, cloudy."

"What are you talking about? Come look at this."

I went back to the window and saw the White Giant, her snow-topped dome stretching above the clouds into a pure blue sky. We threw on some clothes and ran to the Aiguille du Midi, a cable car that takes visitors to a lookout station high above the valley floor. As the tram climbed above the clouds we entered a mystical world. The rising sun shone down on the clouds, which sat like marshmallows between dozens of peaks stretching to the horizon in every direction. It was the most otherworldly, landscape-of the-gods thing that we had ever seen.

"Aren't you glad we came to the mountains?" I asked, as I gave Katy a big hug and a bigger kiss.

"They are beautiful," she responded. "But you know, we haven't had to ride over them yet."

"That's true, but today we'll see how it goes." After we got some good material to post on Instagram, we returned to our hostel, lathered on some sunscreen and ventured off towards Switzerland.

"Katy, our last boulangerie," I remarked as we approached Argentiere, the last town before the Swiss border. We savored each bite, and allowed the perfect flavors to leave an indelible memory on our taste buds as we did not know when we might return to France. When the pastries were gone, we bought a few more and packed them away.

"Katy, we definitely need to stop," I demanded when we reached another boulangerie, on the other side of town. The routine was the same: delicious and memorable first bites, followed by food withdrawal and overwhelming anxiety. We got back on our bike and continued.

"Let me guess, you want to stop again," Katy joked as we came around a corner and saw yet another boulangerie.

"Of course."

Our last pain au chocolat was as delicious as the first, but when Katy suggested it might be wise to not eat three meals before 10:30 am, we left the bakery and continued our ride up the valley. It was hard to leave France, but stuffing our panniers full of pain au chocolat, framboisiers and Camembert, Reblochon, Boursault, Tommes, Brie, Roquefort and Chèvre lessened the pain.

The Col de Forclaz, a 7.5km climb with a 6% gradient, was the first test of our climbing legs. We hit the bottom of the climb fast and instantly my heart pounded in my ears. We were riding above our aerobic thresholds, but it didn't matter. After two weeks of lolly gagging along the Loire, the beautiful snow capped mountains now carried us in a frenzied pace up the mountain.

"Can we take a break?" Katy asked, as I shifted into a harder gear and hammered away at the pedals.

"Nope, we're in a good rhythm," I gasped between breaths.

"Then can we at least slow down?"

"If your legs are tired, just don't pedal as hard."

When my body began to hurt, I doubled my efforts and threw my legs into a rapid cadence. The words of Jens Voigt, a professional cyclist, motivated me: *shut up legs.* Eventually I cracked. My mind gave way to the physical suffering, and I shifted into our easiest gear, dropped to a much lower cadence and finished the climb, without stopping of course, but at half the pace.

"That wasn't so bad," I said, when our bike came to a rolling stop on top of the pass.

"At the beginning I thought you were trying to kill me," she contended. "But once we got into a rhythm it really was a nice climb."

The descent was equally enjoyable. Tandems are twice as heavy as single bikes, but only have to push through a single person's wind resistance. We flew downhill. As we approached each turn Katy politely asked, "Can we go a little bit slower?" so I would sit upright and allow the wind to slow us momentarily, and then return to a more aerodynamic position to continue our 40mph descent. The exhilarating descent took us to Martigny, Switzerland, and then a tailwind blew us along the Rhone, past dozens of apricot orchards to the small village of Chippis.

We stopped in the small village, and pulled out our laptop to look at a Google Maps screenshot for directions. A lady immediately came out of her garden and asked Katy a number of questions. I watched in amusement as Katy tried to converse in French.

"Je parler no France," Katy mumbled.

The lady responded in typical manner, repeating the same questions, only this time louder and slower. I heard the word *boisson* and responded with *merci.* A moment later we were on her back patio, asking if she had any snacks to go with our beverage.

Eventually Madame Favre asked where we were staying that evening. I decided against an attempt to explain the Warmshowers website in French. Instead, I showed her the email and address of our WS host. Immediately her face went blank and her eyes froze, as if she had seen a ghost.

"Ce n'est pas possible," she remarked.

Not possible? I wondered.

We couldn't find out exactly what Madame Favre was trying to tell us, until she pointed to heaven and mimicked cutting her throat with her finger. *Our host is dead? But I emailed her this morning.* Madame Favre insisted we spend the night in her home, but we declined, arguing that we believed our host was alive, and expecting us. We finally convinced her to call our host and minutes later, our host arrived and sorted out the confusion. A different person in town, but with the same name, had recently died. *Phew.*

The next morning, we said our last *mercies* and *au revoires* and followed the Rhone River east. After an hour, everything instantly changed. French road signs were replaced by indecipherable German as we crossed the *linguistic frontier* into German Switzerland. If French is the language of love, German is the sound of a very angry guy with a fur ball caught in the back of his throat. In the town of Brig, we ate a quick power lunch to fuel our bodies for our upcoming climb over the Simplon Pass into Italy.

The Simplon Pass is a 20-kilometer climb that climbs 1,500 meters, with an average gradient of 7.5%. I eagerly awaited the climb. It would be a test of strength I could boast about for years to come. For the next forty years, whether on a Saturday morning group ride or at a bike shop chit chatting about the latest gear, I could always begin my conversation with: *When I climbed the Swiss Alps on a loaded tandem . . .* Katy's ego, however, is less demanding than mine. She approached the climb with cautious optimism, wondering if there was an easier way to the limon gelatos on the other side.

The climb started out steep. A winding switchback brought us high above the village of Brig. The road then pushed into the mountains, climbing higher and higher. As we rode, cattle bells rang in the distance and each passing car slowed down, the drivers shouting encouragement and pumping their fists in support. This only solidified Katy's conviction that we were crazy, but I just imagined we were professional cyclists climbing the Alpe d'Huez or Mont Ventoux.

We got into a good cadence, and we cruised. The gradient was steep, but manageable, and compared to the too-steep hills in England, this climb allowed for a decent cadence that didn't terrorize our quads.

After about two hours the tunnels began, not tunnels that cut through the mountain to the other side, but tunnels carved out of the side of the mountain when there was no room for a road. Expansive bridges carried us over steep gorges, with raging rivers far below. When the summit finally came into view we met our final obstacles, several tunnels under construction. For the last three kilometers, each tunnel narrowed to a single lane, with alternating one-way traffic. We waited for oncoming traffic to pass and then exploded into the dark tunnel, our headlight flashing, and pedaling our hearts out. Adrenaline fueled the fire in our legs.

"Come on Katy, we gotta go faster before some semi-truck comes barreling down toward us."

We pedaled liked we had never pedaled and emerged on the summit victorious. Simplon Pass – 2,048 meters. Victory.

We snapped some photos to document our conquest, and then sat down for lunch in a parking lot behind an abandoned hotel. I had just torn into a baguette-Camembert-sausage sandwich when a Belgian couple and a few Italians emerged from their campers. Casual introductions turned into a more lively conversation, and we finally accepted the Italians' un-turn-down-able offer of a glass of wine with dinner, and to go hiking with them in the morning. Our Italian friends consisted of two separate families, but deciphering which kids belonged to which parents was impossible. Lino, the grandfather and also an older version of Robert de Niro, seemed to hold absolute authority over the group.

After we finished our sandwiches, I went for a swim in a nearby lake and Katy relaxed in the sun and read her book. This is the way man was supposed to live: conquering mountain passes, bathing in alpine lakes, and planning hiking routes for the morning with complete strangers. Back at the parking lot we started boiling some water on our small camping stove, intending to cook some tortellini we had been carrying since Geneva. The Belgians noticed our stove's slow progress and took pity on us (two kids from the States headed to Istanbul via bike often elicited sympathetic behavior). They offered us the use of the stove inside their camper, while Lino, Roberto and Davida (grandfather, father and son) grabbed a picnic table and two chairs for us from the nearby hotel.

I got the tortellini out of our pannier and set it on the table. Placing a package of pasta on a table in front of a lively group of Italians was, I quickly found out, an act with serious ramifications. In an instant, Lino and Roberto started shouting a civilization's worth of culinary knowledge at me, most of it in Italian. Half a dozen other family members formed a half circle around us, frequently nodding in agreement. Italian, I learned, is best spoken when discussing food and, compared to French or German, requires adding an extra vowel to the end of every word – *tortellini . . . cinco minuto . . . molta gustoso . . . buon appetito*. For over an hour, energetic and authentic Italian culture was thrown at us, atop a 2,048 meter pass in the Swiss Alps before we had even reached the Italian border. I suppose it makes sense for Italy to station their citizens at all their borders and ensure any visitor to the country gets a warm welcome in advance of actually entering the country.

We were instructed in all things tortellini – how long it takes to cook, how to tell when the pasta was done, how much I should enjoy it, the legend of Lucrezia Borgia and the origin of tortellini. They also applauded me for having tomatoes with my tortellini – bravo, bravo, bravo. *Glad I didn't blow that one.* They weren't giving me their opinions about tortellini; they were giving me the facts. Facts, it appeared, that any self respecting Italian learns in their youth. Facts which are immutable and non-negotiable.

After covering the basics once, we started over at the beginning, as Roberto tried to explain what seasonings to add to our boiling water. Neither Katy nor I could understand, so a game of charades followed. We first guessed salt and pepper by typical salt and pepper handshaking motions – no, no, no, Roberto replied. Katy's next guess was a bouillon cube, but we struggled to translate or act out the word bouillon.

"Moooooo." I imitated a cow, hoping it would be interpreted as beef bouillon.

"Bravo, bravo, bravo," the Italians shouted in unison. We accepted their offer, and Davida raced off to Lino's van and returned with a bouillon cube. This feat brought us one step closer to dinner.

A rather comical evening followed. To explain our trip, I got out our map of Europe and showed them our route and destination. Lino realized we had a good amount of time to travel, and insisted we visit his home in Florence, what he called the *capital d'Italia*. This erroneous claim led to a long argument, with Lino claiming Florence was the capital, while the rest argued that Rome is the capital. Never argue with an Italian. After dinner, our repeated attempts to decline a glass of wine were refused, so Katy and I turned to each other and said, "When *almost* in Italy?"

The next morning we had tea in their van before setting off on our family hike (we were now part of the family). It was a perfect day for a hike: a warm sun, a blue sky, and the Jungfrau and the Eiger in the distance. We made a valiant attempt to communicate, but our conversations repeatedly hit the language barrier. After this had happened three or four times, Roberto's wife would recite, in slow but perfect British English, the only English sentence she knew, "The cat is on the table." For the rest of the five-hour hike, every time our English-Italian translations failed, we just smiled and said in unison, "The cat is on the table."

Back at the camper, we reluctantly turned down a spaghetti dinner and headed, officially, into Italy. Before our much anticipated descent, we passed a terrifying road sign: a picture of a truck going downhill with flames coming from the tires and the words: 19km – 10% grade. Gnarly. I pulled over and tightened both our brakes in anticipation of the fastest descent of our life. The road started out windy and we leaned into the turns. When traffic disappeared I took up both lanes and imagined we were on a downhill ski course. When the road straightened out, we crept up to 50 and 60mph and I sat up as tall as I could to catch the wind, which would slow us down without using our brakes. I didn't want them to be like the sign, and catch on fire. At this speed, hitting a single rock or hole in the road with tires no more than an inch and a half wide would spell disaster. I gritted my teeth and calculated every turn. We approached semi trucks, crawling down the mountain in their lowest gear, and flew by them in the passing lane. When we reached the Italian border, Katy finally spoke, "Don't ever do that again. I thought I was going to die."

"Hey, I was just starting to get the hang of it," I replied.

I squirted some water onto our brakes and they instantly sizzled. We waited for them to cool off before continuing. We didn't want to add to the horror stories we'd heard of overheated brakes leading to wheel failure and absolute catastrophes.

Two days later, we were in Como, Italy and again discussing Italian cuisine.

"And alfredo? Do you eat this sauce with your pasta?" Katy asked Sileno, our WS host. Sileno's wife was visiting their daughter in the Canary Islands that weekend, so Sileno was in charge of all hosting duties.

"Alfredo? *No capisco*," he answered, and again apologized for his limited English. *What? How can an Italian not know about alfredo? As in Fettucine Alfredo, hello?*

"Al – fred – o?" I repeated the word for the third time, assuming it impossible that an Italian, a man who had just cooked us a homemade pasta dinner, had never heard of alfredo. Sileno served our pasta to us first that evening, before salad or breadsticks, because "pasta is the most important part of the meal."

"No, I never hear of this," Sileno again answered, this time in English, so we wouldn't ask him again.

The moment I saw Sileno, I admired him. He was twice my age, but I instantly knew he was the type of person I wanted to be when I grew up. He wore a pair of sharp slacks, dark leather shoes and a button-up dress shirt. His apartment was clean and welcoming, but not extravagant. As he cooked dinner, he hummed a tune and enjoyed the routine work of boiling water and checking to see if the noodles were done for his twenty-something-year-old visitors. After dinner, we strolled through town. He related its history and showed us the cathedral, where he sings in the choir, and an original stone road built by the Romans 2,000 years prior. In the morning, he rode his bike to work. He lives a simple and meaningful life. He also happens to live in one of the most beautiful cities in Europe, which is a bonus.

After our standstill on Alfredo, I resorted to Wikipedia to clear up the confusion. I pointed to the Italian name for the sauce, *pasta al burro e parmigiano* (pasta with butter and parmesan) and he immediately responded, "Si, si, si, bravo, bravo" as if to say, why didn't you say that in the first place?

On our walk through town, we stopped at Gelateria Lariana (Lungo Lario Trento, 5, Como, Italy – you should go!) and had the best gelato of our entire trip. The scoops were the size of softballs, the limon made Katy's face cringe (as it should), and the nocciola was creamy delicious. An evening stroll with gelato – one of Italy's simple pleasures.

The next day Katy and I split up. Not for good, just for the day. Our ride the previous day had been minimally delightful. On our third or fourth climb of the day, I felt Katy was slacking in her pedaling efforts, again. Instead of asking if she was pedaling (because I knew she'd give me the same answer), I decided to slack on my pedaling efforts. *There, how do **you** like having to do most of the work?* Katy didn't say anything, but responded by also pedaling less. *Well if you're not going to pedal, neither am I.* This silent standoff went back and forth, until we were *barely* moving; it would have been more practical to walk. Or communicate.

Many couples complain that their busy lives don't allow for enough time together. We had the opposite problem – too much time together. Six weeks on a tandem would be long for any couple; we were just getting started. I took the bike and she took the bus and we met 42 kilometers later at a hostel in Mennagio (where eight members of my family had slept in four bunk beds just a few years earlier). Someone once said that distance makes the heart grow fonder. For us, it didn't require very much distance, just more than the three feet between the front and rear seats of our bike.

The next morning's sunny forecast failed and we woke up to a slight drizzle. *Ah, hell. Not this again.* Katy looked out the window and agony melted her usual smile.

"We've done this before," Katy sighed as we pedaled out of town.

The drizzle turned to a steady rain and our squishy toes returned in an instant. We persisted for four hours, until we reached the town of Sondrio and took shelter in a grocery store. We peeled off our wet clothes and checked the weather forecast.

"This isn't going to work," Katy muttered, as onlookers projected their pity onto us.

"What? What's the matter?" I asked.

"The weather channel says ten days of rain. What do you want to do?"

"Ten days?" I asked.

"Yep. It looks like this storm is going to follow us through Italy and into Austria and Germany."

We weighed our options for about five minutes, and made a quick decision. "Let's get out of here."

Two hours later we were on a train, along with our bike, headed south, and away from the dark waterlogged clouds.

"A couple hours in a train is like five days on a bike," Katy mentioned, as our train pulled into the Milan station.

"Then should we keep going?" I asked.

"Might as well."

Three hours later, we arrived in Bologna, Italy, a week's ride to the southeast. I had broken my cardinal rule: never take alternate means of transportation when cycling is possible. In Sondrio, we were only a day's ride from the Stelvio, a legendary Italian pass that makes the Simplon Pass look like a warmup. I do regret not toughing out the bad weather, as climbing the Stelvio would have been wonderful, but on that occasion, another rule – "Don't make this trip utterly miserable" – seemed to have won out.

The next morning, after a hot and stifling night in a cement hostel with no fan and no breeze, we explored the town and Bologna University. Built in 1088, the school is Europe's oldest university, predating Oxford by just 8 years. The surrounding neighborhood is covered in graffiti and was a Jewish ghetto during the Second World War. We spent a bit of time imagining the lives of the many visitors over the past thousand years, before riding off to an LDS church service.

"Sorry, you can't bring your bike inside," two cheery missionaries informed us, "but you can lock it up outside on the fence." The night before, at the Cathedral of St. Peter, an usher let us leave our bike inside. Today, our church's own missionaries were giving us the cold shoulder. So much for hospitality.

Our ride that day was hot, really hot. The thermometers at the Banco Poplare in Bentigovoglio said it was 100 degrees. It did not take long before we started daydreaming of mountains and rain. Dehydrated and defeated, we pulled over and unloaded a handful of Euro coins to a man with a white truck full of giant, juicy watermelons. The corners of our mouths were painted red by the time we polished off our last slice. It's the only time we've ever eaten an entire watermelon in one sitting.

Around dusk, we cycled along the banks of the Po River in search of somewhere to sleep. In typical Mormon fashion, I assumed our search efforts would be blessed for attending church that morning. The riverbank was rural and secluded, but the tall grasses and damp ground weren't conducive to pitching a tent. As we rode along the river, I thought about my Grandpa Dick who had crossed this river valley in the spring of 1945 during World War II.

As I said earlier, I like to think that some of my personality traits come from my Grandpa Dick. My memories of my grandpa are mainly of him sitting quietly at the end of the dining room table during Sunday dinners, and then retreating to his old couch in the basement to watch golf or basketball as soon as the collective noise of his 8 children and 32 grandchildren became overbearing. I always liked that basement; the head of an 8-point elk is mounted on the wall and the TV only comes with 8 channels.

Growing up I was told that my grandpa fought in the "ski troops" during World War II. He was drafted into the army when he was 18 years old, but persuaded the Army to let him join the 10th Mountain Division so he reported to Camp Hale, Colorado where he taught all his senior officers how to ski. He said teaching his officers how to ski was a riot, because every time they were about to fall, instead of falling backwards onto their butt as any skier would, they would instead resort to instincts they mastered in parachute training and jump forward, grab their knees and roll "ass over applecart" down the mountain.

As Katy and I rode down the quiet and peaceful two lane highway, without a person in sight, I thought about my grandpa and how it must have been so much different when he was here 70 years ago. The 10th Mountain Division landed in Naples, Italy, down in the south, and then marched north to Bologna and northeast to Udine. We cycled a route from Bologna to Udine similar to the route they had taken, and I thought it appropriate to spend a couple nights camping out under the stars as I'm sure they did.

"Why not down there," I suggested, pointing to a small dock on the river. "The dock is dry, flat, and the breeze off the river will keep us cool."

"If you say so."

Adjacent to the dock, but no more than thirty feet from the road, was a rusty handheld water pump with a sign, painted in red, that stated: Non Potable. We waited until it was dark and motorists wouldn't be able to see us, and then stripped naked. Not wanting to get our feet muddy, we stood on a half broken wooden crate, filled up water bottles with the Non Potable water and had a nice wash by pouring bottles over us. A shower is a shower, regardless of how it happens. Around 11:30, we retired to the dock and fell asleep.

Clunk, clunk, clunk. The sound of footsteps on the metal walkway woke me up and I turned to face the sound. At first I was nervous, assuming we were in trouble for trespassing, but the full moon showed that the visitors were just four teenagers. *Surely when they see us they'll go on their way, this dock is taken.*

I was wrong. They stepped right over our sleeping bags, sat down about an arm's length away, turned on some music and started snapping their lighters. *Well isn't this great. An entire river for these kids to enjoy their marijuana, and we're bunking up for the night.* After an un-sleepable hour or two, their music decayed further into some sort of Italian Reggae-Techno and I realized any sort of social norms or acceptable public behavior was unlikely to kick in.

"Excuse me, we're sleeping here," I shouted.

I pressed the issue, to leave them with no option other than to get up and leave. Wrong again. They turned the music down, but only slightly, and then pretended to sleep. At 3:45am they finally left and we got a good two hours of uninterrupted sleep before the roar of fishing boats started our day.

We reluctantly got up. I fought off the morning's mosquitoes while Katy wringed the morning dew out of her sleeping bag. I had opted not to sleep in my sleeping bag, but snuck my feet into Katy's when I got cold.

The scenery of the Po River Delta is identical to the Mississippi Delta: flat agricultural farmland flanking a giant, sleepy river. We entered the town of Chioggia, only a couple hours from Venice, when our rear wheel shrieked out a horrific metallic sound.

"What the hell was that?" Katy hollered.

"How the hell would I know," I responded.

"Well you're in charge of our bike?"

"Well you're sitting closer to the rear wheel."

We got off the bike and Katy let out a sigh of defeat – her hopes of an evening walk through the Plaza San Marco in Venice were fading. Assuming we weren't going anywhere anytime soon, she went in search of a hotel while I tried to fix our bike. Katy was convinced we were done for, and I agreed that we probably were, but I still wanted to see what I could do. I flipped the bike over, removed the rear brake caliper and yanked out the brake pad. It was torn and shredded. I'm not sure how it came loose and got ruined, but I replaced it with a spare. After replacing it, I reattached the brake, went for a test ride and adjusted the brake cable tension.

"It's fixed. Let's go," I boasted, as soon as Katy returned.

"What?"

"I said I fixed it, we can go now," I smiled back.

"How?"

"Well, the brake pad got loose somehow, fell out and the brake rotor ruined it. I replaced it with a spare."

"You had a spare?"

"Yeah, I thought it would be a good idea," I stated, feeling like quite the mechanic.

"Wow, I'm so impressed. I never could have done that."

Katy saw a lot of crazy things on our trip, but I never saw a more *Are you kidding?* look on her face than that afternoon in Chioggia. Other, smaller problems had taken me days or weeks to fix but this dreadful shriek was remedied in no time.

* * *

Our repeated attempts to enter Venice were denied by the repeated, monotone shouting of an overweight lady seated at a desk behind a dirty plastic window, "You can't take a bike to Venice, no bikes in Venice." I asked her a fourth time, curious if she was in fact a robot. "You can't take a bike to Venice, no bikes in Venice."

The awful sleep from the previous night, combined with our weakening determination to 'tough it out' (as evidenced by jumping on a train to avoid bad weather), led us to make a terrible decision, at least in my opinion – we checked into a hotel. The hotel was nice, don't get me wrong. The soft bed, immaculate bathroom and air conditioning were all delightful. Choosing these expensive comforts instead of the nearby campground, however, started a trend that proved difficult to reverse – it would be two months before we would again set up our tent.

In Venice we explored the narrow alleyways, marveled at the gondola boat drivers, and ate a delicious dinner at Trattoria alla Madonna. The day before we were downing watermelon in the hot sun and sleeping on a boat dock, but today we were fine dining and cranking up the air conditioning.

Two days later in Udine we enjoyed our last slice of Italian pizza and then 18 kilometers further north in Tarcento had our last gelatos. We said our *arrivedercis* to Italy and began the climb over the Julian Alps into Slovenia.

"Do you know anyone who's been to Slovenia?" I asked, as we crossed the border, and the beautiful Italian landscape turned into the even more beautiful Slovenian landscape.

"I don't think so," she replied.

"Well they're missing out."

That night in Bovec, Slovenia we marveled at all the strange foods we saw, and at the impossible language written in various colors on chalkboard menus throughout town. One menu read: skuta scompami, jagnjetina, divjacina, tatarski, ljubljanski, krafi.

"Which of those do you want? Katy joked.

At a bakery, we asked what new food we should try, and in better English than I expected, a man suggested we try börek. We didn't know it at the time, but börek is a pastry made from phyllo dough and filled with cheese, spinach or meat, which originated in the Anatolian

Provinces of modern day Turkey and spread throughout the Ottoman Empire. Traveling on a bike, one kilometer and one town at a time, allowed us to see the cuisine and the culture change, sometimes dramatically, but usually very slowly. We enjoyed börek for the next couple months in Eastern Europe and Turkey, continually fascinated at how the pastry, and many other foods, would change shape, ingredients and flavors as we got closer and closer to Istanbul. But we will always remember our first börek in Bovec, Slovenia, the western most expanse of the former Yugoslavia and Ottoman Empire.

The Julian Alps are darker, greener and creepier than the French, Swiss or Italian Alps. The next morning we cycled along the Soca River, with its emerald blue wintergreen water, through the densely forested Triglavski National Park, and towards the Vrsic Pass. The pass, which was built by Russian POWs during WWI, is the highest paved road in Slovenia. The POWs managed to express all their ill feelings about being prisoners in the road's construction. It is steep, narrow and contains fifty switchbacks. Not ideal for cycling. As we climbed through the park, we approached a large amphitheater of cliffs. I couldn't imagine how our road would find a way through, but just as the road appeared to dead end into the wall of mountains in front of us, a couple of steep switchbacks sent us in a different direction, climbing up through a side canyon to the official start of our climb. The road sign read 9km, 14% grade – almost twice as steep as Simplon Pass in the Swiss Alps. Just as the going got tough, a cyclist coming down the canyon pulled over and unloaded all his leftover snacks. "You'll need these," he offered, before taking off.

The road punished us. We dropped into our easiest (but not easy enough) gear and barely forced each turn of the pedals. It was as if all the hills in England were stacked into a single climb. Switchbacks turning left offered a slight reprieve as the gradient would lessen momentarily, but turns to the right promised sudden inclines of 20+%. We passed an Australian couple, also on touring bikes, but their easier gearing offered them two or three pedal strokes for each of ours. (Katy would like to draw a little attention to this fact – not only did we climb this absurdly difficult road, but we passed other cyclists in the process.) When the summit was within sight, we both got out of the saddle, a tricky balancing act when battling fatigue on a tandem, and pushed every last ounce of energy into our pedals. Our tires finally found the flat crest of the summit and we collapsed onto our handlebars. The climb was the single greatest physical accomplishment of our trip, not to mention my life.

"Stop, stop, stop," Katy shouted later that afternoon, after our lunch in Kranjska Gora.

"What, what's the matter?"

"My stomach doesn't feel good," she declared as she darted into some trees behind someone's home, toilet paper in hand. As I waited for Katy, a car passed, but then flipped a U-turn and headed back towards me. *This isn't going to be good. Katy caught in the act.*

Two Slovenians, about our age, jumped out of the car and walked towards me. A lady in front led her husband by the hand.

"Nice bike," she exclaimed. "We also ride a tandem, because my husband is blind. Is it okay if he feels your bike?"

"Uh, sure?" I answered, a bit taken back by the uncommon question.

For five minutes, Aleš felt every part of our bike: the pedals, seats, brakes and shifters, the width of our tires, the number of spokes on our wheels and how our panniers attached to our racks. Then his wife Moica pointed out some things unique to our tandem: where the couplers were and how our brake and shifter cables attach underneath our frame.

"If you need somewhere to sleep, you can stay at our house," Moica offered.

"We would love to, thank you so much," Katy responded, feeling a bit more dignified and now out of the woods, both literally and figuratively. We made arrangements to stay with them in a few days when we reached their town of Kamnik in central Slovenia.

We spent the evening in Bled, where we walked around Lake Bled and admired its island and castle. The cover of the *Slovenia Lonely Planet* is a photo of the lake, but like many pictures, it doesn't begin to do justice to the charming town that is Bled, Slovenia. That place is magical.

The next evening we rode to Moica and Aleš' home in Kamnik, a small town about an hour north of Ljubljana.

"You know what's strange?" I asked Katy, as we approached their home.

"What?"

"We rode through a lot of Western Europe, but it wasn't until Slovenia that someone stopped us on the side of the road and invited us to stay in their home."

"Yeah, I really like this place."

We left our shoes at the door, in exchange for some slippers, and dropped our stuff in their master bedroom. They insisted we have a nice bed for the night, and they slept on their couch. Moica cooked vegetarian lasagna, fried chicken and a tomato and cucumber salad for dinner. We talked for hours about tandem cycling and how they compensate for Aleš' vision impairment. Moica always rides in the front, and is in charge of all the shifting, steering and braking. This works fine, until they ride through town and Aleš demands they shift into a harder gear and pick up the pace so everyone will see how fast they are going. Other nuances included knowing when to stop or start, leaning into turns, remembering where they are and bicycle maintenance. Even though he can't see, Aleš still does all of his own bike maintenance. We asked all our questions about Slovenia before Moica asked us a question, "Is there maybe a little more room for you . . . to eat some more?"

"Of course," we said in unison.

Struklji is a typical Slovenian dessert, made with cottage cheese within pastry dough. It's placed in a wet rag and baked in the oven and then topped with sugary breadcrumbs and powdered sugar. It's not too sweet, but quite hearty, like all Slovenian food. The best way to understand Slovenian food, in fact, is to assume it's late Fall and you've just gotten home from a long day working in the field and you're looking for something warm and hearty.

In the morning, we invited ourselves to their Catholic Mass. Compared to a Mormon service, where things can get a bit noisy, a profound reverence filled the cathedral. Their church was a simple place for worship and nothing else. The priest was the spitting image of the priest from *The Princess Bride*, and I was hoping there would be a marriage to announce, preferably of a girl named Princess Buttercup.

After church, we took the bus to Ljubljana, the coolest European capital I had never heard of, and that you probably can't pronounce. The city has everything a great city should have: a river running through town, a pedestrian only downtown area, numerous cafes, street vendors, live music, a castle on a hill, friendly people around every corner, lots of cheap and delicious food to try, and free public WiFi. After a meal or two, we stumbled into Cacao, a little ice cream shop on the bank of the Ljubljanica River, and shared five ice cream cones. Five is a good number when it comes to ice cream cones.

The next day, cycling east from Ljulbljana towards the Austrian border, was picture perfect. Any moment from our ride could have been put on a postcard. All of the usual requirements for a perfect day were present, accented by the dark orange-tiled roofs of traditional Yugoslavian homes and villages throughout the rolling hills. In the morning, we visited the market in Maribor (they don't use the term "farmer's market" because, unlike Americans, they assume all food comes from a farmer). We picked up some homemade cheese, sour cherry yogurt, sausage and a bag of slives (Eastern European plums). Slovenia prides itself on sustainable agriculture and locally sourced food from small farms. To pay for the slives, they were placed on a scale and the register read €1.44.

"No, no, no. €1.20 is okay," a kind old lady demanded.

Katy gave the lady €1.20, and immediately she returned €0.20 as change. That's my kind of shopping.

Before Katy and I left home, one of our goals was to find a country we would live in at some point in the future. Slovenia wins. It wasn't a country we originally planned to visit. Our detour to Slovenia only happened because we had changed our route in Sondrio, Italy to avoid the rain of the Alps. We had taken a train to Bologna and our new route led us to the outdoor recreation town of Bovec, the Vrsic pass, the Julian Alps, warmhearted Slovenes and a charming capital and delicious food that won our hearts, and taste buds. We entered Slovenia with no expectations, but Slovenia delivered consistently great days and became our favorite country (thus far).

A CLUNKING SOUND

"I don't want to go to America," Angela commented after dinner. "I don't want to see Sevi hallucinate."

"That sounds terrible. Will he *actually* hallucinate?" Katy asked.

"I think so. They all do," Angela answered.

Katy and Angela were chatting away in the kitchen, while Sevi and I were in the guest bedroom, looking at his bikes and race trophies.

We were in Graz, Austria, just north of the Slovenian border, discussing Sevi's recent and upcoming races. In contrast to just speculating about racing, as I often do, here I was talking to a pro. Three days before we arrived, Sevi had won the Tortour, a 1,000-kilometer race around Switzerland, in 36 hours and 18 minutes. He thought about quitting as he battled snow and freezing temperatures on the Furka Pass, but found renewed legs a dozen hours later and made a successful final attack. In June 2015, the summer after we arrived in Graz, he was scheduled to compete in the Race Across America.

The Race Across America is "the world's toughest bike race." It's not like the Tour de France or other stage races, where cyclists only compete for a few hours per day, riding as little as 145 kilometers in a day. By contrast, RAAM is a pure endurance event, a race against the clock. The clock starts ticking in Oceanside, CA and the cyclists race for eight to ten days, almost non-stop – sleeping just two or three hours a night – until they reach Annapolis, Maryland, 3,000 miles away. Overexertion mixes synergistically with sleep deprivation, and hallucinations become common.

Christoph Strasser set the course record in 2014 – 7 days 15 hours and 56 minutes, with an average speed of 16.42mph. Jure Robic has won the race five times, also a record. Christoph, a good friend of Sevi's, also lives in Graz, while Jure is from Jesenice, Slovenia, a town just across the border. For reasons I don't understand, the Slovenian-Austrian border is the endurance cycling capital of the world. Americans have nothing on these guys.

Sevi inspired me. It wasn't just his recent victory, racing through the cold over 2,000 meter passes, and it wasn't his meticulous training plans and eating regimen. What inspired me is that Sevi is an otherwise normal thirty-year-old, who lives in a normal apartment with a normal girlfriend and, when he's not on his bike, works as a social worker, helping people to solve problems of poverty and street drug use. His success as a cyclist hasn't come from any magical gifts, but from dedicated, hard work.

I've often talked about being an endurance cyclist, and maybe even riding in the Race Across America one day. But, I've let work and school prevent me from moving beyond casual weekend rides and beginning serious training. Sevi taught me that this should not, and must not, be the case. As Andy Dufresne said, "better get busy living, or get busy dying."

(Update: After we finished our cycling trip and returned to Michigan, Sevi raced and won RAAM, with a time of 8 days 18 hours and 17 minutes. In support, Katy and I got a bucket of red paint and painted the words "Go Sevi Go" underneath an Austrian Flag on a giant white sheet, and nailed it between two giant wooden poles. We drove down to Southern Ohio and met him on an unlit rural road at 11pm to cheer our hearts out, and wave our flag to do our best to motivate him, because he said, "If you come cheer for me I will take a ten-minute break for you." He kept his promise. After our short conversation, (which from a medical standpoint had all the signs of mild delirium) Sevi continued down the road towards Maryland, with his support car following him with a giant spotlight, blaring Michael Jackson from a loudspeaker to keep him awake on his 210-hour bike ride. Our flag and enthusiastic cheering must have been a big hit, because a couple of days later Sevi was featured on Austria's National News and we were seen in the background cheering him on. Sevi is awesome.)

In the morning, we rode northeast towards Vienna, three days away – and if you're familiar with European geography, or happen to be looking at a map, you'll notice it is somewhat in the wrong direction from our ultimate destination. Why ride northeast when Istanbul was southeast? It's a valid question. Our original route, before we decided to ride through the Alps, included Vienna, Budapest, Belgrade, and Sarajevo before reaching the Adriatic Sea. Now that the Alps were behind us, we wanted to get back on our original route. This decision added 700 kilometers to our ride, but over a year of cycling, what's 700 kilometers?

At Sevi's suggestion, we cycled along hilly back roads, and Katy serenaded me with *The Sound of Music*. Katy soon forgot about the unnecessary 700km detour, and her pedaling was now fueled with jubilation for the beautiful ride. For both of us, *The Sound of Music* and Austria are synonymous. I can't think of one without the other. In Austria, however, no one has ever seen the show. They've heard of it, but that's it. Cycling through Austria made me wonder if God, after creating such beautiful European landscapes, got to the Midwest of the United States and said, "I'm really tired. Flat and boring is just going to have to do."

"Shift into an easier gear, please," Katy demanded at the bottom of another hill.

"I can't. The derailleur won't shift," I answered. The derailleur had worked fine in Italy but became progressively worse in Slovenia.

"What do you mean, won't shift?"

"I mean, I push the shifter lever on my handlebars, and the derailleur moves, but it doesn't shift the chain from the middle to small ring."

"Well, why don't you fix it?"

"I tried. It didn't work."

Katy wasn't satisfied with my "I tried once and then gave up" attitude. She confronts problems head on and drops everything else in a heartbeat to solve a problem. Not me. I put problems on the back burner and hope they'll go away. At the next hill she spoke up.

"So are we stuck in the middle ring the rest of the trip?"

"I guess so."

"Well that's ridiculous."

"What's ridiculous is that this derailleur is brand new and doesn't work. What do you want me to do about it?" I asked. It was quiet again. Conversations on a tandem don't have to move quickly, we have all day. After a while I broke the silence. "Unless of course you want to fix it."

"Sure, let's stop."

Katy kneeled down on the cement and attempted to adjust the de-railleur. I started to laugh. I love my wife, but it would have taken a miracle for her to fix this problem. She poked around for a while, and then I manually moved the chain to the small ring in anticipation of the upcoming hill. We got back on. On the other side of the hill, I shifted back to the middle ring so we could ride at a decent pace.

"I have a plan," I stated, as another hill approached.

"What's that?"

"Before we get to the hill, I'll shift the front derailleur into the small ring and then stop pedaling. You unclip your right foot and push the chain onto the small ring, just like our derailleur should be able to do, but isn't. When your foot is in place I'll start pedaling and the small ring will pick up the chain. Then I'll stop pedaling so you can clip back in."

"Are you kidding me? We bought a $5,000 bike, but we're going to use my foot as our front derailleur?"

"Yep."

"Can't we just stay in the small ring?"

"No, the easy gear is too slow for the flats. And try to shift gears real fast, so we don't lose too much momentum."

Our plan took some time to master, but the rolling hills afforded ample practice. After a day or two it became so second nature that the process only took a second or two and required no verbal communica-tion. A common problem turned into a unique, and almost enjoyable, relationship between Katy, the bike, and our shifters and derailleurs. I suppose a better mechanic would have fixed that problem in a couple minutes, but we didn't get the derailleur properly adjusted until we reached Thessaloniki, Greece, a month later.

The next day we reached Wiesmath, a small Austrian town, and stayed with Lucas, an incredibly friendly 28-year-old, who wore a black Rolling Stones t-shirt with a big red tongue on the front. We sat down to dinner on his parents' patio, looking out over the endless green hills, and talked about faith, devotion, and personal testimony. Lucas was raised Catholic, but felt church and religion were rigid and impersonal. He moved to Vienna after high school in search of different people and new ideas. He was very interested in our commitment to faith, and we compared Salt Lake City Mormonism and Wiesmath Catholicism in detail.

When it got cold, Lucas brought out dessert and blankets and our conversation continued. In the morning, Lucas packed our panniers with leftovers from dinner, and we continued towards Vienna.

"Do you hear that?" I asked Katy, as we descended down to Hochwolkersdorf (best pronounced in a German accent.)

"Hear what?"

"That clicking, clunking sound."

"No, I didn't hear anything."

At the next intersection I let up on the pedals to check our map and immediately the strange clunking sound returned.

"Did you hear it that time?" I asked.

"Nope."

I pedaled for ten seconds, then stopped, hoping this would elicit the clunking sound for Katy to hear. But nothing happened. I tried again. Nothing. I inspected the derailleurs, the couplers, and the wheels, but everything seemed okay. When we reached Vienna, the traffic picked up and our steady pace became stop and go. At the third or fourth intersection the clunking sound returned, this time a bit louder.

"I heard it that time," Katy exclaimed as we coasted to a red light. "What was that?"

"I don't know, but it doesn't sound good."

* * *

Vienna is a city with a history. It was a military camp for the Roman Empire, and then the capital of the Babenberg Dynasty, the Austrian Habsburgs, the Austrian Empire, the Austrian-Hungarian Empire, and now the Republic of Austria. In 1913, Adolf Hitler, Sigmund Freud, Joseph Stalin, and Josip Tito all lived in Vienna and visited the same coffeehouses. It was also the home of Beethoven and Mozart. I can only imagine the conversations, and the music. Today, it is ranked the second most livable city in the world. If my brother Eli were with us, everyday items such as benches, buses, and garbage cans would have elicited substantial sarcasm, "Oh wow! This place is so *livable*. And I'm not talking about just staying alive. I'm talking about *really living*."

On our first night in Vienna, Katy and I chased our host Daniel through town on our bike. It was a wild ride – weaving through traffic and dodging trolleys – and a wonderful introduction to a wonderful city. We rode up a cobblestone driveway to a beautiful white building, adorned in sculptures, with a large copper statue and a water fountain out front. "What building is this?" we asked.

"It's our White House," Daniel answered. "Except homeless people bathe in the fountain, and you can ride your bike up to the front door." After a while, these more-splendid-than-anything-back-home buildings became commonplace.

The next day, we went to Zum Figlmüller and had Austria's national dish, Weiner Schnitzel. To make schnitzel, veal is hammered very thin, coated with flour, eggs, and bread crumbs and deep fried. It's incredibly delicious. We washed the fried lunch down with an Almdudler, an Austrian soda, and then stocked up on Manner chocolate wafers (the best) before reaching the market in search of more food.

At first the market was familiar: local produce, French cheeses, Belgian chocolates, gelato, and pizza. But then we turned the corner and entered an entirely new world not previously seen on our trip: olives, hummus, falafel, gyros, and dozens and dozens of spices. WOW! That market had more variety than the past 3,000 kilometers. We walked down the aisle, tongues hanging out of our faces, and drooled over the new foods that awaited us as we rode east. Vienna is the far east of Western Europe or the far west of Eastern Europe. Whichever way you're traveling, it's where things begin to change.

After the food market, we crossed the street and entered the flea market. Here, things really changed. Instead of upscale shops full of crafts or other goods, items for sale were strewn about on blankets that covered the ground. Heaps of clothing sat in an empty parking lot, while middle-aged Middle Eastern and African looking men rifled through piles of tools. Hundreds of books, in half a dozen languages, were stacked on the pavement. A young boy shouted, "Shoes, fifty cents."

That night at dinner, we talked to Daniel about the changes we had seen and the joys of bike touring.

"As a kid I visited London a couple of times, but always by plane," he began. "I got on the plane and magically arrived in London a few hours later. But England is so different from Austria. I always wondered how the culture and architecture and cuisine of Vienna changed into London? When I went on my first bike tour I rode every kilometer from my house to Big Ben and I saw exactly how Vienna turned into London."

Warmshowers hosts are all very different, but they all agree on one thing: the bicycle is the best way to travel. Cycling forces you to go slow. Which is a good thing. When you only cover 80 kilometers in a day, you don't just *stop* to smell the roses, you smell the roses all day long. Cars race to reach their destinations on time, but on a bike, there is no destination. Each moment is why we've come. Going slow allows us ample time to stare at our surroundings and think about the life around us. We stare at facial expressions, and admire the subtle changes in the landscape and agriculture. Often times landscape and culture changes very slow, but other times, as was the case in Vienna, a drastic change of cuisine and outdoor markets stops you in your tracks and lets you know that you're now thousands of kilometers from where you started.

To vacation from our vacation, we took a bus (a serious alternate transportation violation, I know) up to Prague. Weekend highlights included a carnivore's feast at Smíchovský radniční sklípek where we enjoyed an appetizer of deep fried camembert (the French would have disapproved) and a towering pile of venison sausage, roasted pork belly, roast beef, salami, herring and pickled sausage. The food was great. The thick cigarette smoke that hugged the ceiling fans in the dusky basement restaurant was not so great. Each morning we walked the Charles Bridge in a thick fog and then searched for the town's best pastries before our return bus to Vienna. The bus flew past dozens of small towns, and all I could think was, "We're missing the best part of this country."

We got back to Vienna three days later, and that night departed the city under a double rainbow, and rode across the Danube towards Bratislava, Slovakia. We followed the EuroVelo 6 bike route, hoping a signed bike path would be easy to follow in the dark. It wasn't. We got lost, trudged through some mud, and arrived at a hostel in downtown Bratislava sometime after midnight.

The next day we entered Hungary. At the border, Katy quoted our hosts from Maribor, Slovenia: "I cannot recommend for you to cycle in Hungary." Sometimes we follow others advice, sometimes we toss it to the wind. We crossed the border and saw two road signs, both equally scary. MAGYARORSZAG, printed in a bold, white font on a blue background circled by yellow EU stars.

"What is that?" I asked, wondering where Hungary was.

"I don't know, but that word is crazy."

"I guess the Hungarians spell Hungary differently than we do."

The other sign consisted of images that best translate to No Tractors, No Horse Drawn Buggies, No Bicycles. *Great. We've been in Hungary for less than a kilometer and we're already breaking the law.* With no other alternate roads in sight, we pressed on.

That night in Gyor, we ate Fisherman's Stew with catfish, which made us feel like we were back home in the Mississippi Delta. After slurping my last spoonful of broth, we got ice cream cones and meandered through town. It was the third best ice cream of our trip, after Cacao in Ljubljana, and gelato in Como (but who's counting?). Gyor surprised me. I didn't expect much from an unheard of town in northwest Hungary, but Gyor delivered.

The next day was Katy's birthday, so I generously offered her a train ride to Budapest and an afternoon at a spa, instead of a frantic,

140-kilometer race to meet our WS host before she left for the evening. Katy declined. We put our heads down and rode like the wind.

"Did he come into you ass up?" Katy asked, somewhere between Zsámbék and Páty.

"He sure did," I replied. I pulled the giant bee stinger out of my chest and showed it to Katy. I was riding shirtless, as I had done since Venice, in hopes of removing my near-permanent cyclist's tan.

"Man, this hurts like hell," I yelled.

"Now do you believe me?"

"I guess so."

"You laugh at me when I scream and cry about being stung by one of these crazy monster bees, but when it happens to you, you're not so tough yourself," Katy exclaimed.

"Well I've never experienced this type of bee attack before. I mean, we haven't seen any bees our whole trip, and out of nowhere we are both stung ten minutes apart."

We inhaled lunch in fifteen minutes and immediately resumed race mode arriving in Budapest with enough time to spare for second lunch. From a distance I saw a vertical spit, with crispy rotating meat, and a man wielding a three-foot long knife. I ordered "the works" and savored a warm pita stuffed to the brim with lamb, tomatoes, red cabbage, onions, fries, and tzatziki sauce. Heavenly. Cooking meat this way, on a vertical rotisserie, is an invention of the Ottoman Empire. Love those Ottomans. (An entire civilization that, in my opinion, is built on putting your feet up, sitting back, and watching meat spin.)

"What's with the fat people here?" I asked Katy, after another order of the delicious kebab.

Katy shook her head in disgust. "You're having your third lunch of the day, and you're wondering why people here are fat?"

"Well at least I exercise," I replied. "But seriously, this is the first country where we've seen so many fat people. What gives?"

I wasn't being judgmental, merely stating the obvious. For eight weeks, people had been relatively lean and healthy, but in Hungary obesity reared its fat head everywhere we looked – kids at the supermarket, the man driving the mail truck, and folks sitting on the side of the road. At dinner that night, our host Andi offered her thoughts on

Hungary's weight problem, "The poor people just eat a lot of bread, so they get bigger."

In addition to obesity, poverty was also apparent. The day before we had crossed some railroad tracks and observed the familiar, but previously unseen, sights of poverty: dirt paths between homes, corrugated metal fences and roofs, and people bathing in the river. We also hit our first pothole in Hungary. I've read that obesity and poverty correlate, but it was eye opening to see both of these maladies appear overnight, after eight weeks on the road. The night before in Gyor, a kid stuck out his hand and asked me for some money when we bought our ice cream. It was the first time it happened on our trip, but wouldn't be the last.

The next morning we went to a Trek dealer in downtown Budapest to fix the clunking in our rear wheel. I decided the free wheel mechanism inside the rear hub was the culprit, but had no idea how to fix it. We arrived at the shop on a Saturday afternoon, just as it was closing, and were told to return on Monday. Bad planning on our part. We decided against waiting, and planned to stop at the next Trek dealer in Szeged, Hungary, only a couple day's ride to the south.

Sixty kilometers south of Budapest, we approached a carnival style celebration just off the main road, locked our bike to a tree and went to investigate. The crowd was seated at multiple rows of outdoor picnic tables. Large black pots – each one large enough to hold a child – stood at the end of each table. Each pot hung from a teepee of giant wooden sticks, simmering over a pile of red-hot coals. I peered into one of the pots. Giant bubbles burst through a dark red broth, and potatoes, carrots, and meat floated to the surface. *Goulash. Gotta get some of this goulash.* I looked for a cashier, but it appeared the feast wasn't for sale; groups of families and friends were cooking their own meals. *Hmm.*

The simplest option to acquire some goulash would have been to ask a direct question: "Can I have a bowl of that?," however, I rarely muster up such courage. Instead, I lingered at a table, but no goulash was offered, so I went to the next pot. No more than ten seconds passed before a lady pointed to the man at the end of the table and said, "He's the chef." We made eye contact.

"I've never seen such a large pot. What are you cooking?" I asked, playing dumb. I assume it was the equivalent of going to a barbeque in Arkansas and saying, "What's on the grill? Meat?"

I doubt he understood anything I said, but that didn't matter. Five minutes later, Katy and I were part of the family, enjoying a bowl of paprika-spiced goulash, homemade pickles, raisin wine, spicy peppers filled with sauerkraut, and fried fish. People love food. And people love to talk about themselves. Get people talking about themselves and their food, and it leads to a delicious (and complimentary) lunch every time. We arrived as strangers, but when we left two hours later, we said goodbye to friends.

Fifteen kilometers later, we stopped at a grocery store. Katy went inside for some water, and my attention turned to an eight-foot-tall, twenty-foot-wide, white container for donated clothing. Rotating doors, about one foot square, near the top of the container, allowed people to deposit old clothes, but they made it nearly impossible for a person to take something out of the container. *Nearly* impossible. An old black single speed bicycle, with garbage bags hanging from the handlebars and other possessions strapped to the rear rack, leaned against the rusty, white container. Two feet, wearing red flip flops, stood on the bike, one on the seat and the other on the handlebars. The entire upper body of this individual was deep inside the clothing bin. Occasionally the bike would wiggle, but the legs kept their balance. For ten minutes, a face never emerged, but continued the dark search for free clothing. I later inquired about the incident, and was told not to worry: it was only the gypsies.

Ten more kilometers down the road – it was an action packed day – we crossed a levee on a dirt road, and stopped to check directions near a small bar with a ping pong table out front.

"Hey there, where ya from?" a man asked. He was wearing blue shorts above the knee, and his belly protruded into his red t-shirt. His Crocs told me he was a casual fellow.

"The United States," one of us answered.

"Come, let's have a drink."

It wasn't a suggestion. It was a demand. We sipped Coca-Cola Lights in the evening sun and talked and talked. Ernesto had learned

English on multiple fishing trips to Miami and his girlfriend, Victoria, who may have been a Russian mail order bride, also spoke good English – a rarity in rural Hungary. Ernesto offered us his dinner of goose liver and mashed potatoes. I accepted. (Katy doesn't care too much for goose.) Later that evening he called the local restaurant on our behalf, so that we could "taste all of Hungary." During a fierce ping-pong battle, a lady from the restaurant arrived on a motorbike and delivered more goulash, fried fish, and chocolate crepes with chopped almonds. Evening turned to night, and Ernesto and Victoria invited us to their home, to soak in the hot tub and spend the night. The hot tub was lukewarm and itchy; the bed hard, with a previously slept in feel. I guess that's just how some days go.

Hungary was thought provoking. Compared to prior countries, poverty was prevalent throughout Hungary – potholes, corrugated metal, obesity, gypsies, and our first beggar. But at the same time, we were showered with overwhelming hospitality. The kindness became so common we gave it a special name, Hungarian Hospitality. Is it a coincidence that hospitality and poverty coincide? Is there a reason that those who have less are willing to give more?

* * *

We rode for two more days before we reached Szeged and our rendezvous with a bike mechanic. We arrived in town early, and went straight to the Trek dealer. No one was there. It didn't look like anyone was going to be there, either. Frustrated, we went to our guesthouse and began the unpacking and check-in process. As Katy figured out the room, a guy rode by on his mountain bike and I waved him down.

"Hey, is there a bike shop around?" I asked in English, hoping for a response in English.

"Of course. Follow me," he answered.

"I took the rear wheel off our bike and followed him down the street.

"This is the best shop in town," he declared, only three minutes from our guesthouse. I explained the problem to the mechanic, who also happened to speak English, and then played a video from my iPhone that I had recorded the previous day that clearly showed the problem.

"How old is this wheel?" the mechanic asked.

"Maybe four months," I answered, not sure what answer he was looking for.

The mechanic's facial expression changed. "That's not good. We rarely see this problem, and only on really old bikes, after thirty years or tens of thousands of kilometers. You shouldn't be having this problem."

J IS FOR JUGOSLAVIA

When it comes to international travel, the bathroom is the most confusing room in the guesthouse. Bedrooms and kitchens are fairly predictable across the globe, but the bathroom is a wild card – you never know what you'll find in there, or scarier still, how to use what you might find. The first changes were subtle and not a cause for concern. Most toilets in Europe lack a flush handle, but instead contain two buttons, the smaller for liquid waste and the larger for solid waste. These toilets conserve significant amounts of water. Why they aren't common in the States, I don't know.

In Western Turkey we encountered our first squat toilet. Strange at first, they're really not so bad. And you don't have to touch anything. Instead of a bowl, a squat toilet is just a hole in the floor along with two grooved footplates. The footplates tell you where to squat so your hole lines up with the toilet's hole, something not immediately intuitive. In the corner, a bucket of water allows you to manually flush any misaligned or explosive waste. A safety tip: the footplates in Laos assume squatters are of Lao height, adjust accordingly.

Toilet paper never comes standard on the Indian Subcontinent, so I made sure that Katy's supply of TP never ran low. Ever been stranded in India with a bad case of Delhi Belly and no TP? That's some scary shit. A mini spray handle hangs on the wall next to the toilet in the nicer establishments. How someone accomplishes wiping with a Super Soaker, I'm not sure. And frankly, I don't want to find out.

The shower presents its own problem. A functional shower requires four things: water, a showerhead, space to shower and a drain. (Water pressure and hot water lift a shower from functional to delightful.) As soon as we crossed the Great Pond, these items went haywire. The first to go was the wall-mounted showerhead, replaced by the handheld showerhead. At first this was a nice idea – now I could wash those hard to reach areas! – but then we'd occasionally find a handheld showerhead without a wall mount. This complicates things. The simple process of soaping up became a constant battle of washing with one hand, while the other hand holds the water, or a back and forth between turning the water on to rinse and then turning it off again to wash. I don't like to turn the water off in the middle of my shower. The sound of running water protects me as I bathe, and lets me know that being naked is okay. Every time I was forced to turn off the water to free up my hands and lather up, I felt exposed and vulnerable.

Just as I warmed up to the handheld showerhead without a wall mount, the showering fiasco was further complicated when the shower was replaced by a bathtub, although without a shower curtain. This is a lose-lose situation. Do I stand, and risk spraying water throughout the room or do I sit naked in an empty tub? I tried both, but always lost. On too many occasions, I found myself sitting naked in an empty porcelain tub with a handheld shower head in my hand. I was in the Dark Ages. Can't someone tell these people about the shower curtain?

Beginning in Albania, guesthouses got rid of the shower or tub altogether and created the bathroom-shower fusion: a drain in the middle of a room with a shower head on one end and a toilet on the other, the walls covered in tile. Without a separated area for showering, it became possible to shower and sit on the John at the same time. I don't typically recommend this behavior. I can, however, recall one fortunate incident. In Elbasan, Albania Katy was washing her hair when she felt a rumble in her belly, a light bulb went off in her head and she seamlessly transitioned from washing herself to relieving herself. She never even turned off the shower. I knew I married a talented girl.

* * *

"Is the wheel going to work?" Katy asked.

It was a tense moment; our ability to continue cycling hung in the balance. The night before, a mechanic had worked on our hub and found considerable wear and tear. He cleaned the freewheel, removed some grease, which shouldn't have been there, and added some oil, which should be there.

"Only one way to find out," I replied.

We pedaled onto the road and let the bike coast, straining with our ears. Silence. At the next intersection, we again let the bike roll. And again, silence. The clunking that had plagued our bike for the past few weeks was gone.

"Wow," I exclaimed. "Just like that, problem solved."

Before lunch we reached the Romanian border. Romania is part of the EU, but not part of the Schengen Zone. The Schengen Zone allows passport-free travel, and has no visa requirements for many nationalities, including US citizens. Five or six overweight, very stern looking Hungarian border guards checked us out of the Schengen Zone. Why do people who work with passports have a peculiar ability to appear so miserable? I don't know. Then we went to the Romanian border. The Romanian guards resembled athletes. They were friendly and taught us some Romanian. They smiled. I asked why the Hungarian border patrol were all overweight and they burst out in laughter. I suppose that fat people are funny people.

Unfortunately, we only spent one day in Romania, by crossing a tiny area in the far west of the country. It was a slight detour, but a recommendation and favorite country of some WS hosts in France, so we gave it a day's visit. Besides, Katy and I never turn down another stamp in our passports.

"Vair are you going?" a Russian looking man barked the next day at the border to enter Serbia.

"To Belgrade and then Croatia," Katy answered, half apologetic.

The man glared at us and motioned for me to put on a shirt. I obeyed. Gray skies, tumultuous clouds, multiple Duty Free Shops each boarded up behind barbed wire fences, and the echo of this man's scathing voice in our ears was our warm welcome to Serbia.

We raced the tumbling clouds for an hour, hoping our legs would get us to the nearest town before the storm. We put up a good fight, but lost the race, and arrived in Vršac soaking wet. The owner of our guesthouse, an intensely friendly man of 50, yanked us out of the rain, gave us towels to dry off and showed us to a very nice room. It was especially nice for €20, the going rate for a night's sleep in Eastern Europe. These prices kept us out of our tent and under a roof throughout the former Yugoslavia and until we reached Greece where the prices tripled.

"I'm very sorry. My English is very bad," the owner again apologized, as he had done a half dozen times during the check-in process.

"It's okay, my Serbian is much worse," I assured him.

At his suggestion, we went back out into the rain and through the unlit streets to find Etno House Dinar. It's an unassuming restaurant, and you'd miss it if you weren't looking for it. We ordered the combination appetizer for two, more because we couldn't pronounce any of the words describing any individual appetizer, and less to satisfy our ravenous hunger. Foods I've never heard of are often the best.

A stone dish covered with thinly sliced cured meats, fresh bread dripping in gooey white cheese, scoops of kajmak, and a pile of onions, cucumbers and tomatoes were set before us. Kajmak is the Balkan Peninsula's version of the cottled cream we had discovered in the United Kingdom. It's sweet and delicious, but never served in large enough quantities. I would not have guessed that a hidden restaurant in a small town in rural Serbia would leave such a lasting impression on my taste buds, but that kajmak was oh so good. If my dying meal were to finish with Madame Bourthier's plum crumble, then rural Serbia's kajmak, fresh bread, and cured meats would surely be the appetizer to kick-off that meal.

We fell asleep to a steady rain and with a full stomach, but woke up to the shining sun. The good weather, however, wouldn't last. Around 2pm we reached Pancevo, 21km east of Belgrade, and the dark clouds returned. The blue sky turned gray, and a steady rain began to fall. We merged onto the only highway into Belgrade and the traffic intensified. Motorists turned on their lights, just to be able to see through the downpour. Then it rained harder.

At this point in a ride, most cyclists call it quits. The brave ones put on a rain jacket and move as close to the edge of the shoulder as possible. But I've tried this. It's terrifying. When the shoulders are narrow and the roads are good, drivers fly past us at 60mph. It's only a matter of time until someone isn't paying attention. My strategy in this situation is different. I leave my shirt off, let my man-bun down into a ponytail and ride smack dab in the middle of the lane. This forces motorists to slow down and wait to pass. When Katy hears large trucks approaching she turns and glares at the driver. I thought we might get honks of anger, shaken fists or maybe the middle finger or its cultural equivalent. Not so. People were baffled. *What the hell are these two doing out there?* Passengers pumped their fists and sent thumbs-ups out the window to cheer us on. I guess it's not everyday two partially dressed wayward souls ride a tandem bicycle through the pouring rain into Belgrade. I also wonder if my appearance from behind – as a topless Scandinavian female – had anything to do with it.

We crossed the Danube and entered Belgrade. The city is a cyclist's nightmare. After crossing the Danube, we raced up a hill, desperate to keep our pace ahead of a communist-era trolley. Two-inch wide train track grooves, large enough to engulf our bike tires, ran parallel down the street, which created other problems – you've really got to watch where you're going. On the next street, I decided to move onto the shoulder, so we would not obstruct traffic. We rode through a large, innocent-looking puddle and BOOM! We hit a giant pothole and our panniers flew off and tumbled down the wet road. Thankfully, we didn't fly off with our panniers, nor did we break any spokes and no serious harm was done. But I had learned my lesson: never surrender the middle of the road.

* * *

Belgrade and the Balkan Peninsula have a fascinating history. To oversimplify, Slavs migrated from the north, crossed the Danube River (which Belgrade sits on) and settled in the region in the 6th century. In the 15th century, the Ottoman Turks came from the east and conquered Slavic lands all the way to Vienna. The Turks ruled for 400 years. In the 19th century, the failing Ottoman Empire lost control of the northwest of its empire to a Serbian Revolution, and to the competing Austrian-Hungarian Empire. In 1918, at the conclusion of World War I, both the Austrian-Hungarian Empire and the Ottoman Empire were officially dissolved, and Yugoslavia was created. Belgrade became the capital of the new nation and the heart of Communist Yugoslavia.

After World War II, Marshal Josip Broz Tito won a national election (relatively easy to do when you're the only candidate on the ballot) and became the President of Yugoslavia. Yugoslavia consisted of six republics: Serbia, Slovenia, Bosnia and Herzegovina, Croatia, Macedonia and Montenegro; and two autonomous provinces: Kosovo and Vjovodina. In addition to these geographic boundaries, the Southern Slavs can also be divided by ethnicity. The three largest ethnic groups are the Orthodox Serbs, the Catholic Croats and the Muslim Bosniaks. Less populous groups include the Slovenes, Macedonians and Montenegrins. Serbia was predominantly composed of Orthodox Serbs, but ethnic Serbs also lived throughout Yugoslavia. The same was true for the Croats and the Bosniaks. In fact, the geographical intermixing of these groups was primarily responsible for the severity of the wars here in the early 1990s.

Marshal Tito ruled for 35 years. He is often remembered as a benevolent dictator, as he was uniquely able to resolve disputes and calm tensions throughout the multiethnic Yugoslavia. But in 1980 he died and things started to crumble. National separatism swept throughout Yugoslavia; republics wanted to be their own nations.

On June 25, 1991 Slovenia declared independence. They fought and won a relatively easy war against Slobodan Milosevic, the president of Serbia, and his predominantly Serbian Yugoslavian National Army (JNA). (It's JNA instead of YNA, because Yugoslavia is actually Jugoslavia – for the same reason you have Slovenija and Serbija. Slavs love the "j" – although it's either silent or pronounced like a "y".) The war lasted ten days, killing only 62 people. Slovenia was allowed a relatively easy departure from Yugoslavia because, at the time of independence, Slovenia was 83% Slovene. What did this mean? It meant that people living in Slovenia *wanted* independence from a Serb controlled Yugoslavia. Also, Milosevic and the JNA wanted to build an ethnically pure Serb state, and were not very concerned with Slovenia's departure. "What do we care?" was Milosevic's thinking. They're almost all Slovenes anyway.

* * *

Katy and I spent two days in Belgrade, a city the Lonely Planet describes as gritty. It is. It felt a bit like a smaller, poorer New York City – dogs barking all night, the distant sound of cars honking, people begging at busy intersections, and an endless supply of pizza shops. Also, lots of people selling shoelaces. Maybe the communists rationed the shoelace, because people on each block sell these age-old items like a hot commodity. *Shoelace Here!*

For dinner we tried two of Serbia's national dishes, cevapi and pljeskavica. Cevapi is a pita sandwich filled with sausages, onions, sour cream, kajmak and red pepper. Pljeskavica is a Balkan hamburger, although often served without a bun (but perhaps in a pita), topped with chopped onions, tomatoes, and kajmak. After licking the last smidgeon of kajmak off our plates, we walked along Kneza Mihaila, the major pedestrian-only thoroughfare in downtown Belgrade, and munched on street vendor popcorn (which is almost as abundant as the shoelaces).

On our way out of Belgrade we passed a NATO building that the US had bombed during the Kosovo War. It remains in ruins, left intentionally unrepaired since the bombing. At any moment, it seems it may fall and kill the pedestrians on the sidewalk below.

In an effort to avoid Belgrade's difficult to cycle roads, we followed the city's only bike path south, along the Sava River. The Sava is a good reminder to reduce, reuse, and recycle. The banks of the river were lined with abandoned boats and makeshift homes, each of them vacant, in ruins, and in need of a bulldozer. Swimming on the top of the river, between plastic bottles from yesteryear and other filth, was a film of oil. Rivers do not lie. They are the good, the bad, and the ugly of any city. Just outside downtown Belgrade, the Sava ran through a park full of kayakers and rowers, with a lake surrounded by multiple bike paths. The Sava River represents the filth and shame of Belgrade's past, along with its optimistic enthusiasm for the future.

Southwest of Belgrade, we met Miloš. He first passed us on his road bike, headed from Belgrade to his home in the country. At the next intersection, he was waiting for us. An avid cyclist, Miloš works for Herbalife. He answered our questions about the rising generation's views on ethnic tensions and also requested to be Katy's Facebook friend, as everyone did in the Balkans. After a lengthy chat, we parted ways. At the next intersection, he was again waiting for us.

"Can we take a photo?" he asked. "My friends will never believe I met you."

The next day we crossed the Sava and arrived in the Republika Srpska, Bosnia. The countryside was covered in the greens and yellows of six-foot-tall cornfields, punctuated by houses with orange tiled roofs, and white stucco walls. The flat lands of Serbia slowly turned into rolling hills. In the distance, we saw two white towers with black steeples, and a circular balcony with loudspeakers. Minarets. For the first time of our trip, we were in Muslim country.

As we admired the country, beautiful on the outside but struggling inside, I heard the faint ringing of a bell. The ding-ding, ding-ding slowly grew louder. Katy spun around and saw two cyclists we had passed earlier desperately trying to catch up to us.

"Timeout, timeout," an out of breath middle aged man shouted, before reaching us.

It wasn't the greeting I expected, but we pulled off the road anyway.

"Deutschland?" the man asked. Throughout the former Yugoslavia, this was a common question. Because of the Austrian-Hungarian Empire's tie to the area, much of the older generation speaks German and many of them hoped that we did as well.

"No. America."

They smiled, but shrugged their shoulders. They spoke Serbo-Croatian, German, and Albanian, and we speak English and a bit of French and Spanish, but this didn't prevent an invitation for coffee or tea. I sipped my Schweppes Bitter Lemon, Katy her Coca-Cola Light

(Mormons have a hard time with beverages), and we struggled through an enthusiastic, yet impossible conversation.

One of the men introduced himself as Dragon, but I was skeptical. Later he showed us his national identity card, but his name was written in the Cyrillic alphabet: another conversational dead end. Eventually I pulled out Google Maps and zoomed into Utah, to show them where we were from.

"Ahh, Utah Jazz. Karl Malone. John Stockton," they both blurted out. Even in Eastern Bosnia, over a drink with two Serbians, Stockton and Malone are household names. (Surprised at their knowledge of the NBA, I looked into the matter. In 2002, at the FIBA Basketball World Cup, Yugoslavia became the first team to beat Team USA and in 2014, Serbia took 2nd place to Team USA – Serbs are ballers. I suppose that's also why they shouted "timeout" when trying to get our attention.)

At dusk, we entered the small village of Divic in search of the Hostel Soja. We couldn't find the Google Maps address, and booking.com's map was also unhelpful. Technology failed us, which was both frustrating and somewhat refreshing. It's nice to know there are still places on our planet outside of Google's Street View. We went door-to-door and asked if anyone knew of Hostel Soja. We only found adults who laughed at our English and kids with a deer-in-the headlights stare. It seemed we had left Europe and landed on a different planet.

Our search continued, and although Katy grew increasingly impatient, I was quite amused. The Internet's impotence in rural Bosnia reminded me of the two years I spent in Jamaica, where addresses don't exist and children yell "whitie, whitie." But to Katy, inaccurate Google Maps were unacceptable. After more than an hour, the village elected a boy to be our guide, and so we followed him a couple of kilometers past town, until we found Ristorant Soja. And sure enough, Hostel Soja was in the basement.

The next day we rode to Srebrenica. Everyone should know about Srebrenica.

* * *

On April 6, 1992, a year after Slovenian independence, war erupted in Bosnia. Bosnia's quest for independence would not be as easy as Slovenia's had been. At the time, Bosnia was 46% Muslim Bosniak, 37% Orthodox Serb and 15% Catholic Croat. When Bosnian president Alija Izetbegovic, himself a Bosniak, declared independence, half of the country resisted. The Serbs wanted to remain with Yugoslavia and the Croats didn't want to live in a country run by a Bosniak. Civil war followed. Serbs living in Bosnia formed the Republika Srpska (literally: Serbian Republic), whose Republika Srpska army was led by Ratko Mladic and funded and fueled by Slobodan Milosevic and the Jugoslavian National Army from neighboring Serbia. They began an ethnic cleansing of all non-Serbs in the neighboring towns and villages. War against another country is one thing, but killing your neighbors is something entirely different.

Throughout the war, thousands of Bosniak refugees left their homes and settled in Srebrenica, a city that sits in a narrow valley below the mountains and between ridgelines. It has just two mosques, a restaurant or two, a post office, and a couple other shops. It's small and it's isolated. Towards the end of the war, the UN designated Srebrenica a "safe zone," and thousands took shelter here. Living conditions were atrocious. Extreme poverty, starvation, and limited housing were the norm, but the refugees stayed because Srebrenica was safe.

Or so they thought.

On July 11, 1995, Mladic and his Serb forces moved on the town, separated the men from the women and massacred 8,327 Bosniak fathers and sons. They buried the bodies in mass graves. They hid the bodies because even they knew this wasn't war. It was genocide, Europe's worst act of genocide since World War II.

On our ride into Srebrenica, we stopped at the Srebrenica Memorial where a marble wall contains the etched names of the 8,327 deceased. A green field rolls up onto the hillside, with the same number of spotless white tombstones. We walked through the field in silence and reflected on the suffering and cruelty and injustice from not that many years ago. At the marble wall, an elderly man tapped me on the shoulder and insisted we follow him. We stopped at the letter "M".

He looked me in the eyes, pointed at the names and said, "Three brothers." His eyes were dark and heavy. Then he pinched my arm, pinched his own skin, and shook his head. He wasn't blaming me; he wanted my attention. He wanted me to know that Srebrenica isn't just an artifact in history. It was real, and it happened. It happened to him. It's impossible to look into someone's eyes, like this gentleman's, and know what those eyes have seen.

When the Srebrenica Memorial was dedicated, a prayer was offered. The words of that prayer are inscribed next to the marble wall:

> In the Name of God
> The Most Merciful, The Most Compassionate
> We pray to Almighty God
> May grievance become hope!
> May revenge become justice!
> May mothers' tears become prayers
> That Srebrenica never happens again
> To no one and nowhere!

That evening we walked through Srebrenica. It wasn't easy. It was hard to look at the town, or at our waiter, or a kind lady in a shop selling ice cream, without thoughts of separated families and bodies dumped into mass graves. When three women passed us on the street, I didn't think *Just some women walking home from the market* but instead, *Are they widows? Did their husbands die in this town? Or their sons disappear from this street corner?* At dinner, a group of men were having a smoke, but my initial thought wasn't *Just a couple of guys enjoying an evening out,* but instead *Are these men responsible for those widows? Do they still hear the sounds of machine gunfire and tanks coming down the dirt road?*

* * *

At 7:05am we were on our bike, climbing a back road through the mountains. Katy stopped to go to the bathroom, but didn't dare leave the road. And for good reason. During the Bosnian War, the area around Srebrenica was heavily mined. In fact, half a million Bosnians still live near unexploded mines and in the 30 years since the war ended 600 people have died from abandoned mines. The most feared are the jumping mines. They jump three feet into the air and send shrapnel 100 feet in every direction. When the traffic disappeared, Katy squatted on the curb to avoid stepping on any abandoned mines, and I guess you could say she left behind a mine of her own.

There are times when a day in the saddle feels routine. Especially when a day in the saddle *is* the routine. This wasn't one of those days. Sure, it was just another Monday morning, but at 8am I wasn't in class listening to another lecture. I was on a tandem. In Bosnia. Cycling through the mountains on a rural backcountry road. The weather was perfect, the scenery even better and we still had seven more months to pedal. Seven months. Time disappears when you're exploring the back roads of Bosnia on a bicycle.

At the top of the first climb, the road danced along ridgelines and over hilltops. We floated above clouds that smothered the valleys. Around a corner, a man herded his sheep down the road. Houses dotted the hills, each house with its own field. Fourteen foot tall stacks of hay dried in the sun. Occasionally, I have little memory of the road or scenery of a day's ride. Just a few scattered, hard to place images remain. That first climb out of Srebrenica, however, remains forever imbedded in my mind. It was one of those kinds of days. We climbed 10,000 feet, and traversed three mountain passes that day, so Katy and I call Bosnia "our little Switzerland."

Nine hours and 140 kilometers later, after passing countless men on the side of the road selling HUGE jars of honey, we arrived in Sarajevo. Sarajevo and Salt Lake City have some striking similarities. They're both surrounded by mountains. They've both hosted the Winter Olympics. They both start with an S. For these and for other reasons, they are sister cities. I would say that it's impossible to like one city and not the other, but Salt Lake City didn't light the powder keg of WWI, nor has it been stuck in the middle of a civil war.

We burned about 3,500 calories that day, about a pound of love handle fat. After a shower, we hit the streets in search of food to refuel our depleted bodies and to keep a handle on our love. Our first stop – first, because baklava is too good to be eaten last – was at The Baklava

Shop. Baklava is divine. The Baklava Shop, located in the heart of Sarajevo's old bazaar, conjures up hazelnut, coconut, chocolate, nutella and apple cinnamon baklava, in addition to the tried-and-true pistachio and walnut varieties. It was a crispy on top, intensely sweet, lick-your-fingers-clean, indulgence. We shared a dozen pieces.

After dessert, we wandered through town and up a side street, towards a bus park and cemetery, looking for dinner. To find authentic food in any country it's best to look for a restaurant jam-packed with locals, where no one speaks English. If a restaurant has a Lonely Planet or Trip Advisor sticker on the door, you might be in the wrong place. We meandered up a steep cobblestone road until we saw *Pekara Kovaci kod Mahira* written on an old sign above an older building. The line of customers stretched into the road, so we hopped in line. A husband and wife worked at the speed of light, taking orders and handing customers paper sacks and pizza boxes. We were almost to the front of the line, when a man approached us.

"Have you been here before?" the man asked.

"No. We just got to Sarajevo today."

The man's face was confused. "Then how did you find this place?"

It was on odd question, and I wasn't sure my answer would be sufficient. "We walked here?"

"You're lucky. This place has the best pizza in the world. I've had pizza in Italy, the United States, you name it, but this is the best."

"Really?" Katy asked, not convinced. "What should we order?"

"Well they only have one flavor. You can get a small or a large."

A restaurant without a menu is my type of restaurant. The chef is the one who has been in the kitchen for half a century, surely he knows best. We ordered a small. It might have been wise to get a large, but the first rule of grazing in a new city is this: don't fill up too fast. As soon as your expanding stomach cries out in pain, your evening of cheap eats comes to a crashing halt.

The man took our money. His wife went to work. She tossed dough into the air, loaded it with mushrooms, cured meat, and cheese, and threw it into the fiery depths of a wood-burning oven with a fourteen-foot wooden spatula. The handle of the spatula stuck out of the oven, through the window where customers ordered, and into the road.

When you make the world's best pizza, I guess you're allowed to dangle your dirty kitchenware wherever you like.

The pizza emerged with flowing cheese, but crisp edges, and received a ladleful of kajmak and tomato sauce before being boxed up and handed to two drooling customers. We sat on the curb across the street and had *thee* best pizza. When the last slice was finished, I licked the box clean – because you know how the center of a sliced pizza will ooze toppings – while Katy went back across the street for a repeat order. We're big fans of the repeat order. Cycling across the world and eating on our A-game every night requires it. *And another one of those.*

The next day we took a taxi to visit the bobsled track from the 1984 Winter Olympics. Unlike other bobsled tracks from other Winter Olympics, the bobsled track in Sarajevo is in ruins. During the war, Republika Srpska soldiers gathered in the hills around Sarajevo and besieged the city. For almost four years, heavy artillery shelled the city, and snipers killed anyone in the streets. The besiegers used the bobsled track as a bunker. More recently it has been used as a canvas for graffiti artists, and as a downhill track for the X-games.

Before reaching the track, we passed a couple of hotels, each of them built specifically for the Olympics, each of them now in ruins. Roofs were missing, wooden boards were strewn amidst piles of bricks, and trees and shrubs grew where world-class athletes had once slept. We walked down the bobsled track and admired the graffiti, but thought twice about the many holes in the buildings, from machine gun fire or artillery shelling only decades earlier. Our taxi guide showed us a spot where Bosniaks were routinely tortured and killed. On the ride back home, we asked him about growing up in Sarajevo.

"I was only seven when war broke out," he began. "But it feels like yesterday. For four years, I only attended school one day a week. We could only leave home at night, and then only to get water from a nearby spigot. My older brother went to war. A couple of my neighbors were shot by snipers in the middle of the afternoon when they walked down our street." Sarajevo's recent history is very much apart of the day to day life of everyone who lives there.

The next day we continued our journey towards the Adriatic Sea, and spent the night in a bungalow on Lake Jablanica. Of all the types of paying accommodations: hotel, motel, hostel, guesthouse, campground, cabin, haveli, lofts, or bungalows, Katy and I would opt for the bungalow every time. What is a bungalow? I'm not exactly sure. As we traveled across the world, the accepted standard of what constituted a "bungalow" seemed to vary dramatically. The unifying theme, however, was an overwhelming feeling of comfort and homeliness.

The next night we arrived in Mostar. Mostar's claim to fame is the Stari Most. Stari: old and Most: bridge. And it is old. The Ottomans built the bridge in 1557, during the reign of Suleiman. The bridge, like the Sultan who commissioned it, is magnificent. The bridge we saw, however, isn't the original. While Bosniak and Serb forces fought throughout Bosnia, Croat forces in the south of the country also joined the fighting. They laid siege to Mostar, and destroyed the bridge on November 9, 1993. A cable bridge had hung in its place until the bridge was rebuilt in 2004, using the same technology and materials used by the Ottomans centuries earlier.

As we approached the bridge, the stench of tourism was foul. Vendors hawked cheap jewelry, knick-knacks, trinkets, and other keepsakes you are sure to find wherever tour bus drivers put on the brakes and unleash the hordes. It was a difficult contrast to the night before with our taxi driver. The Stari Most and its immediate vicinity cater well to the tourists, but only two streets away, Mostar still shows the scars of war. Buildings are pocked with baseball size holes from artillery shells. A homeless man scavenged for dinner out of a dumpster. It's interesting to see what is worth fixing and what has been left broken for the last twenty years.

The next morning there was a buzz in the air. For the past ten weeks, our eyes had been set on Dubrovnik, where we planned to meet my two sisters, Jessica and Elizabeth, and Jessica's son Charlie. Every time we sat down to map out our route, we asked ourselves three questions: How many kilometers to Dubrovnik? How many days until Charlie and Co. arrive? Can we afford a rest day? Today the answers were easy. 140 kilometers. One more day. No time to rest.

We were two hours into our ride when Katy shouted the best one-liner of our trip: "You're getting fucked one way or another." I laughed out loud. Katy's timing was perfect. Her use of a great line from *My Cousin Vinny* shocked me. To explain, half an hour earlier we reached a crossroads and had to choose between two roads that both led to Dubrovnik. After a couple of kilometers down one road, dark clouds covered the horizon, so we turned around and started down the other road in search of sunnier skies. It wasn't long before another gray sky appeared. The rain came in a downpour and Katy's movie quote was delivered with impeccable timing.

At the Bosnia-Croatia border, traffic came to a standstill. We slowly made our way past the long line of cars, and were surprised to see the weary, dejected facial expressions of the passengers in each car. Stuck in traffic, and confined to their cars, they had nowhere to go. They were in a hurry to arrive at their destinations, but couldn't get there. But for us, stuck in the rain and trying to cross another border, our journey was our destination and each moment was why we had come. Such is the life of a touring cyclist. Sometimes it is pristine mountains, blue skies and all-you-can-eat baklava – and other times it is pouring rain.

BAKLAVA

If I were to imagine an enchanted city, it would have narrow walk-ways, a chimney on every rooftop and an impregnable city wall. An unforgiving, mountainous coastline would crash into an endless sea, where I could spend a lifetime of summers watching the warm sun sink into the cool ocean. A city like Dubrovnik. Dubrovnik, Croatia. It has the unique ability to make your hometown laughable and your dream city mundane. We spent a week in this fairytale dreamland with Jessi-ca, Elizabeth, and Charlie, and I wish we were still there, licking melt-ed ice cream on cobbled walkways and dipping our feet into the emer-ald sea.

We wasted no time; the party began at the airport. Katy, Eliza-beth and Charlie got in a rental car, while Jessica and I rode the bike. A strong tailwind blew all day and we flew along the Adriatic Coast to Kotor, Montenegro. Every twenty minutes Jessica hollered, "It's so beautiful here. This place feels so foreign. I can't believe you do this all day, everyday." Later that week she wrote in our blog:

"Leaving the confines of 170 South Main and hauling down the highway of a foreign country with my brother on a tandem bicycle, ocean breeze blowing in our faces and burning in our thighs, was noth-ing short of exhilarating, an adrenaline rush, and feelings of gratitude for the perfect moment." Jessica is the epitome of enthusiasm. Spending time with her was a great reminder to enjoy every moment, and to be grateful for every day.

Elizabeth is my twin. Not only are we the same age, we also share similar interests: new people, new places and swimming in really cold water. After spending a day on the beach, we took a day trip to Bosnia and stopped at Kravica Falls. Were such a beautiful waterfall in any other country, it would have been packed with people. But we had the falls to ourselves. I jumped into the empty river below the falls and the air in my lungs vanished. I couldn't breathe. I cried in pain and my frozen limbs awkwardly pulled my body out of *thee* coldest water I've ever swam in. Then Elizabeth jumped in, quickly caught her breath, casually swam towards the falls, and yelled, "Come on, you'll get used to it." Never wanting to be outdone, I reluctantly followed. We had a numbing, but gorgeous, swim under a magical waterfall. Elizabeth is an adventurist.

Charlie, of course, was the delight of the trip. A five-year-old would spice up any trip to the Balkans. He excels everywhere, but he flourished in Bosnia: on dark unlit alleys in Trebinje, buying honey from a roadside bee farm in rural Republika Srpska and earlier that afternoon in Mostar, taking the rearguard 20 meters behind us, sword in hand, fighting off the bad guys to make it safe for us to cross the Stari Most. (The bad guys, if you must know, are the people that break through Dubrovnik's and Kotor's city walls.) I'm sure this was a sight for others – a five-year-old without adults at his side, wandering down the street, swinging his sword and shouting sound effects. *Hae-yah.* That night in Trebinje, he tried to maintain his superhero status, but occasionally a stray cat would appear and he'd turn and run. He also had ice cream smeared across his face each day, from dawn until dusk. A kindergartener vacationing in Bosnia, no big deal.

Trebinje is Bosnia unfiltered. It isn't on anyone's to-visit list. You won't find it in any guidebooks. These types of towns, rural and over-looked, are the real gems of bicycle travel. Without any tourist attractions, we just show up and see what happens. We wanted Charlie and Co. to get a feel for what our trip had been like, so that's what we did. A maze of unlit alleyways weaved through the old city and foreigners were nowhere to be found. On one of these alleyways, I saw the bright lights of a corner shop and above the doorway hung a sign: пѐкара. Пѐкара is the Cyrillic spelling of pekara, the Serbo-Croatian word for bakery. After learning how to say thank you in a foreign language, the next word I always learn is bakery. You have to be on your foreign-language, different-alphabet A-game if you want to eat well in rural Bosnia.

"Two Baklava," I stated, as I held up two fingers.

The lady behind the counter just stared at me. She had no idea what I had said or what I wanted. *Oh great. I've told my sisters I'm a pro at this, but when it really counts I'm coming up short.*

"Two baklava?" I again stated, this time pointing at the perfect squares of sweet, nutty crunchiness.

"Aaah, baklava," she answered.

At first her pronunciation seemed identical to mine, so I pressed her on the issue. As it turns out, Baklava (my pronunciation, accent on the ba) and baKlava (her pronunciation, accent on the klava) are two very different things. One is a well-loved regional dessert, the other is nothing.

My ordering may have been mediocre, but the baklava was divine. After a literal feeding frenzy, where pieces of walnuts, pistachios and honey-laden Filo dough could be seen flying in any direction, Jessica went back to the pekara for refills. To pay, Jessica fumbled with the Euros, Croatian Kuna and Bosnian Convertible Marks in her pocket. Telling them apart, especially under the gun of hunger, can be difficult. Desperate to get to the walnut and pistachio dessert, Jessica grabbed a handful of coins and held them up to the counter. The lady selected her country's currency, and in the right amount, and we had another round of baklava. It was an amusing end to a wonderful week.

The next morning our three visitors packed and drove to the airport. Just like that, they were gone. Katy and I, however, were still in Croatia. We looked at each other and said, "I guess we'll keep biking?"

We battled headwinds and grotesque humidity all day. I'm not sure which was worse, barely crawling into a wall of wind or peeling my clothes off at the end of the day, hoping never to see them again. Our guesthouse owner told us we were her first American guests, ever, which was a nice boost to my wanderlust ego. The next day we reached Albania. Our touring lifestyle returned in full swing.

The moment we entered Albania, things changed. First were the animals – we may have heard them before we saw them. Rowdy pigs rummaged through roadside dumpsters, bells tied to cattle echoed down the country road, herds of sheep blocked the road, and the rooster – that egotistical, louder than necessary nuisance – made his small self heard at every turn of the road. (I mean honestly, we have seedless watermelon. Can't we get a mute rooster?) Then, the kids came out. They saw us from a distance and sprinted to the side of the road, the younger siblings a step behind, and stuck out their hands for high-fives. We were star athletes celebrating a monumental victory. The last peculiarity was the number of cars with the word AUTOSHKOLLA painted across the side, often with a middle-aged man or woman in the driver's seat. *It's 2014, why are all these old folks just now learning to drive?*

That's a good question. From 1947 to 1985, Albania's Supreme Comrade was Enver Hoxha, who ran a very strict Communist regime. Among other things, he banned religion and Albania became the world's first atheist country. He severed ties with all other countries, and eventually distanced Albania from the world's other Communist countries, Yugoslavia, Russia, and China. Massive economic stagnation followed. And, he outlawed the private ownership of vehicles. When communism ended in 1992, a country of three million people only had five thousand cars. Twenty years later, fifty- and sixty-year-olds were in the AUTOSHKOLLA getting their driver's licenses for the first time.

We spent our first night in Shkoder and feasted on sausage, steak, grilled eggplant, stuffed peppers, goat cheese, and drinks – for $13. Prices were starting to fall our way.

For the next three days we took a detour. We left our bike in Shkoder and ventured into the Accursed Mountains of Northern Albania (they are cursed, you should see them) and hiked between the mountain villages of Valbona and Theti. Time in the mountains is always enjoyable, but a ferry built out of an old school bus, a candlelit dinner in the freezing cold, clothed in thick Albanian wool coats, and a bumpy bus ride through the mountain fog accompanied by two British fellows who kept on saying, "When The Guardian writes an article about this place, everyone in the UK will be here," will make those three days memorable.

The next day we were back on our bike and halfway to Tirana when road conditions rapidly deteriorated. The highway turned into dirt, potholes appeared and then a stream ran down the road.

"This road is terrible. Where are you taking us?" Katy wondered aloud.

"I have no idea. You said the main highway was too scary, this is the only other road to Tirana. And according to Google Maps, this is the second largest road in the country," I answered.

"So Google led us astray?" Katy questioned me.

"Yeah, I guess you could say that. Someone needs to call Google and tell them that dirt roads with rivers running down the middle of them shouldn't look like highways on Google Maps."

"Blame it on Google."

In addition to rocks and streams, the dirt road was full of barking dogs, who were impossible to out-pedal on the bumpy road. At my suggestion, Katy preemptively armed herself with an arsenal of rocks. She put most of them in her frame bag but tucked a couple in her spandex shorts for quick access. The dogs must have sensed Katy's weapons, because they disappeared as soon as she armed herself. As we approached Tirana, another conversation occurred.

"From how long do it take you to ride from Shkoder?" a man in a truck yelled, his head hanging out the window. "I see you in Shkoder this morning."

"Four hours," we hollered back.

"That is very good. Very strong," he shouted. When he said the word "strong," his hand motions of two feet pedaling a bicycle intensified. "Welcome to Albania," he hollered as the truck sped off.

We entered Tirana and driving rules deteriorated in the same way our road had, law and order turned into chaos and confusion. Life on the road was a celebration. For the first time in fifty years, a growing economy, along with the right to own cars, put ordinary people behind the steering wheel. Their time in the AUTOSHKOLLA, however, hadn't been sufficient. They sped. They followed too closely. They ran through stop signs. They sped some more. They failed to yield at a round-a-bout. They changed lanes in an intersection. They changed lanes while running a red light and speeding. It was an every-man-for-himself battle and I reverted to the driving rules I had learned in Jamaica: if you are in the way you have the right of way.

Further down the road a bus pulled up next to us. Kids whipped out their iPhones to take our picture and I waved a peace sign at them as they passed. A couple of minutes later we caught up to the bus and I whipped out my iPhone to take a picture of them. They shot peace signs right back at us.

I welcome lawless traffic. To be completely honest, I prefer it. It makes cycling interesting. It allows mini conversations with everyone on the road and on that day it lifted our spirits after a rough argument on a rougher road. Why argue with each other when everyone we meet thinks we're awesome?

South of Tirana, the main highway enters a long tunnel that cuts through the mountain, but we stuck to the old secondary road that switchbacks up that mountain and traverses the ridgeline. After an hour or two of rolling along the ridgeline, the mountains abruptly ended and the road plummeted. A flying descent commenced. We were a third of the way off the mountain, when a loud, grinding sound forced me to slam on the brakes.

"What was that?" I yelled.

Katy didn't say a word.

We got off the bike and I rotated the pedals backwards, simulating the coasting of our rear wheel. The clunking returned, much worse than before. I walked the bike a couple steps down the road, more clunking.

"Shit!" I screamed, as loud and as long as I could muster. My anger echoed off the mountains.

Katy still didn't say a word.

Our rear hub problem, it seemed, had returned with a vengeance. Every rotation of the wheel clunked and pushed the chain and pedals forward. Our free wheel mechanism on our rear wheel was locking up.

"I guess we're walking," I declared.

"What?" Katy asked in disbelief.

"Walking. You know, put one step in front of the other."

"But Elbasan is fifteen kilometers away."

"Then we better get started."

We started the long walk down the mountain. Far away on the valley floor, we could see Elbasan. It was so close, but so far away. I thought it might be the last town on our ride. Each step, and the wrenching noise from our wheel, was one step closer to our trip's grave. Our bike was finished and our cycling was over. The nearest town with a decent bike shop was Thessaloniki, Greece, 240 miles away. I had no idea how we'd get there.

We would have tried to hitchhike, but all of the cars were on the main highway. Walking would have taken forever.

"Our hub is broken, right?" I asked Katy.

"I guess."

"And we have to replace it, right?"

"I guess."

"Then what difference does it make if we ride into town and completely ruin it? Will it even matter?"

"I guess not?" Katy answered, rather timid.

We got on our bike, which I hated at the moment, and started to pedal downhill. After five seconds our speed picked up and I shouted, "Here goes nothing." I stopped pedaling, expecting the awful noise and speedy destruction of our rear wheel. But the sound never came. I pedaled again, and then stopped. No clunking. *Great. Now our bike works only when it wants to.* We flew down the steep road. And after a minute or two, the clunking resumed.

We came up with a plan. I shifted into our biggest gear and each time we heard the sound we pedaled as fast as we could. Sounds easy, but it's awkward to descend a 10% grade and, while braking, simultaneously pedal fast enough to not let the rear wheel coast, all on a 450-pound loaded tandem. But we got used to it. Half of the time this would "reset" something in the rear hub and the sound would disappear, at least until we went around another corner and stopped pedaling. The clunking would then return and the process would repeat. Comical? Maddening? Memorable? Whatever it was, we finally got off the mountain and hobbled into Elbasan.

The next day was Sunday; we went to church, keeping alive our go-to-church-once-a-month streak. This might, just might entice God to smile on our situation and allow our journey to continue. Lunch was sufllaqes, Albania's version of the kebab. We had three or four, because when a tasty sandwich of meat and french fries, crispy onion and tomatoes, (extra tzatziki sauce please!) wrapped up in a pita is only $1.50, it's hard to not have thirds and fourths.

After lunch we crossed our fingers and said our prayers. *How will our bike do today?* It worked fine. Maybe God smiled on us. Maybe our wheel just needed some rest, whatever that means for an inanimate, mechanical object. We rode east towards Macedonia, crossed the border at sunset (it was freezing) and arrived at Lake Ohrid just after dark.

Our three days in Macedonia gave us the best weather we had in Europe. In the mountains, traffic and houses disappeared. Macedonia reminded me of Utah; for long stretches at a time, I was at home, riding up Millcreek or Emigration Canyon. Good riding was complemented with good food. Kebabs and hamburgers hovered at $1.50, and the autumn harvest brought the juiciest, crunchiest green apples I've ever sunk my teeth into. At a restaurant in town, we met a 10-year-old kid who spoke perfect English with a perfect American accent.

"Where did you learn English?" Katy asked.

"I think TV was probably my first teacher," he answered, without hesitation. "I watch a lot of cartoons."

We entered Greece on October 1st, our trip's three month anniversary and decided to celebrate with a return to wild camping. We found a spot tucked away in an apple orchard, but then a shepherd (well a man with a herd of sheep) and his ferocious sheep dogs came around the corner. Katy asked if we could camp, but the guy didn't know a word of English – and Katy's Greek is sub-par. Instead of answering, he reached into his dirty pockets and offered us a heaping handful of unshelled walnuts. Images of Katy using the bathroom in the dark, wandering into a herd of sheep and being attacked by dogs suggested we would be better off continuing our search.

In the next town, we got lost. We passed by a group of ladies multiple times on our way back to the highway and eventually they waved us over. I asked if there was a campground nearby, and we had another lost in translation moment – only this time we were given two apples.

Two very delicious apples. More smiles, more waves and we continued our search for a free place to camp.

In Edessa, we passed a hotel and Katy ran inside to ask about a room.

"How much?" I asked, when she returned.

"Forty euros."

"Nope. That's not going to work," I answered.

"Why not?" Katy asked.

"Why not? Well, do you want to sleep in a bed tonight or eat two gyros a day for a week?" Traveling on a budget always raises interesting price comparisons.

It started to get dark, but we continued our search. Below Edessa, we searched for a park at the base of a waterfall, which Katy located on Google Maps. We were almost there when a pack of wolves, or maybe they were just dogs, came out of nowhere and chased us out of town. Blinded by the dark, Katy hurled her rocks into the howling, and pedaled her heart out. The only time I *really* know Katy is pedaling is when dogs are nipping at her heels. And boy can she pedal.

We returned to Edessa and checked into a hotel for €30. It brought a mix of emotions: anger that we had wasted the money on the simple process of falling asleep, and disappointment that we couldn't find a place to put up a tent in the countryside. But after a couple hours wondering what field or orchard we might sleep in, and how we would wash the dirt and sweat from our bodies, a simple bed and shower were a welcome relief. These are two luxuries I take for granted almost every day of my life.

The next day, as we rode to Thessaloniki, our rear hub further deteriorated. *I'm done, find me a replacement!* it cried. We could pedal just fine, but coasting was impossible. And not just impossible once in a while, as before, but now entirely impossible. Each time we stopped pedaling, the free wheel mechanism caught, threw our chain forward, and clunked and clunked and clunked. It's painful to ride a tandem without the luxury of coasting. On a typical day, we stand and stretch at the top of each hill, on every descent, when we come to a stop, and countless other times. But with our failing hub, we could never stop pedaling and could never stand up to stretch. Our butts quickly went numb. We tried to pedal while standing up, but balancing all of our weight was not easy. But when your butt is numb and blood flow is marginalized, you do what you have to do.

Thessaloniki's stop and go traffic at rush hour only exacerbated the problem. Buses stopped in our lane with no warning, so I slammed on the brakes while forcing myself to keep pedaling. A couple of kilometers took an hour, but we finally reached our Airbnb host and I went in search of a bike mechanic.

Just around the corner, I met Angelos at his bike shop. It was a lucky find. He spoke decent English, and his store was still open at 8pm. More importantly, his shop was stocked with Park Tool bike tools – a sign of high-end bicycle competence and my only essential requirement for a mechanic. Five minutes later, our bike was on the repair stand. Angelos carefully listened to the wheel and decided a loose hub, and not the freewheel, was our problem. He thought a bumpy road, such as the dirt road into Tirana, had loosened our hub. I was skeptical, but after tightening our hub, a simple procedure requiring a wrench and thirty seconds, the problem disappeared. *How could I be so stupid? For days we've suffered numb asses and mental frustration for that. A simple turn of the wrench?* Here I was, a self-proclaimed world bike tourer, but apparently I was oblivious to simple bike maintenance.

We returned to the shop the next day at 11am. Angelos had cleaned our bike, trued the front wheel, adjusted the derailleurs, and replaced the chain and gear cassette. Before departing, however, I wanted to make sure that Angelos had in fact fixed our problem. Katy waited at the shop while I rode up and down the oceanfront walkway a half dozen times, pedaling as hard as I could and then letting the bike coast. I tried my best to elicit the clunking problem, but try as I might, the clunking never returned.

"Are we good to go?" Katy asked, when I arrived back at the shop.

"I guess so. No problems."

It was a miracle. Our rear wheel worked. We departed Thessaloniki with our eyes set on Istanbul. For the first time in many days we were confident we'd reach our destination, and Istanbul was just a week away. We climbed out of town and reflected on our fortunate circumstance – of the many places we could have stayed in Thessaloniki, we stayed around the corner from a knowledgeable, English-speaking bike mechanic. We were elated. And then I heard something.

I wasn't sure what I heard. A bike can make many sounds and most of them resemble each other. I didn't say anything. Maybe it was just my imagination. For half an hour my mind was at war. *Keep going? Turn back? Did I really hear something, or was it a phantom noise?* When the gradient relaxed I stopped pedaling. Clunk.

Katy heard it too. I know she did.

In that moment, our bicycle died. But we didn't say a thing, we couldn't. The first stage of grief is denial. Denial is easier than defeat. For ten more minutes, my legs pedaled and my mind asked questions I couldn't answer: *Why now? Two hours ago it was fine. If we turn around will we ever reach Istanbul?* Eventually I made a decision. If I heard the sound one more time, I told myself, no matter how faint it was, we would stop. Minutes later, we were parked on the side of the road. I was fuming. Anger follows denial. We sat in silence for an eternity, and then Katy spoke.

"What do you want to do?" Katy asked.

"What the hell does it matter," I responded.

More silence. Eventually Katy left. I think she went to find some hot chocolate. I got on the bike and funneled my rage into the pedals, hammering up a nearby hill and coasting back down. I think I was trying to break the bicycle. I was so frustrated by its unpredictable behavior – fine yesterday, but not today, okay in the morning, but worthless at lunch – I thought if I could destroy our bike, the problem would be solved. I rode for half an hour but the clunking never returned. We continued on our journey.

At the top of the climb out of Thessaloniki we waved goodbye to the city and started a long, steep descent. We were almost to the bottom when a clunk-clunk-clunk-clunk-what-the-fuck exploded from our rear wheel. I cursed every foul word the good Lord frowns upon before pulling off the road.

"What do you want to do?" Katy asked.

She defers to me in these types of moments. I'd prefer for her to be in charge, that way I could blame her for our bad luck.

"It seems the problem only happens when you're on the bike," I answered.

"You're blaming *me?*"

"This morning on the oceanfront and for the past half hour I was by myself and it worked fine. Now you get on and look what happens."

Infuriated, Katy grabbed the bike and started walking up a very steep and very long hill back to Thessaloniki. With each step the rear wheel coasted and the rear hub clunked.

"You're never gonna make it," I shouted.

"You're right. Take your stupid bike."

I held the bike while Katy stuck out her thumb. Katy is a great hitch-hiker. Three minutes later we were in a truck headed back to Thessaloniki. Halfway to town our disaster became comical and we started laughing. "I guess this means more gyros and donuts," Katy suggested.

Just a few hours after we had left Angelos's shop, we were back. I told him a loose hub was not our problem. We opened up the rear hub and carefully cleaned and lubricated the freewheel mechanism. With the bicycle on the repair stand we let the wheel coast for ten minutes. It appeared the problem was fixed. When I decided there was nothing else we could do, we went for dinner. The gyro, a wrapped-up-nicely-in-a-pita sandwich, is drippingly delicious every night. But that night it was a lifesaver.

Our previous Airbnb host was booked, so we searched the city for urban wild camping. I found a nice spot (nice to some, I suppose) near the ocean, and told Katy to check into the hostel, which only had one bed left. She declined. We kept searching. At 10pm, we spent €70 and checked into the Metropolitan Hotel. Rip off. To show our disgust, we each took very long, hot baths and ate an army's worth of food at the continental breakfast. *We'll show you.*

Morning came. We got on our bike and were almost to the top of the same hill, and clunk-clunk-clunk-clunk. Fury overwhelmed my ability to curse. I stopped the bike.

In my politest voice, and in great contrast to the storm brewing inside me, I said, "Katy, take the bike from me." If I had a sledgehammer, or if we were standing next to a cliff, I would have fixed our problem once and for all.

I sat down on a cement retaining wall, and Katy sat thirty feet away. We didn't speak. Neither of us had the strength to approach our obvious problem. I inhaled and exhaled. Five minutes passed. Then twenty.

And then something strange happened. My frustration and anger melted away. For the past ten days my mind was consumed by a single thought: *I hope our bike is okay. I hope our bike is okay. I hope our bike is okay.* But it wasn't a thought – it was just a worry, much less than a thought. Worrying is the opposite of action, it is counterproductive and consuming. It aggravates the problems it wants to solve. In that moment, my worries of *what if our bike is broken* and *what will we do if our bike is broken* were replaced by an absolute: our bike is broken, now what? We were able to move past the worrying, and start talking about options. A sense of optimism came. It was refreshing, and I embraced the moment. Sitting on the cement wall, high above the Aegean Sea, frustration and anger turned into possibilities, possibilities that weren't *that* bad.

"We've got a couple of options," I stated.

"Which are?"

"Go back to Thessaloniki, order a new hub online and sail through the Greek islands for a week until it arrives."

"Not bad." Katy replied.

"Or, we can keep going, hitchhike if necessary. If we order a hub tomorrow it will probably reach Istanbul before we do."

Or?"

"Or we can send this stupid piece of shit home, wander around the Himalayas until we get tired and then fly to Thailand, sit on the beach for four months and drink piña coladas."

"I like the sound of that."

We took the second option. We were in determination mode, and resolved to let nothing stand in our way of reaching Turkey. We ordered a new hub that night, and had it shipped to a Warmshowers host in Istanbul. The next morning, bright and early, Katy was on the side of the road with her thumb out. We were going to reach Istanbul, one way or another. But no one stopped. An hour passed. Still no one.

We took it as a sign. The idea of giving up and accepting a ride to Istanbul, when we were so close, was unbearable. So I changed my mind. "Let's just ride there."

"But what about our hub?"

"We're replacing it anyways. If it breaks, it breaks."

"And if it does break?"

"If it's entirely useless and we can't cycle at all, then we can walk."

"Okay, let's go for it," Katy agreed. "It's only 600 kilometers. If the hub doesn't explode, we could be there in a week."

We climbed on our bike as we had a thousand times before, but this time we were renegades, riding on borrowed time. More importantly, we were going to Istanbul baby!

Over the next seven days, our rear hub deteriorated, but never gave out. Coasting, of course, was not an option. We were in continuous pedaling mode for the entire week. By the third day, even normal pedaling created unhealthy sounds. Sounds best described as follows: the squeaks and creaks when your nephew jumps on a trampoline with rusty springs, combined with the moans and groans of an attic door hinge at your grandmother's house – both to the cadence of a galloping horse. When one cadence and squeaky rhythm became obnoxious, I shifted gears and another song would begin. At 30mph descents, the symphony of strange sounds emanating from our rear hub became so frantic that it seemed an explosion was imminent.

In the next four days we camped in Northern Greece (because we were tough now), rode our longest day thus far of 172km, got our first flat tire, chatted with some bread folk, who have been making the same bread from the same recipe in the same oven since 1818, and enjoyed delicious 10% fat Greek yogurt – thick deliciousness. It was much better than any other yogurt related product I had ever had. If you fill a container and then turn it upside down, it won't fall out.

And through it all, we battled relentless head-cross-winds of 20-30mph. Headwinds slow you down. Crosswinds blow you over. Especially when your tandem's frame bag doubles as a parachute. I leaned into the crosswind so we wouldn't be blown off the road. But then a semi would pass, blocking the wind and creating a vacuum, sucking the bike into the road. I'd quickly steer the other direction, but then the semi would pass and the wind would return. We barely stayed on the highway. Semi trucks passed all day. When we crossed the border into Turkey, the wind picked up.

Throughout Europe, touring cyclists we met had claimed the Turks, after the Iranians, are the most hospitable people. This was first mentioned to us by Peter, in Leeds, England and then again by Ale, in Geneva, Switzerland. We were optimistic that our experience would support their claims, and we wasted no time in putting the Turks to the test.

On our first day in Turkey, we pulled into the very small town of Kocaçeşme around dusk and stopped at the town's only restaurant. We were welcomed inside, but were not given menus. Instead, we were beckoned to the glass display case. It was full of fish, of all shapes and sizes. Katy asked for a menu, but our waiter just pointed at the fish. She motioned with her hands for a menu, but again, was directed towards the display case and a myriad of different types of fish.

"So what are you going to have?" Katy asked.

I thought about it for a moment and then responded, "Fish?"

After dinner, I returned to our bike, curious where we might camp, while Katy paid our bill. She exited the restaurant with a smile on her face.

"We can camp in their yard," she stated.

"Whose yard?"

"I'm not quite sure," she answered. "The restaurant's yard, I suppose."

"Where?"

Katy pointed to the only grass underneath the restaurant's outdoor seating and said, "Here?"

"How did you communicate in Turkish?" I asked. "You weren't even able to ask for a menu, let alone explain camping."

"Some guy in there actually speaks German."

"Oh, so you speak German now?"

Katy just smiled, so I didn't question her further. A free campsite is a free campsite. We moved the patio tables and chairs out of the way and pitched our tent fifteen feet from the restaurant, next to a wall that hid us from the town square, and under the minarets of the town's mosque. *I guess we'll be waking up early.* After a cold bucket shower, and our first squat toilet, I got out our giant, foldable map of Europe and updated our route with a black Sharpie. Our waiter and a few others gathered to admire our journey's progress.

The man pointed to Istanbul, our next destination, and in very limited English said, "And?"

I pointed to Izmir and then Antalya. The men applauded our choice. (We were a couple weeks ahead of our original schedule, mostly because we had hurried to meet family in Dubrovnik, and we planned to spend a month riding through Turkey after we replaced our hub.)

"And?" the man again asked.

At that question, I made a split second decision. I already determined the Turks were a friendly bunch, offering us the use of their restaurant's lawn to camp was unprecedented. But I wanted to probe their personality deeper, so I pointed to northern Syria, the site of the recent terrorist attacks by ISIS. Back home in the States, ISIS had plagued the news and there was significant discussion about how to deal with the matter. I had heard a lot about what Westerners think about ISIS, but I wanted to know what Turks – other Muslims in a neighboring country – thought about ISIS.

Without hesitation, the man grabbed his friend next to him and held him tightly in front of him. Then he slowly, and with much facial expression, pulled an imaginary sword from a sheath at his waist and in a drawn out, animated manner, slit his friend's throat. They joked and they laughed. It was readily apparent that they viewed ISIS the same way that I did.

In the morning, just after the Call to Prayer, but before the restaurant opened, some townsfolk appeared to confirm that we had slept well and would get on the road safely. Just after lunch, we stopped at a gas station for a snack. We sat down on the curb, as we've routinely done in every other country, but two minutes into our snack a man emerged from the gas station with two chairs. He insisted we have somewhere to sit. We sat. Then he brought out tea. We drank. The Turkish çay glass (pronounced chai) is small, shaped like an hourglass, and always served on a small dish with two sugar cubes. I take two sugars with my çay, Katy takes one. When we finished our tea, the gas station attendant brought another glass. And then another. Let me remind you, this wasn't at a fancy restaurant. This was at a gas station, sitting on a sidewalk.

"I could get used to this," Katy stated, as I thought about Greg Mortenson's *Three Cups of Tea*.

"I know. Can you imagine this happening back home?"

"Maybe there's more to Islam than what's on CNN."

The next day the wind continued to rage. But it was an enjoyable battle. It was the last battle in a long war, and I knew we had won. That evening we would be in Istanbul. We couldn't have known it at the time or maybe we should have, I don't know, but it would be our last day on the bike for a long time. We cycled to Bandirma, a small town on the south coast of the Marmara Sea, and at noon we boarded a ferry to Istanbul.

Just before the ferry docked in Istanbul, a spectacular sound of wonderful worship, the familiar prayers that one-fourth of our planet's inhabitants must know by heart, rang out from the cities' minarets, and filled the air:

Allahu Akbar
Ash-hadu an la ilaha illa Allah
Ash-hadu anna Muhammadan-Rasul ullah
Hayya'alas-Salah
Hayya 'alal-Falah
Allahu Akbar
La ilaha illa-Allah

Allah is the greatest.
I acknowledge that there is no god but Allah.
I acknowledge that Muhammad is the Messenger of Allah.
Hasten to prayer.
Hasten to success.
God is greatest.
There is no god but Allah.

BULLETPROOF

Istanbul means *to the city*. And to the city we had come. It's quite the city. It's the link between Europe and Asia, the city of Constantine, which fell to Sultan Ahmet II to become Istanbul, and the home of fifteen million. Just one of these fifteen million, however, taught me everything I needed to know about Istanbul.

We were at the Sirkeci metro station, just below the Hagia Sophia, looking at a giant map of Istanbul on the wall. A man approached. He was short, thin, and dressed in a tweed suit, with a striped shirt and a polyester tie. His face was dark and wrinkled – he'd worked hard all his life – and although there was a spring in his step, he walked slower than the rush-hour crowd racing to catch the metro.

He stopped in front of me and stared at the map. Before I could say *merhaba* he put the tips of the five fingers on his right hand together, raised his hand high and said, "Istanbul." The gesture was familiar, done to signify great worth. His pronunciation was slow and deliberate: ee-stan-bul. He again pointed to the map on the wall and again repeated the word, but slower and with greater energy, "Istanbul." He pointed at himself and again spoke, "Istanbul." Had he built the city himself, he could not have spoken more passionately.

I pointed to myself and mimicked his enthusiasm. I brought my right hand together, just as he had, and said, "America."

Great delight swept over his face and we embraced. It wasn't a transient hug – we really hugged. He stepped back, locked his right hand with his left, held them high over his head and said, "America. Istanbul." We hugged again.

* * *

Friday, October 10th 2014: Our first night in Istanbul

After ferrying to Istanbul, we took another boat across the Bosphorous Strait and arrived at the Üsküdar ferry station on Istanbul's Asian side. Asia. We were a long way from London. We arrived late, but Başar, our WS host and soon-to-be best friend, was still waiting. Başar is a bit shorter than me, and completely bald. If you had to pick him out of a crowd, however, look for the man with a smile on his face. It's his defining feature. Başar is a smiler.

He led us to his simple apartment – one room had a bed, some cupboards and a fridge, and the other room had a small bathroom-shower fusion – where we dropped off our stuff. We then went to dinner at his nearby feel-good restaurant. He ordered for us – fish soup, fish sandwiches and a salad, and then gave us the key to his apartment. When he was convinced we were comfortable, he raced to catch the last bus to his other home in the country. During the week he stays in Üsküdar, but he returns to the country each weekend.

We arrived in Istanbul with only one goal: to replace our rear hub. Once that was done, we planned to cycle to Izmir, and then to the Mediterranean, and to reach Antalya before an onward flight. An onward flight where? We weren't sure, but India, most likely.

Our hub was supposed to be delivered to Başar's office the day we arrived, but it never came. Oh well. We'll get it on Monday and take it to the shop Tuesday. It will be fixed Thursday, and we'll be on the road in a week. For now, let's see Istanbul.

10/11/2014: Istanbul

Cycling 40 hours a week makes Katy and I hungry. Real hungry. Our bodies, however, react to hunger differently. An eight-hour ride will make Katy hungry for the whole day. After two hours she'll need a snack, then a decent lunch, a bigger dinner and a treat at the end of the day (anything that resembles an Oreo will do). It's just how her body works. I'm different. An eight hour ride curbs my short-term appetite but plants the seeds of hunger deep within. I can ride most of the day without eating, have a small lunch and occasionally skip dinner. If the next day is equally demanding, my eating will be the same.

A rest day changes everything. The seeds of hunger have had time to grow, and, without exercise, the seeds blossom into giant flowers. I become ravenous. Some days, before I even get out of bed I know it's going to be a 10,000 calorie day. Saturday morning I woke up and said, "Hunger! Hunger! Hunger!"

But first, an item of food history. Hundreds of years ago, the Sultans of the Ottoman Empire were also hungry. They demanded the world's finest food to accompany the world's greatest Empire. Terrified of the Sultans' hanger (anger fueled by hunger), the Sultans' chefs retreated to the kitchens of the Topkapi Palace. They worked all day and all night and by morning they created a thin dough. They called it filo dough. Filo was then used to make baklava, börek, gibanica, and spanakopita: the world's finest foods. We toured the Topkapi Palace, and while everyone was fascinated with the living quarters of the Sultans, I spent my time in the kitchen staring at the marble tables. "Look Katy," I whispered. "This is where it happened. Baklava genesis." It was a spiritual moment.

What did we eat in Istanbul? What didn't we eat? Fish sandwiches on the Galata Bridge, Turkish Delight in the old Bazaar, roasted chestnuts on every street corner and a kebab or three.

I love the kebab. Love it. Rotating meat is mesmerizing. Like waves crashing in the ocean, or the dying embers of a fire, I could stare at that rotating meat forever. I've never been able to find out what animal grows in that shape, so I refer to the kebab as meat-plywood.

Then we discovered sütlaç – Turkish rice pudding. It's served in rectangular tinfoil containers. I like mine cold; Katy prefers hers warm. I wish I could have shared each bite with my Grandma Ann. She was a connoisseur of fine rice pudding. Just around the corner from Başar's is a little dessert shop, so we got sütlaç every night.

The strangest of Turkish desserts is tavuk göğsü. It's white and sweet and full of stringy chicken. I never really got the hang of it.

To accompany these new foods, I searched for a Turkish beverage. I found ayran, Turkey's national beverage. It comes in a plastic cup, with a tear-away paper lid and a pointy straw. The Turks never tear-way; they jab. They send the straw right through the lid the same way the "cool kids" put their pointy straws through the bottoms of Capri Suns. I wanted to be cool, so I jabbed.

If you ask a Turk to describe ayran, they hesitate. It's like asking a thirsty person to describe water. At our first kebab shop, I ordered a Diet Coke and everyone at the shop stared at me: *Hello? You're doing it wrong.* With my second kebab, I ordered my first ayran. It was awful. Putrid in fact. I couldn't finish it.

Ayran translates to diluted, salty yogurt drink. And it's just that – watered down, salty yogurt. But everywhere we went, there it was, taunting me: *if you want to experience Turkey, learn to love me.* I figured it must be an acquired taste, and with only a month in Turkey, I decided I better hurry up and start acquiring. Each jab of the cup brought me closer and closer to my all-time favorite beverage. My third ayran left me feeling uncomfortable, but when I finished my fifth I was left wanting more. Ayran number eight and nine went down smooth and after ten of those drinks a light went off in my head and the drink was divine. When I reflect on Turkish cuisine, there are many foods I miss. But if I could have anything, it would be ayran. It is watered down, salty yogurt. And it is delicious.

10/12/14: Istanbul

Başar took us to Kadıköy, a neighborhood adjacent to Üsküdar, and taught us about local foods, the history of the city, and current events. New places are great; new places with locals are even better. As we passed a Starbucks, he said, "The stuff in there is awful, I would never drink it." We ate at Ciya Sofrasi, the "best restaurant in Istanbul," and enjoyed incredible flavors and textures not found elsewhere in Europe. For dessert we had kabak tatlısı, candied pumpkin topped with walnuts and kaymak. Mmm.

10/13/14: Istanbul

Başar spent hours calling and emailing FedEx about our hub, only to learn it was stuck in customs. We planned to find other accommodations so Başar could return to his apartment, but he insisted we stay in his home until our wheel was fixed. We were his guests and he happily took the long bus ride each day from work to his home in the country.

10/14/14: Istanbul

We trekked across town to the FedEx customs office, filled out their form, paid an $87 import fee and were told our hub would arrive in two days.

10/16/14 Istanbul

No delivery. No hub.

10/17/14: Istanbul

Friday is Islam's holy day. Katy arranged for us to attend the 1pm sermon at the Sultan Ahmed Mosque, the Blue Mosque. We followed our chaperone, Shadid, past security and left our shoes at the door, while all other foreigners were turned away. If you're going to visit one of the most famous mosques in the world during Friday worship, you have to arrive with someone who knows what they're doing!

Allah commands Muslims to pray in a clean place, so we removed our shoes before entering. The mosque was packed. Katy followed other women to the balcony, and I followed Shadid in search of an empty patch of carpet. An usher directed Shadid to the front of the mosque, so we carefully tiptoed over hundreds of men preparing for worship. Suddenly, my blonde ponytail felt slightly out of place. The many stares, however, were friendly, welcoming stares. Islam is the fastest growing major religion in the world; they must be used to newcomers.

Before the Imam began his sermon, the mood was spiritual, but casual. Some took photos and others whispered to friends, but most performed *salat*, the Islamic ritual prayer. *Salat* is a complex sequence of Arabic phrases, combined with hand movements and prostrations.

Stand erect. Hands to the ears. A full bow and then back to standing. Fall to the knees. Prostrate with hands and forehead on the ground. Return to kneeling. Back to prostrating. Return to standing. Shadid told me I could pray as I pleased.

Then the Iman appeared. Instantly, *salat* was performed in unison and the mosque got hot. It was spiritual Bikram Yoga – sweating, poses, and devotion to Allah. I did my best to follow along. Stand, bow, stand, kneel, prostrate, kneel, prostrate, kneel, stand. Repeat. I've prayed before, in many places and in many circumstances, but never have I had such a powerful reminder of the necessity for humility and devotion towards God, as I did in The Blue Mosque, fully prostrated on the floor, surrounded by thousands of devoted Muslims. The word *Muslim* means surrender, and on that day these Muslims surrendered to Allah.

After the sermon, the *muezzin* sang the call to prayer. I was familiar with the call to prayer. It's always performed live and is always the same (except in the morning when the phrase "prayer is better than sleep" is added). It occasionally feels a bit creepy, like Big Brother is watching you, but for the most part I enjoy it. Inside the Blue Mosque, however, the call to prayer was one of the most intensely spiritual, awesome moments I've ever had. The voice was angelic and the devotion real.

One in four people on Earth call themselves Muslim. Muslims are peaceful and kind. I love their mosques. They are clean and simple, decorated only with Arabic verses from the Quran, because to make any art or interpretation of Allah or Muhammad is forbidden. Mosques are for worship, and nothing else.

In contrast to my Mormon background, where, in addition to religious services, churches are used for basketball games, Ward Christmas dinners, Boy Scouts meetings, Young Women cake auctions and a host of other events, mosques exist for one reason and one reason alone – to worship Allah. I admire Muslims' devotion to Allah. They don't feel the need to justify their actions, but instead say, "Allah forbids it" when defending their religious beliefs. If you tried to build a basketball court or host a Pinewood Derby in a mosque, many would protest and someone would cry out, "Allah forbids it."

10/18/14: Istanbul

Başar called FedEx a dozen times but was unable to find out when our hub would be delivered. We hailed down an MNGKargo (Turkey's FedEx partner) delivery truck and asked the driver the same question. He told us to call customer service. We decided our hub "will come when it comes" so we left everything at Başar's, packed a backpack and took a train to Ankara and then a bus to Cappadocia.

10/19 – 10/22: Cappadocia, Pammukale and Efes

Cappadocia is incredible, a wonderland of red rock, with thousand-year-old homes carved into the volcanic rock. After Cappadocia we visited Pammukale and Ephesus before flying back to Istanbul. We realized two things on this mini-vacation. First, flights in and around Turkey are cheap. Second, traditional tourism – on public transportation to all the recommended sites – is exhausting. In Pammukale, desperate to avoid more tour buses, we hunkered down and planned the next ten weeks of our trip.

Because flights in Turkey were so cheap, and also because our hub still hadn't arrived, we decided against more cycling in Turkey. Instead, we planned five days of hiking in the Kaçkar Mountains of Eastern Turkey, getting there by a round-trip flight out of Istanbul. Then a week in Israel and Jordan, also flying out of Istanbul. Then we planned to fly to Kathmandu, Nepal, with an intentional 36 hour layover in Dubai. We planned for a week trekking in the Himalayas before getting back on our bike and cycling south into India.

India had always been on our itinerary. In 2012, we spent three days there on our way to Nepal and Tibet. India had shocked and terrified us. We couldn't wait to go back. We originally planned to travel through India by train because we believed, like everyone else we had met, that cycling through India would be insane. We asked many WS hosts what they thought about cycling in India and always got the same answer, "Have you been to India?" Only the lunatic or arrogant would venture into the Subcontinent on a bicycle. But in Cappadocia, that decision changed.

In Cappadocia, Pammukale, and Ephesus we were tourists. We

arrived by bus, got harangued by touts, ate in restaurants with English menus, and read free copies of the Lonely Planet in coffee shops. It was exhausting. The Lonely Planet is the "Bible" for most do-it-yourself tourists. It's a great guidebook, with suggestions on how to navigate public transportation, where to go, what to eat, and where to sleep. In essence, what Lonely Planet says, goes. Everyone uses it. (Except for the French, of course, they use Le Routard.) And that is, unfortunately, exactly the problem with it. For example, to get to Cappadocia, we followed LP travel suggestions. They were good, but the bus was full of foreigners. Then we went to the suggested guesthouse. More foreigners. At night we heard conversations in German, French, and English, but no Turkish. We made a reservation at the suggested restaurant (we had to make a reservation, Lonely Planet said so) and it, too, was full of foreigners. We went to Kaymaklı, the recommended underground city, and were met by a dozen tour buses. We even went *early*, just like LP said, but so did everyone else. *We're in Turkey, where are all the Turks? If I wanted to meet Germans I would have gone to Germany.*

Not only did it feel like Disneyland, lining up for the next tourist attraction, but the behavior of the few locals we met was also very different. They were businesslike, not friendly. They deal with hundreds of tourists each day, how could they possibly offer tea to all of them? Instead of a guest in their country, I felt more like a bank account. There was limited generosity and certainly no offers to "sleep in my restaurant's garden." It was business as usual. But I didn't want usual. I didn't even expect usual. I expected kindness and genuine friendship, because that is what Başar (and all our other WS hosts) showered upon us. It's what a family of Italians on Simplon Pass, fellow tandemists in Slovenia, goulash-loving Hungarians, and ordinary folks across rural Turkey had offered.

These anti-tourism feelings didn't begin in Cappadocia. They boiled over there. They probably started years ago as a missionary in Port Antonio, Jamaica but more recently resurfaced in Venice and Prague. Venice is one of the most beautiful cities in the world; no one will dispute that. After that, however, I thought it felt hollow. It's 50,000 people a day corralled down narrow streets. We saw what everyone else saw. But I don't want what everyone else sees. I want a unique experience. To me, going with the flow and obeying the LP commandments is boring. Prague is also a beautiful city. But it's really creepy when my morning walk to the Charles Bridge is interrupted by half a dozen offers for a Thai massage. Fast forward a couple months into the future: Angkor Wat is absolutely magnificent, one of the most incredible structures on this planet, but if you spend the night in Siem Reap be prepared to turn down massages performed by fish nibbling at your feet.

The best thing about the stench of tourism – if it has a redeeming quality – is that its foul odor doesn't blow far. You can usually find quiet solitude just a couple streets away from 50,000 tourists. I guess it's nice that Lonely Planet exists; it ensures tourists never wander too far, and thus makes sure that most of a country remains authentic and unspoiled. And it's those quiet streets that we do our best to find. If there were a straight road between two cities, that's not the road we want to cycle. We want the one that winds and wanders and adds an extra hour to our ride. That's where things happen.

In Pammukale, we decided the only way we could visit India would be by bike. The decision frightened me and terrified Katy. But, if we wanted to embrace India – hate it and love it – we knew we had to be on our Brooks saddles, far away from the air-conditioned tour buses.

10/23/14: Back in Istanbul

The day we'd been waiting for. We took our wheel and replacement hub (which finally came!) to Bisiklet Gezgini. Bisiklet Gezgini is the only capable, high-end bike touring shop between Istanbul and Bangkok. For cyclists venturing from Europe into Asia, it's the last chance for repairs and supplies. We explained our problem to Alexios, the owner and mechanic, and he told us he'd take care of it.

What ruined our wheel? The simple answer is that Katy and I are too strong. We rode too many kilometers, on roads too steep, in a gear too hard, pulling too heavy a load. Four legs pounded on the pedals and our rear hub couldn't take the abuse. At least, that's what I tell myself. I'm not exactly sure why our hub failed prematurely. We were told our replacement hub would be much tougher. I hoped so.

10/24 –10/28: Trabzon, Turkey

We flew from Istanbul to Trabzon, a city in Eastern Turkey and then took a bus to Ayder in the Kaçkar Mountains. We enjoyed marvelous weather, stunning mountains, and a spontaneous dance session with some Turkish medical students. Each night, in the mountain town of Ayder, we went to the single-room grocery store and each night the owner brought out a table and chairs. We sat and drank tea. In a mountain lodge we were offered *muhlama,* a cheese fondue dish popular in the Eastern Black Sea region of Turkey. After an eight hour hike, it got dark and we resorted to hitchhiking back to town. We were picked up in no time. Thirsty, hungry, or lost in Turkey? Never fear, the Turks are here.

The week was a smashing success, until the following email arrived:

> Ahoy there dear Clayton,
>
> I had a closer look on the hub you got here and am sorry to have to tell you it cannot be used for your wheel, as there is no place for a disc brake rotor. The attachment is missing. It certainly is not a good idea to use a tandem with only the front brake!
>
> Greetings,
>
> Alexios

Holy mother of hell! Three weeks after we ordered a new hub we were back at square one – stranded in Turkey with a bogus wheel. I emailed my bike mechanic in Ann Arbor, told him of his egregious error, and he profusely apologized and put the disc brake attachment in the mail the next day. But I couldn't risk the attachment also being the wrong size, or this package also getting stuck in customs, so I devised a backup plan. I ordered an entirely new hub and sent it to my sister Elizabeth in Utah. She was going to visit us in Kathmandu in a couple of weeks. If the brake attachment didn't arrive in Turkey, we'd have a new hub brought to Kathmandu. I wasn't sure if we'd find a decent mechanic in Nepal, but what other option did we have?

10/30 – 11/5: Israel and Jordan

Jerusalem is an intersection of Judaism, Christianity, and Islam. It's where King David established the Kingdom of Israel, where Solomon built his temple, where Christ was crucified, and where Mohammad ascended to heaven. We arrived in Jerusalem amidst escalating Palestinian-Israeli tensions. The day before, a Palestinian had shot and killed a Rabbi who had campaigned for Jews to visit the Temple Mount. (Most Jews avoid the Temple Mount, because they don't know the exact location of Solomon's Temple and the Holy of Holies, and to enter that area would be heretical.) Throughout the week, Israeli Police prevented Muslims from entering the Temple Mount and visiting the Dome of the Rock or the Al-Aqsa Mosque.

In the midst of the protest, a Muslim lady explained the situation to us. "They won't let us go in and pray. It's been like this for weeks. Today they say only men can go in. The women talk back to the police because if men do they will be arrested."

Israeli soldiers were decked out in their uniforms, armed with weapons, and Muslim women nearby chanted "*Allahu Akbar*" or "Allah is the Greatest". You can learn a lot about cruelty and oppression by watching the news or reading books, but standing in the Old City and watching it happen in real-time left a much more meaningful impact.

That evening at a roadside restaurant Katy asked two Arab girls where we could find some dessert.

"Come with us," they answered.

Twenty minutes and one unexpected bus ride later we arrived at Jafar's Sweets in Beit Hanina where their friend, Aladeen, joined us. In addition to baklava with cream, they had us try kanafa and basbousa. All week the Palestinians were as friendly as can be.

Jordan was awesome. Wadi Rum is vast. Petra is unbelievable. Another of our favorite stops we didn't originally plan on visiting.

11/6/14: Istanbul

Our flight landed in Istanbul and we went straight to Bisiklet Gezgini . . . but got bad news. The disc brake attachment had not arrived. After almost four weeks in Istanbul, with only one tangible goal to accomplish, we left Istanbul no better off than when we had arrived. That evening we would leave Turkey and fly east to Dubai and then Kathmandu. It was hard to say goodbye to Istanbul. It's an incredible place. I miss everything about it. Everything, of course, but the cats.

As the story goes, the Prophet Muhammad was taking a nap when a cat fell asleep on the edge of his garment. When the Prophet awoke, he noticed the cat and, not wanting to trouble the animal, cut off a portion of his garment so the cat could remain asleep and the Prophet could go on his way. Because of this, Muslims treat cats – most of them strays – with great respect. They leave out food and milk, and place little boxes next to their front door for the cats to sleep in. It's not uncommon to see a businessman pick one up, scratch its back, and offer it a snack. Not me. Cats are nasty little creatures when they belong to someone. But stray ones? Don't get me started.

11/7/14: Dubai

Dubai is wild. And, thank goodness, most of it is air-conditioned.

11/8 – 11/15: Langtang National Park, Nepal

Before our Himalayan trek began, while Katy enjoyed her continental breakfast with my mother and sister, I raced off to Himalayan Single Track to . . . get our rear hub fixed. (I feel like a broken record.) Before we arrived in Nepal I did a thorough internet search and decided this was the best bike shop in the country. I dropped off our wheel and our new, new hub – the one Elizabeth had brought out – and was promised the wheel would be fixed by the time we returned from our Himalayan trek. I crossed my fingers.

Trekking in the Himalayas never disappoints. Along with my sister, my mother Charlotte also joined us for our time in Nepal and a weeklong trek in the Langtang Valley. Here are their own words about our trek.

Charlotte:

"At 10,000 feet, after an eight-hour hike, we chose Hotel Potala for our evening stay. Before I could even think of sitting down and taking in my bedroom's view, I jumped at the invitation to have a solar-powered hot shower. The promise that it would be hot caught my attention and I rallied my last bit of energy. Standing inside a corrugated metal square box, atop a rock floor, I turned on the hot faucet.

It was the most scenic, most memorable, hottest hot shower of my entire life. Sizzling hot water, fabulous spray, and a scenic view out a rusty square window. I could have stayed for hours. My gratitude for a hot shower took on a whole new meaning! I was rejuvenated beyond belief. Warm, clean, and cozy, I put on my ski underwear, sat next to a warm wood-choked stove and spent the evening with three of my wonderful children."

Elizabeth:

"The day after we arrived at Kyanjin Gompa, Clayton, Katy, Valerie, and I set off to conquer Tsergo Ri. Tsergo Ri, a 16,450 foot peak at the end of the Langtang Valley, can be summited in a day from Kyanjin Gompa. But don't get me wrong, just because it was a day hike doesn't mean it was easy. The first challenge was crossing a river covered in ice. Once that was accomplished it was up, up, up, and up. Straight up.

I consider myself to be in decent shape, but this was a challenge. At times I felt like all I could do was put one foot in front of the other. Apparently high altitude and the lack of oxygen is a real thing. But the views kept me going – my goodness. They were stunning! And the higher we got the more spectacular they were. Once we passed the rock fields and all the Koreans in their fancy pansy gear, and up the icy, snowy ridge, we made it to the top! The peak was covered in beautiful prayer flags, exactly how I imagined it."

The colors of the prayer flags correspond to the syllables in the Tibetan Buddhist chant, Om Mani Padme Hum, as follows. Om – White – Generosity, Ma – Green – Ethics, Ni – Yellow – Patience, Pad – Blue – Diligence, Me – Red – Renunciation, Hum – Black – Wisdom. It's best sung as a mantra: Om Mani Padme Hum, Om Mani Padme Hum, Om Mani Padme Hum, Om Mani Padme Hum. When the wind blows, and it does blow, the prayers are sent to the heavens.

11/16: Back in Kathmandu

I was nervous. I returned to Himalayan Single Track and was consumed by a single thought. I entered the shop, hoping to see a beautiful new wheel, but instead found a haphazard pile of spokes, two hubs and a rim. My heart sank. I tried to argue with the mechanic. He fumbled and he mumbled, and said something about the spokes not being the right size. He was wrong. I demanded he start building the wheel. He said okay, it will be done tonight.

I returned half an hour later, after telling Katy the bad news. The mechanic was gone and the pile remained. *Forget this.* I found my rim and my two hubs, carefully counted all the spokes and nipples I had brought and returned to my guesthouse.

Relax Clayton, you can do this. You've never built a wheel before, but surely you can figure it out. In eighteen hours, Charlotte and Elizabeth were flying home. If I couldn't rebuild the wheel by then, or at least convince myself that I could, I decided I would send the bike home and my mother could return with it in two months when she'd visit us in Laos. We'd see India by train. But, if I managed to rebuild the wheel, or convince myself that I could, we could continue our journey and cycle through India. Time to get to work.

I started online. I read everything Sheldon Brown and Park Tool have written about wheel building and I watched half a dozen YouTube videos. Then I read and watched everything again. I learned fast.

A wheel has three pieces: the hub, the spokes, and the rim. To replace our hub, the spokes needed to be removed. Then the wheel could be rebuilt using the new hub with the original spokes and rim. In theory it's easy. I was just swapping out one piece. But I wasn't just building any wheel. I was building the rear wheel of a loaded tandem that would spend the next two months on the bumpiest, roughest roads of our trip. I couldn't build an okay wheel. I had to build a damn good one.

First I chose a lacing pattern. An old picture of our wheel showed a 3 cross pattern. I decided to replicate it. If I tried to use a 2 or 4 cross pattern the spokes would be too long or too short. I found a piece of cardboard and drew the pattern again and again until it made sense. Then I began.

Spokes enter the hub on two different sides, in an alternating pattern, in, out, in, out. The 3 cross pattern means each spoke crosses 3 other spokes before attaching to the rim. When spokes cross, they strengthen a wheel. I laced each spoke to the rim, careful to follow the pattern, and cross the spokes correctly, over, over, under. Then I started tightening. My spoke wrench is basic. It comes standard on a multi-tool, but it does the job.

When building a wheel, little things matter. I marked a spoke with my Sharpie (to know where I started) and tightened each spoke half a turn. Then another half turn. Then a quarter turn. And another quarter turn. Once the spokes felt tight, and the wheel began to take shape, the hard part started: truing the wheel. Just because each spoke had an identical amount of tightening, did not mean the wheel was true. Far from it.

Wheels are "true" in two dimensions: horizontally and vertically. A wheel that isn't horizontally true wobbles side to side, and the brakes may rub. A wheel that isn't vertically true is slightly oval. You probably won't be able to tell by looking at it, but you will feel a little bump when you ride down the road each time the oval part comes in contact with the pavement. Professional wheel builders use truing stands to build and true wheels. The slightest deviation from perfectly true can be detected as the rim spins next to precise calipers. I didn't have a truing stand. I used six inches of fabric ruler, some electrical tape, a disposable Glide flosser (it had a straight edge), and the rear triangle of my bike.

I placed the bike upside down, taped the fabric ruler to the frame right next to the rim, and spun my new wheel. It wobbled like crazy. I turned the wheel slowly, and found the spot on the rim with the greatest lateral deviation to the right (as measured by the ruler). To "pull" the rim back to the left, I found that spot on the rim and tightened the two adjacent spokes going into the left side of the hub, half a turn each, and then loosened the two adjacent spokes going into the right side of the hub. You must be careful to tighten and loosen the same amount. If you only tighten, then you'll create a vertically out-of-true problem.

I spun the wheel again, looking for the greatest deviation to the left. Then I tightened spokes to the right side of the hub, and loosened spokes to the left side. I repeated this process for a couple of hours. When the ruler could no longer detect a wobble, perhaps because my eyes were going blurry, I put the disposable Glide flosser up to the rim and listened. If I heard a scrape, that was my next spot to fix. I repeated this process for a couple of hours.

Then I checked for vertical out-of-trueness. I held the disposable flosser just on top of the rim and spun the wheel. If the rim scraped in one place, but not another, it meant the wheel was slightly oval there. This problem is fixed by tightening two adjacent spokes, one to the right side and one to the left side. If you don't tighten spokes to both sides you create a horizontal out-of-true problem.

Once the wheel was true and tight, I checked spoke tension. A wheel can be perfectly true, but it also needs tight, strong spokes. Most mechanics use a tension meter, but I didn't have one. I used my ear. I plucked the spokes, just like guitar strings. Low notes were not tight enough. I plucked and tightened, again and again. I plucked and tightened until notes on the rear wheel matched notes on the front wheel. Of course, tightening spokes created a wheel that wasn't true. I re-trued.

11/18: Kathmandu

Almost six weeks after arriving in Istanbul, my wheel looked brand new. But looks can be deceiving, so I went for a test ride. Better to have the wheel crumple around the block than in Uttar Pradesh, the most populated state in Northern India. I needed a bulletproof wheel, not a good-looking wheel.

I waited until night, when most of the traffic was gone. Katy wished me luck and off I went. Halfway down the street the craziest thing happened – I realized, for the first time since somewhere in Austria, I was riding a perfectly functional bike. I stopped pedaling and let the rear wheel coast. It was quiet and smooth. It didn't wobble one bit. I circled around town and picked up Katy. I hit every pothole I could find. The wheel was bulletproof.

Bicycle Assembly, Heathrow International Airport

Mark Cavendish, Marcel Kittel, Peter Sagan – The Tour de France

Camping in Malham, Yorkshire Dales National Park, England

Katy, our tandem, and the Chateau de Chambord

Above:
Madame Bourthier
and her legendary
plum crumble

Right:
Leaving France for
Switzerland, with
baguettes and
fromage in tow

Left:
The Vrsic Pass,
Triglavski
National Park,
Slovenia

Below:
The Stari Most,
Mostar,
Bosnia and
Herzegovina

Arriving in Turkey

Dinner with Basar in Uskudar, Istanbul

Sultan for a Day, Topkapi Palace, Istanbul

Another Cup of Tea, Ayder, Kackar Mountains, Turkey

PART THREE

"Life is like riding a bicycle.
To keep your balance, you must keep moving."

Albert Einstein

TIBET
PAKISTAN
RAJASTHAN
NEW DELHI
RISHIKESH
UTTAR
PRADESH
NEPAL
LANGTANG VALLEY
KATHMANDU
JAISALMER
JODHPUR
JAIPUR
AGRA
LUCKNOW
GORAKHPUR
VARANASI
BICYCLE
TRAIN
INDIA
INDORE
KOLKATA

ONCOMING TRAFFIC

When you're recovering from a bout of diarrhea – and Kathmandu is two-for-two on giving me the runs – the best sign of recovery is fearfully pushing out a fart, nervous as hell that something wet might escape, but when you check, it's dry as can be back there. *Phew*. No more nasty, squirty liquid and no more compulsory change of undergarments. I'm okay with a transient episode of loose stools. In fact, I welcome it. When I arrive in a third world country I hit the street food early and often. The sooner my bowels learn who's boss, the better.

After I built our rear wheel, and before I was able to declare it bulletproof, I had to reassemble our bike. We break it down into a myriad of pieces and box it up each time we fly, so it must be reassembled. I tossed two custom-sized cardboard boxes aside and removed bubble wrap and packaging tape from a dozen or more items. We had three sections of frame, two wheels, two seat posts with their saddles, four cranks, two handlebars, front and rear racks, fenders, a timing chain, a rear derailleur taped inside the rear triangle, Katy's water bottle holder, two disc brake rotors, and an assortment of screws, nuts, and washers. I'm in charge of the bicycle; Katy attends to the rest of our belongings.

I assemble the entire bike with a basic multi-tool, three separate

Allen wrenches and an adjustable wrench. *Clayton, put your tools HERE when you're not using them,* I told myself. I enjoy working on our bike but I hate looking for misplaced items. I hate it.

The building process takes two or three hours. First, I assemble the frame with four couplers and attach my handlebars. Katy's handlebars slide through my seat post before I can set my seat to the proper height. Once the frame, handlebars and seats are attached, I turn the bike upside down and the real fun begins.

Next are the cranksets. These "moving parts" require a little more attention. The right and left cranks connect through the frame's bottom bracket by a spindle, and they are screwed tight with an 8mm Allen wrench. Every time we pedal this spindle rotates – a couple million rotations over the course of our travels. The smallest amount of dirt or grime left on the cranks will wear and tear at the bottom bracket until it is ruined. I clean each surface. Then I clean them again. After I blow it clean, I add grease to the crankset washers and attach the right and left cranks.

"Hey Katy, be quiet for a moment," I hollered across the room.

When the room is silent, I spin the cranks and listen. If I can't hear any grinding then I feel with my hands. The smallest foreign particles can often be felt when the pedals rotate but not heard. If I feel nothing then I move on to Katy's crank.

The rear derailleur attaches to the frame with a single bolt. I'm careful not to strip the threads on that bolt or in the frame. Stripped threads would end our party real fast.

Fenders go on before the racks. They're easy to assemble, but tedious. They have metal rods, which attach to the frame, allowing the fender to be centered over the wheel. The racks are simple; I always triple check that the screws are tight because our Edinburgh WS host's story of his front rack catastrophe replays in my mind every time I reattach our racks.

When we pack up our bike I remove the disc brake rotors and pack them in a sturdy cardboard cutout inside the wheels. This might not be necessary, but a bent rotor would rub on our brakes for thousands of kilometers, so I spend ten minutes to remove them and not take any chances. They attach with 6 star shaped screws and are often a job for Katy (which I double check).

Three cables, one for the rear brake and one for each derailleur, connect under the frame with little screw connectors. Individual pieces of sand, dirt or miscellaneous filth from a dirty floor often get stuck in the threads of these connectors, so I scrape the threads clean with my fingernail. Screwing the connectors entirely closed ensures our cable tension is nearly identical to what it was before the bike was disassembled, which means the derailleurs and brakes shouldn't need significant adjustment. I secure the wheels and tighten their skewers to ensure that the brake cables are taut and the brakes don't rub. Sounds easy, but getting the brakes just right can be a lengthy process. Last are the pedals, each secured with a little grease on the screw threads. Right pedals tighten by turning clockwise and left pedals by turning counter-clockwise, so the pedaling motion will further tighten, rather than loosen, the pedals once we start riding.

This entire process went without difficulty until I snapped the head of a screw off while trying to attach the front rack to our frame. Except for the one broken screw, we performed the three hour task without error. That one error, however, was a showstopper. It prevented our front rack from attaching and made it impossible to carry half of our gear.

I sent Katy to search Kathmandu for some vise-grips. She returned an hour later with a broken pair. I told her I would go find some, which I did, but that screw wouldn't budge. No matter how hard I squeezed, the vise-grip would slip. I returned to the auto mechanic and asked for a file. If I make straight edges on this screw, I thought, the vise-grips won't slip. I filed for an hour and squeezed with all my might. No dice. I went in search of a professional.

At first glance, Gopal isn't the type of guy I would usually let work on my bike. His bicycle repair shop was no more than some dirty tools strewn about on the dirty asphalt and a large bowl of dirty water. There was no "inside" to his shop; he worked on the side of the street. But he worked frantically to help other customers and spoke a little English, so I went with him. I didn't explain my problem. I just pointed to the screw stuck in our frame and Gopal went to work.

First he tried vise-grips. No luck. Then he tried placing two nuts on the screw, the second one to lock the first, which could then remove the screw with a wrench. He couldn't place the nuts on the screw, however, because I had filed the threads off. He looked up at me like I was an idiot and shook his head. *Sorry.*

Finally he got out a chisel, a hammer and some WD40. Not your typical bike shop tools. He soaked the screw in the lubricant and started tapping. I winced each time he struck the chisel with the hammer, but I didn't stop him. If he had swung too hard and cracked our frame we would have had a serious problem, but I assumed he'd done this before. After a series of taps and whacks he felt a little give and carefully removed the screw with the vise grips. Then he inserted and removed an identical screw five or six times to create clean, unobstructed threads in our fork.

"In Nepal, we can't buy a replacement anytime something breaks," he told me when his work was finished. "We find a way to fix everything."

We were grateful for his resourcefulness, and paid him $4 or $5 for his repairs, a small price to pay in exchange for the use of our front rack. After the screw was fixed we got a side view mirror, nine spare spokes (to prepare for India's roads) and a bell for Katy. Further down the street we bought a pair of super groovy green and blue parachute pants to be worn over our spandex to cut down on the "out of town" look we already carried with us, and also for Katy to be more culturally sensitive.

"Yeah, you blend," Katy joked when she saw me put on my new outfit.

Last but not least, we bought a flag with the word Om, written in Sanskrit, and thumbtacked it to a wooden flagpole. For Hindus, Om is the greatest of all mantras. It represents the earth, the atmosphere, and the heavens. It represents Brahma, Vishnu and Shiva. To create the universe, God spoke. And the sound He spoke was Om.

Om is also closely related to the Hindu deity Ganesha. Ganesha is the remover (and placer) of obstacles and should be worshipped before the beginning of any undertaking. Everyone – and not just Hindus – loves Ganesha. Why? Because Ganesha has an elephant's head.

As legend has it, Parvati (Ganesha's mother) asked Ganesha to guard the door of their home while she took a bath. Shiva (Parvati's husband, who had been away for a very long time) returned home to find a young boy guarding his own front door. Ganesha told Shiva he could not enter. Enraged, Shiva sent his army to kill Ganesha. Ganesha killed the entire army. Shiva then fought Ganesha and cut off Ganesha's head.

Parvati was furious that her husband had killed their son. She went to Brahma (the Creator) and threatened to destroy all of Creation unless Ganesha was brought back to life. Brahma and Shiva agreed. Brahma instructed Shiva to go and find the first living creature with its head pointed north. He returned with an elephant. Ganesha was brought back to life, given the head of the elephant, and became the most beloved of all of the Hindu Gods.

Of course I didn't know any of this when I bought the Om flag. I thought it looked nice. But when you're trapped in India, sick, and unwilling to battle the curious throngs, *and* you have decent WiFi for the first time in a week, you spend your time on Wikipedia and learn the fascinating beliefs of a billion of the people on your planet.

* * *

Our alarm went off early. At 4:30am I usually press snooze, but on our last morning in Kathmandu I jumped out of bed. By five-fifteen we were packed, dressed in our parachute pants and out the door. Breakfast could wait. I looked at Google Maps one last time, committing the first five or six turns of our route to memory and released the front brake. I heard Katy's cleats click into her pedals and we were back – back on the road, and the left side of the road – after a long six-week hiatus.

I thought we'd have the roads to ourselves on that dark and cold morning, but the city was already stirring. Motorbikes raced by. Roosters stood on their tiptoes to wake others long before dawn. A man pushed a fruit-filled wooden trolley down a dark alley. At the intersection of Tridevi Sadak and Thamel Marg, the main intersection in Thamel, men set out their Hindu statues, wall masks, Gurkha knives, and other trinkets.

"Ugghhem." Katy cleared her throat for the sixth time in what seemed like the same number of minutes. As we rode west out of the Kathmandu valley towards Pokhara our lungs filled with smog and air pollution. Diesel engines blew black clouds of soot into our faces and I wondered if this was one of those "outdoor exercise not recommended" kind of days. Kathmandu is the gateway to the pristine Himalayas, but it isn't pristine itself.

Morning's darkness hid us, and our tandem, from the eyes of a thousand pedestrians and we escaped the city unnoticed. As we climbed out of the Kathmandu valley dozens of small fires burned along the sides of the road. Around each fire, men and women huddled together and sipped their morning tea. We were in a different world now, one without climate control. Staying warm meant blankets and fire and hot tea. There was no longer a thermostat on the wall.

At the edge of the Kathmandu valley, we saw the lights of the city to our east and nothing but darkness to the west. From there it was a two day descent to the Terai in southern Nepal, and then nothing but flatlands for ten days to Varanasi, India on the Ganges River.

The road was decent, but not ideal – a simple two lane highway, without a shoulder of course and, instead of paved asphalt, sections of concrete. In a car, this makes no difference, but on a bike it makes a rhythmic ka-bump . . . ka-bump . . . ka-bump for hours. No shoulder? No problem. We rode right in the middle of the lane.

The morning traffic leaving Kathmandu was light, but rush-hour traffic crawling up the windy mountain towards Kathmandu was bumper-to-bumper. Most of this traffic was Nepal's transportation workhorse: the over-loaded semi-truck, painted with a myriad of Hindu gods and goddesses. The words "Horn Please" or "Blow Horn" are painted on the back of each truck. Trucks that might some day enter India have the words "All India Permit" painted on the front. It's kind of like stamping a US Visa on your forehead, and expecting entrance into the States. My favorite, however, are the trucks that say "Road King", especially the ones, and there are many, that break down on the side of the road. As their overused, weak engines try with all their might to climb the steep roads, breakdowns are the norm, not the exception. But it's not the broken trucks that scare us; the tip overs and the trucks in the bottom of ravines are what catch our attention.

Three minutes into our descent, we came around a switchback and a truck was in our lane, overtaking the standstill traffic, and headed right at us. The driver and I made eye contact and I assumed he'd merge. It was obvious we had the right of way, as it was *our* lane. I slowed down but held our course. He didn't flinch. Katy rang her bell to alert the driver, but I assumed her $2 *ting-ting* wouldn't alter the course of this climbing, inertial mammoth. A spot opened up for him to merge, but he didn't take it. Just before we were about to collide I swerved off the road and into the dirt.

Katy was silent, which usually signifies anger or fear, or both. I congratulated myself on my expert bike handling and on successfully evading a near death experience. Were another cyclist in my position, I reasoned, it might have been fatal. I assumed the unique event was due to a deranged driver, and so I etched it in my mind so I'd have stories to tell later. Surely this won't happen again.

But it did, ninety seconds later. Another truck coming right at us in our lane didn't bother to slow down, or move over, or even honk. He just headed right for us. *Oh I get it. We're the smallest guy on the road so we'll just get pushed around.* And then it happened again.

Things were different now. Ideas like "my lane" and "your lane" or "safety" and "reasonable" were gone. It was every man for himself, and the small guy always lost. The rules had changed, or maybe vanished. I wasn't sure which. If there were any rules of the road here, I couldn't decipher them. On our first day cycling in Nepal I just tried to not run into anyone, or be run over by anything.

At 8am we stopped for breakfast and to warm up. Morning sweat from our climb had turned our dry clothes wet and damp on our chilly descent.

"Curry, curry?" A little man asked from behind a giant pot.

I shook my head. Curry for lunch and curry for breakfast are two very different things. We settled on two bowls of rice pudding, four chapatti, two golden brown biscuits and two glasses of tea. $3.10.

After breakfast the road straightened out and I let up on the brakes. The sun was out, the breeze was cool, and we were cruising. But something didn't feel right.

"Do you feel that?" I asked Katy.

"Feel what?"

"That, that, that, that, that," I repeated the word as quickly as the thumping feeling repeated.

Further down the road our front tire went flat. As I replaced the tube I realized something was also wrong with the tire. A "flat tire" is easily fixed with a spare tube, but our problem was also with the tire itself. A pocket of air had collected in between layers of the tire, delaminating individual layers of rubber, and was responsible for the recent and rhythmic thumping.

"That's not good," Katy exclaimed after I explained the problem to her.

"Correct," I answered. "Flat, ruined tires aren't good. I've never seen, or even heard of, anything like this."

I replaced the tube with one of our extras and replaced the tire with our only spare tire. I bungeed the delaminated tire onto our rear rack, in case we'd need it later. Four months in Europe: one flat tire. One day in Nepal: one flat tire and one ruined tire.

At lunch, a dozen schoolgirls surrounded Katy and gave her handfuls of flowers for her hair and then taught us the basics of Nepali. For lunch we ate two veg chowmeins and two samosas. $1.20. It was delicious home cooking, with local ingredients and fresh vegetables. *Do these people have any idea . . . what the prices are . . . everywhere else in the world?*

On the next long descent, our Om flag, which we had attached to our rear rack, started to fray so we stopped at a roadside tailor. I asked a 15 year old boy if he could hem the edges. He did a quick and professional job.

"How much?" I asked.

The boy shook his head to say no. I thought maybe he didn't understand, so I offered him a fifty rupee note, just less than a dollar. Again he shook his head. I tried to force it into his hand. He put his hands behind his back. Finally I left it on the counter, said *Namaste* and walked away.

I'll always remember those fifty rupees. In third world countries I'm prepared to haggle. But I'm used to bartering for *lower* prices. There isn't a Nepali in Thamel or an Indian in Varanasi who wouldn't accept *more* of my money. And no one refuses a tip. But out in the country – away from the city's hustle and the frequent foreigners – things were different. This young tailor lives in a world where people are more than customers. Foreigners weren't wallets or business as usual. They were people. Our appearance in their town was rare and so they treated us as guests.

This scenario stood in stark contrast to the familiar fight-for-dollars and barter-for-nickels I had grown accustomed to from the week before in Kathmandu. Guesthouse prices were always negotiable, taxi drivers always charged 300% of what was fair, and purchasing anything off the street for face value was unheard-of. Barter, barter, barter. But this kid was just the opposite.

After a steep descent the wind snapped our wooden flagpole in half. I taped it together with black electrical tape but after the next descent it had bent to ninety degrees. I then found two sticks and taped them to the flagpole as splints. The flagpole still bent in the wind. At last I found a long rusty nail in the road and banged it straight with a large rock. I taped it next to the two sticks, and it held our flag sturdy for the next six weeks. Gopal was right. Westerners repair things with their wallet, but Nepalis must find a way to fix everything.

That evening we stayed in Mugling and enjoyed an all-fried dinner of samosas, deep fried hardboiled eggs, chapatti, and pakora. The next day we rode to Pragatinagar, pulled off the highway onto the town's only paved road, and stopped at the town's only accommodations – Hotel Namaste.

Across from the hotel (the word hotel is a bit generous for a room with filthy, stained walls, a squat toilet and bed sheets capable of transmitting illness) there was a simple bike shop. Out in front, a fifteen year old kid sat on the ground with a hub, a rim, and piles of spokes. He was building a wheel, lots of them. But he was simultaneously chatting with friends and watching the ox carts and motorbikes fly up and down the road. My heroic effort from just a few days ago was his daily routine. Hmm. Maybe my self-congratulations were uncalled for.

At a food cart, built of four bicycle wheels and a couple of boards, we picked up a snack of excessively-spiced popped rice, chopped up cabbage and some other bits and pieces all mixed together and served on a piece of lined paper. At the top of the lined paper, in legible handwriting, it read: Subject English. At the bottom, below the chili spice stains of my snack, it read: 4) How did he feel when he was released from prison? In rural Nepal, old homework was not discarded as trash; it was reused. But not as homework. Whoever said old homework was garbage? When used instead of a plate, it saves a worker a fraction of a cent per serving (which might make or break the business), and removes one piece of garbage from a country with a serious garbage problem.

As I munched on my new favorite snack, we wandered down a dirt street into some fields. Children were everywhere. They ran barefoot through the dirt. They chased each other through the fields and finished games of badminton just before dark. A couple of girls played hopscotch with a rock on a course drawn on the dirt road. I thought about my childhood. Hopscotch in the middle of the road was impossible. Night games required a monstrous effort to organize. I had the feeling, however, that these kids do this every night. They're kids, so they play. They didn't care – or maybe didn't know – they couldn't afford a hoppy-taw or a soccer ball. Shoes were unnecessary.

"Can we play?" Katy asked.

News spread like wildfire and forty kids formed a circle around us. Katy put forth her strongest hopscotch efforts, but was defeated by a barefoot seven year old girl in a dirty pink dress. Her small feet and uncanny intuition of the lopsided bounces of the rock she was using as a makeshift hoppy-taw were too much for Katy to even compete.

When it became too dark for hopscotch we turned to foot races and when I was thoroughly exhausted, we collapsed onto a nearby porch. We sipped tea, were garlanded in flowers, and posed for dozens of photos taken on their Nokia cellphones. One of the girls disappeared and returned minutes later with an English storybook. She insisted we read Rapunzel, in honor of Katy's golden hair. After the story we sang their national anthem and then quizzed them on general school knowledge. The kids all spoke English and were very smart.

"What's the tallest mountain in the world?" Katy asked.

In perfect unison twenty children belted, "The tallest mountain in the world is Mount Everest."

That was an easy question, since Nepal is home to Everest, so I decided to ask a harder question, "And how tall is it?"

"Mount Everest is 8,848 meters tall," they all responded.

"Okay, well what are the tallest trees in the world?" I asked jokingly, surprised they all knew the height of Mt. Everest.

Without dropping a beat, they all sung, "The Redwood Trees in California are the tallest trees in the world."

Whoa. These kids know their stuff. After many questions with only one correct answer I asked a question they would surely argue over.

"What is your favorite food from McDonalds?"

Silence. Not a word.

"What's McDonalds?" one of the older kids eventually asked.

Wow! We really are in a different world.

In the morning, before we braved the chaotic highway, we stopped at the town intersection and Katy went to get some water. Water is her job. In the two minutes she was gone, a crowd of twenty men gathered and formed a semicircle around our bike. Then they stared. Not at Katy. Not at me. And not at matching blonde ponytails. They stared at our tandem. They couldn't wrap their mind around it. It was red, shiny, had strange yellow bags, gears, shifters and disc brakes. Unlike the children in town, none of the adults spoke English, so they couldn't ask any questions. Instead, they stared.

That day we rode to Siddhartanagar, the birthplace of The Buddha – the Enlightened One. It was our last stop in Nepal before venturing further south into India. After a walk around town we returned to our guesthouse to find some bad news. Both our tires were flat.

"Well this isn't good," I muttered to Katy, after checking the front and rear tire.

"Not good at all, what do you think happened?" she asked.

"I don't know."

"I guess it's a good thing we got those two extra tubes in Istanbul," Katy reminded me.

Fixing a flat tire is easy, but obnoxious. Remove the panniers, flip the bike over, release the wheel skewers, remove each wheel, pull one side of the tire off the rim with a tire lever, pull the tube out. Then it's the reverse order to put the wheel back together. I replaced one tube with an original spare tube and then got out a tube we bought in Istanbul. I tried to push the valve through the rim, but it wouldn't fit. I wiggled it to no avail. I inspected the tube carefully and realized it had a Schrader valve, not a Presta valve. The valve was too thick and wouldn't fit through the valve-hole in our wheel's rim.

"Damn it," I yelled.

A week earlier, rear hub issues almost brought our cycling to a screeching halt. After that mishap I imagined smooth sailing. But now, three flat tubes in two days presented a similar problem. Our two new tubes we bought in Istanbul wouldn't work; it was time to patch one of those flat tubes.

Reluctantly, I fumbled through our bag for a patch kit. I don't like patching tubes. Never have. A good road tire and tube should rarely flat, so I usually replace flat tubes instead of patching them. They're only $7, so in the States I live by the "just buy a new one" philosophy. The worst flats have tiny leaks and go flat over a couple of hours, which seemed to be the problem we were dealing with. Tiny leaks mean tiny punctures. Punctures so small that you can't see them with your eyes. Or even worse, two tiny punctures. If you patch one your problem still isn't solved.

I searched the tube and found a small hole. I buffed with sandpaper, dabbed on some cement, let it dry, and applied the patch. It held air. I reinstalled the tube and reassembled the tire and bike, but the next morning it was flat again.

"Wish me luck?" I asked.

"Luck? Where are you going?" Katy asked.

"My patch job failed. Instead of trying again, I'm going to go and see if I can't find another Gopal to fix this flat tire for us. Wish me luck."

"Good luck."

TUBES AND HOLES

The developed world loves law and order. Nowhere is this more apparent than while driving. Traffic signs display the laws to facilitate order. More signs means more laws, so a sign has been created for everything: Stop Signs, Red Lights, Speed Limit, Yield Signs, One Way, Do Not Enter, Carpool Lane, No Turn on Red, No U-Turn, No Left Turn, No Parking, Two-Hour Parking, Buckle Up: It's the Law, and the list goes on. Other signs aren't laws per se, but attempts to increase safety: Windy Road, Deer Crossing, Railroad Crossing, Steep Grade – Use Lower Gear, School Zone, Dip. It seems that we've created a sign and a law for everything.

Other signs make me wonder, such as the State Law: Yield to Pedestrians in Crosswalk or the Share the Road sign above a bicycle. If it weren't for these signs, would drivers hit pedestrians in crosswalks and run cyclists off the road? "But officer, I ran the cyclist off the road because I didn't see a sign that said to share!"

In India things are . . . well, let's say . . . different. During our first five days in India, we cycled through the most densely populated area on Earth, but we saw zero stop signs and zero traffic lights. There were no speed limit signs. Paint on the road to designate lanes was also a rarity, and even where it existed, its compliance appeared to be optional. The only signs we saw pointed the direction and mileage to the next town.

The lack of signs appeared to accompany a lack of rules. Motorists drove into oncoming traffic, often for ten or fifteen minutes, and parked in the middle of the road. Goatherds herded their flocks down the highway. Fathers carried families of three, four or often five people on a single motorbike, and merged onto the highway without looking. No helmets. No seatbelts. Infants held in arms. Was it chaos? Was it lawlessness? It sure seemed that way.

After scrupulous observation of the Subcontinent's driving situation, the chaos intensified but my perception of it changed. The chaos seemed to organize and the central theme to that organization was one very simple idea: don't get in an accident. I believe that it's the only driving rule in India – don't run into anyone. More specifically, don't run into anyone in front of you. The human mind can only pay attention to so many things, and with so much happening on the roads in India, drivers are only able to pay attention to, and are therefore only responsible for, what's directly in front of them. Side view mirrors are often permanently swung closed, because they are more of a liability than an asset.

As long as we followed that simple rule, everything else seemed to be okay. A two-door truck bouncing down the road packed full of 18 women in vibrant, flowing saris. No problem. A camel plods down the center of the highway pulling a cart full of cabbage. Why not? A bicycle rickshaw pulls into an intersection and obstructs traffic for half an hour. Sure thing. Carrying sheep in burlap sacks, draped over the rear seat of a motorcycle. Economical. Anything is allowed and nothing is off limits. But remember the golden rule: don't run into anyone in front of you. Also, don't run into any cows; that's worse than hitting a human.

To be fair, some cities are trying to put up signs and get with the law and order program. After two weeks, we saw our first traffic light – although the Indians apparently did not. It didn't matter if it was red, yellow or green. They were going for it. On the way to the Delhi airport we saw our favorite sign. It read: "Lane Driving is Sane Driving." Our taxi driver, however, managed to take up two lanes all the way to the airport. To him, the painted lines on the road were a foreign language.

How does a country with over a billion people and no traffic rules get by? I'll suggest two simple answers. First, only 5% of Indians own a car. 20% drive a motorbike, 50% ride a bicycle, and the rest walk. The second answer is love. That might sound cliché or absurd, but when road rage filled my body with violent anger, which was not an infrequent occurrence, all the Indians were still smiling and waving and enjoying life.

On the roads of India, we were just one more bicycle trying to fit in. I learned the ebbs and flows of the road similar to how a toddler learns to use an iPhone, through intuition and trial and error. I studied the behavior of others. Responding to the chaos with love was difficult, but we tried our best. Once we were able to fit in – to dissolve into the sea of commotion – India was a delightful country for cycling. The road was a party. The collective energy that is India energized us, and we were happy to join the madness.

* * *

Back in Siddhartanagar, Nepal, I stopped at the first bike shop in town. It had a cement floor, and no front door. A pile of boxes clung to the wall and a rusty red propane tank sat in the corner. A little girl was getting dressed for school. If I were in the States, Yelp and Google Maps would have directed me to the best shop in town, but alone in Siddhartanagar I put my trust in a small barefoot man working out of the front oh his house.

I pumped up my two flat tubes with my bike pump (my presta valves weren't compatible with any pumps east of Istanbul) and gestured that the tube was flat and needed patching. The man was confused, either because I had awoken him, or because he'd never met a foreigner on his front porch at 8am. I put my tube into a bowl of dirty water on the floor, mimed air bubbles floating to the surface and the sleepy Nepali exploded into action.

With the tube submerged, he located three holes on the two tubes and marked them with some wax. Other bubbles leaked from my previously failed patch job. The man then squat on his haunches and got to work. It's the way people sit, over there on the Subcontinent. They sit with their feet flat on the floor, butt on their heels, perfectly balanced. I've tried to sit like them; it's not easy. It feels more like yoga than sitting. Years behind a desk and in a chair make this simple child's posture difficult for westerners, but when he sat on his haunches his entire body relaxed.

He covered my patch in a black liquid, pulled out a lighter and set in on fire. *Fire? What the hell is he doing?* My nervous instinct almost made me yell at the man. If this bozo screwed up, we'd be out a tube and our bike would be non-operational. Somehow, my trust prevailed. *Don't worry. He's done this before,* I told myself. He watched the flame closely and, at the perfect moment, blew it out and peeled the faulty patch off the tube. He patched the leaks, banged the new patches multiple times between two metal rods and checked and double-checked his work in the bowl of water. When he was convinced no bubbles formed, he handed them to me and I thanked him and paid him for his work. Fifteen minutes later, Katy and I were off.

* * *

We saw India from a distance. To be honest, we heard India before we could see it. A combination of haze, dust, exhaust and smoke reduced visibility to about 100 meters, but when the collective rumble of thousands of people, and the thundering of oversized, overladen steel trucks fumbling down pothole riddled roads grew louder, we knew we had arrived.

Uttar Pradesh, the madness across the border, is the most populous state in India. If it were a country itself, it would be the 6th most populated in the world. It's slightly larger than Utah and has 200,000,000 people, nearly two-thirds of the entire United States. Six thousand years ago, the Indus River Valley civilization built its home along the Ganges River and people have been around ever since. France had cheese. Turkey had tea. India has people. For a week in Uttar Pradesh, we were never more than ten feet away from another person. Whether cycling down the highway, at a hotel, or "trying to get away from it all," we were surrounded. Our route planning was no longer dictated by percent grade or total elevation change, but rather by population density and estimated vehicles per person.

At the Indian border, Katy went inside a small government building to deal with paperwork while I stayed in the street with the bike. Two Indian gentlemen, well dressed and middle-aged, approached.

"Ooh, fantastic double cycle," they said in unison, in perfect Indian accents. Apu from The Simpsons flashed into my mind. They stared at our bike – something I had grown used to – but then they rang the bell on my handlebars and started to played with our brakes and shifters.

"No, no, no. Don't do that," I shouted. Our bike was our baby; we didn't let others poke or prod. They continued to touch and fiddle so I asserted some authority and tried to push them away. Their poking and prodding continued. I breathed a sigh of relief when two men in military uniforms approached, comforted that these officers would restrain the growing crowd.

"Will you tell these people to . . ." I was halfway through my request when the two officers began to play with my bell. *So that's how it's gonna be, huh?* Then the officers posed for pictures.

Three kilometers down the road – after we had passed the last of hundreds of overloaded trucks, most of them with All India Permits painted on the front – a policeman assisted an elderly man across the road. The old man was dark, frail, and wore a lungi, a single white cloth beautifully wrapped around his waist, designating his place within India's caste system. He hobbled across the road on a single crutch and as we passed, he whipped his head around toward our tandem and shouted, "Good, good."

And just like that, we were in India. We were in love with India. It's difficult to describe what Katy and I saw from the seats of our tandem over the next six weeks. To quote *Shantaram*, essential reading for any traveler to India, we were "unnerved by the density of purposes, the carnival of needs and greeds, the sheer intensity of the pleading and scheming on the street. I knew nothing of the cultures there, clothed in robes and saris and turbans. It was as if I'd found myself in a performance of some extravagant, complex drama, and I didn't have a script. But I smiled, and smiling was easy, no matter how strange and disorienting the street seemed to be."

The highway, a narrow road with a narrower dirt shoulder, didn't resemble a road. Rather, it was a pulsating artery. It traversed the landscape and delivered thousands of pedestrians, age-old oxcarts, bicyclists who carried everything you could and wouldn't imagine, lovely rickshaws, huge lumbering trucks that miraculously passed without incident, a scrambling of goats, and the holy cows with their right of way to their destinations. When the road entered town, local markets spilled into the streets, and tire-destroying cobblestones brought traffic to a halt. We got off our bike and walked.

We stopped in Kolhui Bazar at dusk and asked if there was a guesthouse in town. Buried in the crowd, a single English speaker informed us that the nearest guesthouse was in Pharenda, 28 kilometers down the road. We didn't want to end our first day in India cycling in the dark, but we pressed on.

The red sun dropped into the haze, and set well above the horizon over endless rice fields. Uttar Pradesh is poor, rural, and dense. Without electricity, sunset turned into darkness, but busy lives continued working without interruption. Corrugated metal shops were lit by old kerosene lanterns. Thousands of people flocked to the highway for a samosa or the day's final cup of chai.

Kerosene lanterns, ox carts, dinner on the side of the street, living on $2 a day. It might sound like poverty, but I don't think it is. It's dangerous to project Western ideas onto other cultures. It's easy to say *we are so blessed* because we don't understand how they can thrive without air conditioning, carpet, a microwave, a car and the other unnecessaries of life. But that's our problem, not theirs. If they came to the States they'd likely say *we are so blessed* because we don't have to sit behind a desk all day, eat bland food, and worry about getting fat. They live a simple, arduous, and enjoyable life. They work in the fields, eat what they can grow, and trade their goods for the rest. They smile. They aren't poor people living in the 21st century. They are regular people, living mostly in the 12th century, with the occasional cell phone and Twitter account.

In the dark, we cycled through the crowds unnoticed until we arrived at Susham's Haveli Hotel. We were, of course, the only guests that evening. By Western standards our room was a bit subpar. We debated whether or not we'd lie down on the less-than-clean bed, and if the bathroom was safe to use. In front of our room two giant car batteries hooked up to a long electrical cord that ran out the window (not closable of course, let's let all the mosquitos in) to the generator out back. It ensured somewhat consistent electricity and definitely consistent engine buzz which lasted all night.

In the morning I packed up our bike while the hotel owner asked Katy where we were from.

"We're from America," she answered.

"Ooh, America. Very good country," he chimed back. "My sister is in America. California."

The man grabbed his phone and immediately called his sister, unconcerned about the difference in time zones. She answered and they spoke briefly in Hindi before he handed the phone to Katy. Unsure how to handle the unfamiliar situation, Katy hesitantly spoke, "Hello. My name's Katy. I'm from America."

I continued laughing, but kept it to myself.

"Yeah, I'm here in Pharenda. My husband and I are riding across India on a push bicycle," she continued. The conversation lasted half an hour. Katy can talk to anyone about anything.

Cycling in India is great for the mildly narcissistic. A minute doesn't pass without waves and smiles and camera flashes. It's life on the red carpet, and everyone has come to see us. After we finished a fifty-cent breakfast of chai and roti and were back on the road, a white car pulled up alongside us and launched into conversation.

"That's a fantastic double cycle. I never see one before."

"Oh, thank you," Katy answered. Katy's spot on the back of the tandem put her in prime position to fend off the paparazzi while I focused on the road.

"And what is your good name, ma'am?"

"My name is Katy."

"Oh, very good name, isn't it?"

"Yes. Very good."

"And from which country you are coming?"

"America."

"Oh America. Very good country, isn't it?"

"Yes. Very good."

After that brief introduction we knew it was only a matter of time until the passenger and three others in the backseat each got out their phones and started to take our picture as we cycled down the road. The car obstructed all traffic behind us, and each time I swerved around an obstacle in the road I made sure to not hit their car, which was driving just a little too close. Eventually the car sped off and a motorbike pulled up alongside us.

"What is your good name?" the motorcyclist asked.

"My name is Katy."

"Oh, very good name, isn't it."

"Yes. Very good."

"And from which country you are coming?"

"America."

"Oh America. Very good country, isn't it?"

"Yes. Very good."

I glanced back at Katy and laughed. "You're gonna be famous!"

Three minutes later we saw the white car from earlier pulled over on the side of the road. We passed and waved and twenty seconds later they were back on the road, driving alongside us. Again.

"Oh hey, you're back," I hollered sarcastically, not sure how we could be of assistance.

"Can we have a photo with you?"

With us? You already spent five minutes taking photos of us. Now you need photos with us? I obliged. We posed for photo after photo. Every possible permutation of I stand here, you stand there, photo alone, photo in a group, hats on, hats off, sunglasses on and etc. India redefined our idea of personal space.

That afternoon we rolled into the outskirts of Gorakhpur. Traffic quickly came to a standstill, as you might imagine it would in a town of half a million with no traffic lights and dozens of cows wandering through each intersection. Google Maps failed to locate our hotel so we wrote Hotel Vivek on a square of toilet paper and showed it to anyone willing to aid in our search. Two ten-year-old school boys – either best friends or brothers, I'm not sure which – in gray dress pants and white button-up shirts, their long sleeves rolled up in the heat, read the name of the hotel and motioned for us to follow them. One boy jumped on his bike seat, the other jumped on the rear rack of the same bike, and they took off. We followed.

They dashed off the main road and down an alley. Our cumbersome slightly-too-long-for-Indian-traffic-jams tandem was no match for their cycling dexterity and familiarity with the city. We raced around rickshaws, through lanes of traffic, and over multiple speed bumps. When the road was tight and narrow they'd get ahead and the boy on the back of the bike would tap the driver on the shoulder and they'd stop and wait. When they'd see us coming they'd take off again.

Ten minutes into our frantic race I noticed that at each intersection the boys stopped and asked others for directions. They didn't know exactly where they were going, but they were determined to find out and help us get there. When we finally arrived at our hotel, I congratulated myself on the finest bike handling of our trip, and Katy offered each of them enough rupees, about $0.25 worth, to buy a couple of snacks. They refused. Like the tailor in southern Nepal, they weren't accustomed to tourists and were happy to lend a hand.

We spent $7 on lunch, $6.50 more than breakfast, so we were optimistic about what might be served. Three men emerged from the kitchen with our meal: a large platter overflowing with naan that was crispy, garlicky and buttery on the outside but warm and chewy on the inside, a steaming bowl of Jazeera rice, a side of "spicy pickle" and chopped onions and peppers and three large silver bowls, with matching lids and brass handles. With a flair of flamboyance, each waiter gracefully removed the lid on his silver bowl to revealed butter paneer, dal makhani, and vegetable coconut korma, and then wafted the aromas towards us. (There are some times in my life when I wish I could smell.) To describe the flavors with words would be blasphemous. To put it simply, when I'm on my deathbed many years from now, fly me in some food from Hotel Vivek in Gorakhpur.

That evening we meandered through town and I saw a sign that read *Physics, Chemistry, Maths,* printed on a large banner which hung from some rebar on an unfinished brick building. I hopped over the sludge-filled gutter onto the dirt driveway, ducked under some power lines and went to investigate. I was curious to compare the science standards of rural India with the Mississippi Delta, where I had taught High School physics years earlier.

A tall man (because any Indian as tall as me is tall) introduced himself, and I asked if I could observe his class for a minute. We crept up a precarious set of stairs, ducked under more rebar, and entered a small cement room. Forty pairs of dark brown eyes, packed into a classroom for 12 or 15, stopped what they were doing and stared at us.

"Here is a Physics Professor from America," the man introduced me.

It wasn't true, but I wasn't going to argue with my only chance to ever be introduced as a professor. The classroom was silent for a moment, but then someone from the back corner yelled, "Teach us something."

Oh no, this isn't good. I'm here to observe, not to teach. My mind brainstormed excuses, but my right hand grabbed the dry erase marker and started writing – THE CONSERVATION OF MOMENTUM. I suppose I am a teacher at heart, and I'd never turn down the opportunity to teach kids some basic science. I started off slowly, with frequent checks for understanding, and occasional jokes to gauge their English proficiency.

"What will happen if Katy and I collide with the truck?" I asked, as I drew an overloaded truck coming down the road towards our tandem.

"You'll die." "You'll get run over," the students shouted.

"You are all correct," I answered. "But why?"

It was silent. The students were unsure how to justify what seemed to be so obvious.

A male student in the front row, wearing a green vest over a blue, button-up dress shirt and tie, carefully raised his hand. "The truck has more mass?" he asked.

"The truck does have more mass, but when we talk about collisions it isn't just mass we are interested in," I answered.

"Oh," he quickly shot back, "then it's momentum."

"Of course," I answered, as I pointed to the words I had written on the board. I made up some masses and velocities, and let the students use physics to explain common sense. After this problem, we moved on to projectile motion and before we left they instructed Katy and I on how to count to ten in Hindi. I taught them physics and they taught us how to count. We must have looked real smart.

"How are you feeling in India?" the student in the green vest asked. Indians were always more concerned with how we were feeling and less concerned with how we were doing.

"Very nice," I answered. The entire class let out a sigh of relief.

As the students filed out of the room, they touched their own chests with the palms of their hands and then the leg of their teacher, just below the knee. After this unusual custom, they offered small bows and were on their way. The teachers invited us to return the next morning for breakfast and to meet, and teach, their other class.

Breakfast was a spread of rotis, curries, chai, jelebi and curd. It was a welcome change from the yogurt and muesli we'd been eating every morning for the past 5 months. Immersed in a foreign culture, while sharing a delicious meal, we asked these teachers many of the questions we had about their country.

"When the students left last night, they touched you below the knee. Why do they do that?" Katy asked.

"In India, a teacher is just below God. Without teachers we would not know anything," one of the teachers answered. "It is to show respect."

It's true, without teachers we wouldn't know anything. Public school teachers in the States, however, are rarely given this type of respect. After two years teaching in rural Arkansas, the number of times a student cursed at me significantly outnumbered the number of times anyone bowed before me.

"Is anybody else right below God?" I asked.

"Yes," he answered, without hesitation. "Guests to our country are also right below God."

After our last bite of jelebi and curd we said our goodbyes, stepped back into the noise of India and started back to Hotel Vivek. We were halfway home when one of the boys who helped us find our hotel spotted us from across the street and came running.

"Good morning," he sang.

"Yes, good morning," we replied. And it was a good morning.

"You will come and visit my school?"

Katy and I exchanged what-in-the-world glances before I answered, "Of course, we do school visits."

We followed him into a strip mall, past a barbershop and into his third-story, two-room school.

"Can I offer you some chai," the teacher asked.

"Of course."

The teacher made a quick call on her phone and two minutes later a teenage boy entered with a large plastic bag filled with the intensely flavored and always delicious chai and enough earthenware one-use cups for those in the room. Compared to Turkey, where tea is always on hand, tea in India is just a phone call and a chai-wallah away.

When we finally left Gorakhpur, and headed south towards Varanasi, Katy and I were in love. With India. And also in love with each other. We were seasoned travelers, global nomads. We'd had our ups and our downs, our highs and lows, but we had stuck it out and we were better because of it. We were right smack dab in the middle of the grittiest country on the grittiest trip we'd ever take, and we loved it. Our trip was happening. Each moment was a memory we would carry with us for the next fifty years. Our trip was real and it was raw. We were doing it.

We departed the city amidst a dense traffic of rickshaws, pedestrians and motorbikes. Twenty-four hours earlier, the garbage that covered the streets had shocked and appalled us, but now it seemed to make sense. Every moment on the bike was an out-of-body experience that challenged our expectations and left us grasping for words. We loved India and India was love. But love can be a rollercoaster.

As we rode south, we passed dozens of small towns and at each town, the road turned from pavement to giant cobblestones – cobblestones with huge gaps that devoured bicycle wheels and threatened to puncture tubes and break spokes. I tried to keep our front tire in the dirt on the narrow shoulder, but our path was obstructed by mud, animals and their dung, piles of garbage and the like. We decided to walk. This was amusing the first time it happened. But four hours later, when my neck got sore, when my mental and emotional stability waned, and we got off our bike to walk for the seventh time, I wanted to scream.

"Can't someone pave these damn roads?" The honking and waving turned from amusing and friendly to obnoxious and incessant. India didn't change but I fumed with anger. "Can't I get a little peace and quiet?"

Our hotel room in Barhalganj was infected with a blanket of filth, and we hoped we wouldn't contract anything if we slept on our own sheets, didn't touch the walls, didn't sit on the toilet seat, and didn't stay longer than twelve hours. We leaned our bags against each other in the center of the room and went in search of food.

From the moment we entered town, a pack of children followed. Occasionally, a few brave ones would dart ahead of us, exclaiming to the town, "Look what we've found! White people." We stopped at a wooden cart built out of a piece of plywood and four bicycle tires, with no less than a hundred eggs stacked on it, and ordered some sort of fried egg, tortilla snack. The teenage chef worked his magic while a crowd – forty intensely curious folks – congregated behind us. *How did these foreigners get here? Do you really think they'll eat our food? I wonder how they are feeling?* the crowd must have wondered.

With each bite, the crowd held their breath and waited for our facial expressions to show satisfaction. We smiled and they smiled back. These weren't transient smiles, but bright-eyed, beaming Indian smiles.

"How much?" Katy asked, wondering how much our snack cost. Ordering food before knowing its price is often a dangerous game where you can get slammed with ridiculous foreigner prices, but lost in rural India we were safe.

The man behind the wooden cart waggled his head.

"How much did he say?" I asked Katy.

"He didn't say anything. He just did that head thing."

"How much?" I asked, hoping to get an answer.

He again waggled his head. We negotiated for a moment before surrendering to India and accepting a free meal from a stranger. Later that evening we were enjoying our day's final roti and chai when a gentleman insisted he pay for our meal. The rollercoaster had come full circle.

It's easy to hate India. It's dirty. It's noisy. And it's in your face, all day, everyday. You could hate everything about India, but that would be futile. It's exhausting trying to fight an uphill, unwinnable battle. We tried and we failed. India gave us another chance, so we tried to love India. We let go of any preconceived ideas of how things should or ought to be. We surrendered to India.

It wasn't easy, to forfeit our notion of how things ought to be – to say to hell with modern comforts and common sense – but we did our best. A yogi in Rishikish helped us out. He said, "Your body is a block. You are not your body. Your body will only cause you suffering. You are not your body. Your body is a block." He repeated it a hundred times. Our physical bodies, and the comforts of our Salt Lake City homes, always got in the way of embracing India. India is sensory overload, and our physical bodies, inundated by the overflow of sights and smells and sounds, were unable to keep pace with the fury of energy on the Subcontinent. Our bodies lost their ability to fight an impossible battle.

But all the sounds and cows and noises, they're just distractions. They are a facade that covers the real India, the beautiful India. India isn't in your face. India is curious. It isn't noisy; it's an orchestra. Nothing is what it seems, and you always have to look a little deeper. It's one billion, two hundred million people crawling all over each other with more love in their hearts than anywhere else in this world. If you can't surrender, India is apocalyptic chaos. But if you can find a way to just let it all be, and to enjoy the show, then India is the greatest place on Earth.

* * *

The next day we rode six hours south to Ghazipur. It's difficult to be "in" India for six hours. The mornings are the easiest, when our bodies and minds are fresh and we respond to the endless waves and hellos with enthusiasm of our own. But no one can perform at 100% forever. It's impossible to be everyone's best friend. It's hard to have the same conversation, over and over again, with every passing motorbike. It's even harder when these conversations are in Hindi and you just learned how to count to ten.

As we entered Ghazipur, the paved road turned to cobblestones and then to dust. The road narrowed and motorbikes, rickshaws, cars, cows, and cyclists packed tighter and tighter together until we all reached a dead halt. The road was being "fixed". A couple of men dug up the highway with shovels and picks made with bamboo handles while dozens of idle men looked on. You might think repairing a road by hand would be a slow process. It's slower.

The sole piece of heavy machinery was wedged into the rick-shaw:cow:pedestrian:mud traffic jam and was entirely incapable of moving (and working), due to the frantic race of each person edging their way an inch here and an inch there through the traffic. Thick mud made half the road impassable and compounded the problem. Our tandem fell into the mess, and we didn't move for five . . . ten . . . fifteen minutes.

In the midst of the madness, and while crammed shoulder to shoulder with a thousand frenzied Indians, a logical thought came to my mind: "What if someone had the bright idea of hiring a flagger to stand in the road and direct one lane of traffic at a time through this construction? Or maybe, since this road is under construction, they could close the road and put up some detour signs to direct traffic around this mess. It seems to work pretty well in *every other country in the world*, maybe they could try it here."

I took a deep breath. I looked at the smiles on everyone's faces. I tried to not let my blood boil.

VARANASI

India attracts three types of tourists: Hippies, Photographers, and Safe From a Distance tourists.

The best of the hippies left home in the late 1960s on a very groovy across-the-world trek to follow the Beatles, and maybe to meet the band's newest mentor, Maharishi Mahesh Yogi. They hitchhiked, bussed and trained to The Freak Street (aptly named) in Kathmandu, Nepal and having "made it" they then wandered towards India or South East Asia. The disciplined hippie follows the path of least resistance. The strictest disciples are easily recognized but difficult to spot – they've been stained the color of India and resemble Mother Earth. At first glance it's impossible to tell where they end and the street begins. Gristly, flowing dreadlocks are worn as trophies. Shoes are a major faux pas. When we cross paths with them I do a quick double take to ensure I've seen a holy man and not the walking dead. Freshly lit cannabis is a sure sign that this hippie is hard at work.

The photographers are easier to spot. They carry a camera, or two, around their neck. They travel in pairs, husband and wife, and prefer to see life through a circular, telephoto lens. It's best to avoid conversation with these folks, because they're always the same:

"How do you like India?" Katy or I will ask a seemingly innocent question.

"Well," the wife begins. "This is our 13ᵗʰ trip to India. We just love it here."

If the Hippies' claim to fame is a resemblance to India, the Photographers' badge of honor, which they proudly wear around their neck, are their dozens of photos of their repeated trips to the Subcontinent. They've plodded up and down India so many times (and they're anxious to tell you about it). After a healthy dose of self-centered rambling I'll blurt out, "Great, gotta go," and we escape mid-sentence.

Why do they talk so much? Forty years ago they visited India. They loved it. They returned home and told *everyone* about it. Then they made a mistake – they invited neighbors over to look at their pictures. Fifteen trips later, no one at home wants to hear about holy cows or overnight train rides, or look at photos that haven't changed in half a century. Their only outlet is talking the ear off of any new visitor to India. And boy do they talk.

Safe-From-A-Distance tourists prefer to see India from within a bubble, which keeps them a safe distance from actual India. They travel in large, pre-arranged tours, on buses with private drivers and follow guides (who carry nice little flags) through Safe For Tourist attractions. The India they see is climate controlled, and doesn't make too much noise. Katy and I rarely saw these folks. They occasionally looked up from their smartphones or iPads, and waved from their giant vehicles as their buses flew down the road, desperate to stay on schedule in a country that hasn't checked the time in a thousand years, where farmers still tend to their fields and shepherds to their flocks. Or perhaps we'd see them at Lonely Planet's Top Attractions. When you go to India, as you should, they'll be easy to spot. Just look for some sheep and their shepherd. Baaaaa.

* * *

After Ghazipur, we rode one more day south and arrived in Varanasi at the Ganges River. For Hindus, the Ganges is the Goddess Ganga descended from heaven, which makes Varanasi the spiritual capital of India. The holiest site on the Ganga, thousands of pilgrims come to Varanasi each day to bathe in the river and be cleansed of their sin.

After we got settled at the Alka Hotel, I got on Wikipedia to begin my foray into Hinduism. I read, "Hinduism is a diverse system of thought with beliefs spanning monotheism, polytheism, panentheism, pantheism, pandeism, monism, and atheism among others; and its concept of God is complex and depends upon each individual and the tradition and philosophy followed."

"Katy, what's panentheism?" I asked, as Katy returned from a hot shower in our shared bathroom across the garden.

"Pan-what?"

"Panentheism."

"Never heard of it," she answered.

"What about pandeism?" Or monism?"

"What are you reading?"

I quickly decided that Hinduism, at least for us, would be less about understanding doctrine and more about statue and name recognition. We stayed in Varanasi for a week and learned some of the basics. For starters, Hinduism has three main deities: Brahma – the creator, Vishnu – the preserver, and Shiva – the destroyer.

Brahma is the progenitor of all human beings. In paintings and statues he has four heads, which represent the four Vedas (spiritual texts): the Rigveda, the Yajurveda, the Samaveda and the Atharvaveda, and four arms that represent the four cardinal directions.

Vishnu is colored blue, clothed in yellow and also has four or more arms. His many hands hold a conch shell, a mace, a lotus flower and other objects that represent his divine attributes. Vishnu has manifested himself on Earth as ten different avatars, three of which are Rama, Krishna and Buddha. (Krishna is the Supreme Being for the Hare Krishnas and Buddha is . . . well . . the Buddha. How did an avatar of a Hindu deity become the founder of Buddhism? That's a good question, which I don't have the answer to.) Vishnu takes a nap from July to November, so Indians are wise to not marry during these months – it would be inauspicious. They instead wait until December.

Shiva has three eyes. The center eye only opens during acts of destruction. Shiva's consort is Parvati, and they are the parents of Ganesha, Hinduism's favorite deity. With his long hair, Shiva supports the

Ganga River and his favorite city, Varanasi.

"According to the World Wide Web, Shiva's favorite city is Varanasi," I mentioned to Katy.

"Then we better get out there and see what all the fuss is about."

We attempted to retrace our steps back to Dashaswmedh Ghat Road, but instead got lost in the narrow alleyways, often jammed with cows and speckled with manure. Indians have a unique ability, maybe it's a sixth sense, to walk through the crowded streets with their heads held high without plunging their feet into steamy manure. For us it was quite the task. As we approached the Ganga the merciless touts disappeared and the streets filled with beggars. Homeless and downtrodden, they prostrated their amputated limbs and emaciated bodies into the frantic flow of pedestrian traffic, hoping to capitalize on the good Karma of freshly cleansed Hindu pilgrims just out of the Ganga.

Karma is a word that is casually tossed around in Western culture, but it is an integral part of life on the Subcontinent. Hindus believe good intent and good deeds will not only return to create happiness in this life, but also in their future lives. They believe the soul is eternal and that after the mortal body dies, the soul is free to begin another life in a new body. The beggars know this, and their cries of distress and forlorn faces claw at those headed to the Dashaswmedh Ghat. They provide the righteous with an opportunity to increase their Karma.

That evening the Dashaswmedh Ghat was ablaze with worship. Thousands of devotees sang and chanted while priests, standing beneath bright lights near the bank of the river, lit candles and incense, tossed flowers into the river and danced with six foot long peacock feathers. It was an intensely religious worship service for those present but Katy and I just stared at each other and said, "What are they doing? Peacock feathers? Little banana leaf boats carrying candles into the Ganga?"

The next morning, a gray-haired, barefooted man, about 60 years old, wearing a long sleeve pink dress shirt and reading glasses took the two of us on a rowboat tour of the river. He rowed slowly, not because he was frail, but because our agreement was $1.50 per hour, not $3 for the trip. Our mistake. As the sun rose over the horizon a different Ganga was exposed, one hardly worth worshipping. The river was filthy. It wasn't just dark, bubbly and murky. All sorts of plastic, old bike tires, the debris of candles and flowers from last night's worship, old clothes, and any other sort of filth covered the banks of the river. A thick scum on top of the water glimmered with its own life force.

This filth, however, did not stop dozens of pilgrims from bathing in the river. It also didn't prevent countless women from doing their morning laundry. After the laundry was "washed", the women laid their maybe-cleaner items out to dry on the cement steps of the ghats. The best way to describe India is to take two ideas that are the exact opposites and fuse them. On this morning, Varanasi and the Ganga were intensely filthy and supremely clean, all at the same time.

The one thing we didn't see – but believe me, I looked for them – were dead bodies in the river. I suppose this needs some explanation. One of the goals in the life of a Hindu is *moksha* – liberation from reincarnation. Bad Karma, the bad deeds and intents common to all, ensures a constant cycle of death and rebirth. Hindus want to be freed from this cycle. One way to attain moksha requires coming to Varanasi to die. When a soul is about to depart the body, Lord Shiva may whisper the name Rama into the person's ear. If that person then chants the name Rama in return, Shiva receives this individual to himself, breaking the cycle of death and rebirth. Many Hindus come to Varanasi to die and be cremated, with hopes of attaining moksha.

Hindus have been cremated at Varanasi's Manikarnika Ghat, or the Burning Ghat, for thousands of years. The ghat is an ongoing funeral procession. At any moment, but typically every hour or so, a dozen men march through the streets with a corpse lying on a makeshift bamboo bed hoisted above their shoulders. The body is wrapped in orange cloth, sprinkled with flowers, and the men chant and sing funeral songs as they make their way through the busy city to the Ganga. When they reach the river, the body is dipped in the holy water before being placed on wooden pyres.

As we approached the Manikarnika Ghat, the sun was high in the sky and smoke swirled into the air. We marveled at the twelve foot high stacks of wood, stacked along the narrow alleyways, a necessary supply for around-the-clock cremations. We purchased some chai, found a seat on the cement steps and watched bodies set on fire on wooden pyres, their ashes then washed into the Ganga. The bodies are covered in orange cloth and white robes, but occasionally we'd watch an uncovered foot or arm or head consumed in the flames. If the amount of wood purchased is insufficient, the body will only be partially cremated. Hence the stories of dead bodies floating down the river. After the cremation the bamboo poles, orange cloth and flowers were tossed aside, making the largest pile of post-cremation trash I've ever seen. Cows congregate near the flames because the smoke soaks their hides and works as a natural insect repellent. Cow shit was everywhere, right next to someone's grandpa burning in public. It was somber and exciting, beautiful and disgusting. All at the same time.

For most people and circumstances, the site of public cremation removes any possible appetite. But for me, in a country that defies all odds, a long morning of cremation viewing fueled my hunger and we decided to head to lunch. Food and India are two of my favorite topics. Together, they're my favorite topic. Months later, back in Utah or Michigan, we were occasionally asked about our trip. These conversations were typically as follows:

"What was your favorite country?" someone would ask.

"India."

"Really? How come."

"The people were so nice," Katy would answer.

"And they have the best food in the world," I'd add.

"Did you eat the street food?" they would continue.

"Of course. It's the best."

Indian food is the delicious meal at the end of a filthy street. And the food is as delicious as the streets are filthy. In most of India, street food is the only option, and I'm okay with that. When you can watch your food prepared in front of you, you know exactly what's in it, and what's not in it. It is cheap, spicy, delicious, authentic and cooked while you wait. For the most part, it's all vegetarian. Indian restaurants in the States regularly serve chicken tikka masala or lamb korma, but in Uttar Pradesh we were more likely to find dal, paneer, paratha, roti, saag, aloo, gobi, makhani, gulab jamun, curd and fresh lime soda. Meat does exist, but mostly at tourist hotels, in modern cities, or wherever Muslims have a strong influence.

"Why don't Indians eat meat?" my father once asked a Krishna Consciousness devotee.

"Are you Christian?" the man answered, with a question of his own.

"Yes, I am," my father responded, although a bit confused.

"And doesn't *your* Bible say thou shalt not kill?"

They have a good point. I had never before considered that the commandment given by Moses to include animals, but who's to say it doesn't? Mormon doctrine counsels to eat meat only "in times of winter, or of cold, or of famine," but I suppose Mormons are more accustomed to skipping Starbucks than skipping Café Rio.

I digress. We were in Varanasi for a week, and quickly developed our go-to places for delicious eats. Shree Café Vegetarian Restaurant served up 41 different versions of paneer, the multipurpose, cottage cheese chameleon that can absorb any flavor. When we had a hankering for Masala Dosas, a south-Indian dish made from a crispy crepe filled with potatoes, onions, peas, carrots, and the mysteriously delicious masala, we stopped at Dosa Cafe.

The crème-de-la-crème of Indian street food, the deliciousness that justifies the international flight, is the samosa, a triangular prism pastry stuffed with spices, vegetarian delights and all that is delicious. Our best samosas of the trip were served to us hot off the street in Old Delhi. A group of men, one rolling out pastry dough, another chopping up veggies and mixing them with curries, and another stirring the not-yet fried pastries in a giant caldron of sizzling hot oil, worked frantically at a street corner and a throng surrounded them. I fought my way to the front of the line, and pushed a twenty rupee note into the chef's hands, securing my order. I stepped aside, and moments later was handed a small bowl made out of banana leaves, containing two samosas. If you are "in-the-know" they come with a free curry refill from the street chef. It was lunch as usual for that crowd, but for me it was a meal I'll always remember. The pain au chocolats of France were divine and the gelato of Italy heavenly, but Indian street food is in a cosmos of its own. And it only costs a dime and a nickel.

On a walk through town later that week I glanced down an alley and saw a dozen or more thirty year old men huddled around a small fire. "I want what they're eating," I told Katy, as I departed off the main street.

Katy rolled her eyes. *I wonder what Clayton's going to eat today?*

I was optimistic I had stumbled upon a new delicacy, only served to those foreigners daring enough to enter the dark alleyways of off-the-beaten-path India. But, I was met by a man with eight slices of white bread inside a metal roaster contraption. The man roasted, or toasted, the bread over the hot charcoal coals, identical to a kid roasting marshmallows. Once the bread was sufficiently browned it was doused with a thick square of ghee cut from a gigantic cube, and then delivered to one of the many hungry men sitting on benches lining the alley. *Great. Instead of a secret Indian delicacy, I've found roasted bread – aka toast.*

The next day we ventured north of Varanasi to the sacred town of Sarnath, where Lord Buddha gave his first sermon after his enlightenment. The Buddhist monasteries in Sarnath were a drastic and welcome contrast to the Hindu temples and ghats. They were immaculate and, except for a few chanting monks seated on the floor, incredibly quiet. Quiet cleanliness, in contrast to the collage of India, was much appreciated.

We left our shoes at the steps, entered the front door and took a seat on the tile floor at the back of the monastery. We listened to the fervent devotion of the chanting monks. Everything was as expected until an overwhelming feeling of peace descended on me. It was, without a doubt, the Holy Spirit.

My thoughts quickly jumped to Istanbul's Blue Mosque, the last place I had felt the Spirit so strongly. In the quiet calm, my mind spun and raced to make sense of the spiritual experience I was immersed in.

I believe the Holy Ghost testifies of truth. As a missionary for The Church of Jesus Christ of Latter-day Saints, I taught Jamaicans that God would send His Spirit to teach of Christ and lead them back to their Father in Heaven. But this was different. This was Islam and Buddhism.

If God sent his Only Begotten Son into the world, why would he also send His Spirit to me when I was worshipping with Muslims and Buddhists? Doesn't God want me to be Christian, or will any faith do? It was a difficult question, and one I couldn't readily answer. Since this event, I've thought about this question a lot, a whole lot. My best answer comes from a talk my younger brother Elijah gave in church when he was just old enough to speak in full sentences. It reads:

"People are everywhere. People are different. Heavenly Father made them all. Heavenly Father loves them all. Heavenly Father and Jesus want us to love everyone. In the name of Jesus Christ, Amen."

On our cycling trip, I saw firsthand that people are everywhere, and that people are different. Throughout the world, different faiths and cultures teach different religious doctrines, and have different names for their God. Some worship Jesus, others Allah, and some Krishna etc. I think God is okay with that, because I believe these different names represent one individual.

When you strip any of the world's major religions down to its very core, one thing always remains: a Supreme Being worthy of our worship. We should focus less on our differences and more on what unites us, and that is a desire to love and serve God. When this life has ended, our relationship with God and how we've treated others will be more important than what religion we belong to, or whether we call God by the name of Jesus, Allah, Buddha, Krishna or anything else. My membership in The Church of Jesus Christ of Latter-day Saints shouldn't be any reason to think less of others' religious beliefs, but a constant reminder that, if I am going to live a Christ-like life, I better do as Christ did, and as my brother said, and love everyone.

* * *

At 2am the next morning, I woke up to a river of fluid parading out of my left nostril, possibly grimier than the Ganges. I always find it odd that, when a voluminous runny nose hits, it first attacks from a single nostril. Aren't the two connected? Is there something they're not teaching me in medical school? In the four hours before waking, I wiped or blew my left nostril every five minutes, but my right nostril somehow, miraculously, remained untouched by the pathogens invading my body.

Morning finally came. We went to the train station to buy tickets, one ticket for a twenty four hour journey from Varanasi to Jodhpur, then a six hour layover, and another ticket for a six hour ride from Jodhpur to Jaisalmer. This would land us in Rajasthan, in the far west of India, and would give us four weeks to cycle from Rajasthan to Delhi. From Delhi we'd catch a plane to Vientiane, Laos to start the South East Asia leg of our journey. We opted for a train ride across the country, instead of continuous cycling, because India has so much to see and covering all the ground by bike seemed impractical.

Later that evening, as we sat in a rickshaw, clunking through the dense traffic and thoroughly grossed out by the masala flavored chewing tobacco and thick red spit that our driver shot onto the street every time he had a free moment, I noticed a mounting headache. I rarely get headaches, so I attributed the splitting pain to the multitude of noises and possible dehydration.

The next day the headache was full force. I blamed Katy. She was sick the day prior and must have gotten me sick. As the day rolled on body aches, fever, chills and fatigue had their way with me. I slept mostly. The day's physical accomplishment was descending two flights of stairs to lie on some grass because I was going crazy laying in that tiny hotel room. That night I got online and did what medical students do best: I came up with a differential diagnosis for my illness and speculated about viable treatment options.

My differential diagnosis included the flu, malaria, dengue fever, food poisoning or the wrath of Lord Shiva for not paying my devotion and rupees to the sadhus, in that order. So what to do? Malaria and the flu present identical symptoms: fever, chills, headache, nausea and vomiting, body aches and general malaise. The flu is much more common, but malaria is endemic in rural Nepal and India. Unfortunately, I counted nine mosquito bites on my left kneecap alone – mosquitos carry the parasite *Plasmodium* (of which there are five sub-types) in their saliva, which is the infectious agent in Malaria – and I supposed it was possible that I had missed a day or two of our anti-malarials.

"If we have Malaria, what's the treatment?" Katy asked. She said we, because by this point she was concerned her illness the prior day wasn't the flu, but a simultaneous case of malaria.

"I don't know, let me see," I answered, as I continued my search about malaria on the Center for Disease Control's website. "Perfect."

"What's perfect?"

"Treatment for malaria is the same as prevention for malaria. We just need to quadruple our dose of Malarone for the next few days and we should be good."

"That's it?"

"Unless . . . " I mumbled as my eyes drifted to the Nepal and India section.

"Unless what?"

"It says here that if we are infected with *Plasmodium vivax*, which is less common than the other types, then the Malarone will kill the parasites in our blood, but not if they've gotten into our livers. These parasites can live dormant in our liver and may reactivate at some point in the future."

"So what should we do?" Katy asked. I wasn't sure if she was asking for my opinion as a fledgling medical student, a sick and agitated cyclist in India, or as a husband.

"First, I don't think we have malaria. But, if we do, then chances are that Malarone alone will be sufficient treatment. I'm going to quadruple my Malarone for the next four days and see what happens."

"So if we take these meds for four days and we get better that means we had malaria?"

"Probably not."

"What do you mean, probably not?"

"If we get better it's probably because the flu happened to go away on its own."

"So how will we know whether or not we got malaria?"

"I guess we won't."

I popped three extra pills and made a mental note to give ten rupees to the next sadhu or beggar on the street. That would cover the treatable illnesses on my differential.

The next day we arrived at the train station at 3pm, two hours before our scheduled departure so we could put our bike in parcel service to be transported with larger luggage. I was a bit hesitant about leaving our bike in others' hands, but 36 hours later we collected our bike in Jaisalmer, Rajasthan after only two what-in-the-world incidents.

The first occurred in Varanasi. A man at the parcel service, with a paintbrush and a 2-Liter Coke bottle filled with a vile black substance, approached our bike. He was painting destination codes on the burlap and plastic coverings of other parcels, and when his paintbrush got within an inch of Katy's seat Katy grabbed his hand and politely demanded, "Actually I'd prefer it if you didn't paint on my bike seat."

"Yeah, that seat costs more than what you will make this month and we'd like to keep it as clean as possible," I added. It wasn't the kindest comment, but illness and India don't mix well – and this guy didn't speak a word of English. Sometimes I lose my patience.

Thirty six hours later – that's a long time in an Indian train – another parcel carrier refused to let Katy and me walk our bike from the train to the storage room. We followed behind him closely. Our bike had made the journey without any damage, and now we just had to get possession of it. We reached a flight of stairs and without hesitating, the man lifted our bike onto his head and began climbing the stairs.

"Whoa, whoa, whoa there," I shouted. To any rational person, a head might not be the best way to carry a tandem bicycle. "In America we carry things with our hands. Let me help you out." I grabbed the bike and forced it back down to the ground.

My favorite part of sitting on a train for 36 hours, besides the chai-wallahs, eavesdropping on Hindi conversations, fresh food served every few hours and listening to the mesmerizing rhythm of the rails, was my visit to the restroom. Situated between passenger cars, the toilet consists of two footplates lined up over a hole with a slightly angled tube below that. Through the hole and the tube you can see the whizzing railroad tracks below. It's a careful, balanced act to stand on those footplates while the train bounces down the track, not touch anything, and send your feces splatting onto the railroad track below.

Indian Railways is one of the world's largest employers with 1.4 million employees, and they serve nine billion passengers per year. Nine billion passengers? What happens to all that splat on the railroad tracks? It's the logical question to ask, and the answer is fascinating. Along the railroad tracks are a surprisingly large number of pigs, especially for a vegetarian country. If the pigs don't end up on a dinner plate, why are they there? It's simple. Pigs will eat . . . well . . . just about anything (we don't say people "eat like a pig" for nothing), and they patrol the tracks, providing a unique and environmentally friendly solution to a potentially catastrophic human waste disaster.

TWO GORAS

     This chapter is a short memoir. I wrote it on the rooftop terrace of the Shahi Guest House in Jodhpur, India, and I wrote it in the third person, instead of the first, because I can't believe that it happened. And that it happened to me.

    Travel, we agreed, was a litmus test: if we could make the best of the chaos and serendipity that we'd inevitably meet in transit, then surely we'd be able to sail through the rest of life together just fine. So far, we'd done pretty well.
    – Julia Child, My Life in France

I saw the two of them, the *goras*, or foreigners, sitting at breakfast on the rooftop terrace of the Shahi Guest House in Jodhpur. It was 10:45am, a little late for tourists to be having breakfast. Katy wore a long sleeve flannel shirt and a pair of black and white paisley pants cut off around the calf. Clayton's hair was pulled back into a ponytail and he wore a lemon colored shirt that said ISTANBUL across the front, and had a picture of a man in a small boat fishing a bicycle out of the sea. His shirt made me wonder whether the double-cycle parked in the open air lobby of the guesthouse, along with the local kids' noise and commotion at 11pm last night, was their doing. They looked tired but well rested at the same time, as though they had had a good night sleep, but that sleep alone wasn't enough to rejuvenate their battered bodies. Then they spoke.

"Well, yesterday definitely goes down as the worst day of our trip," Clayton declared in a half-accusatory, half-nonchalant way. He rubbed his eyes, yawned, tried to remove some earwax with his right pinky finger, and then reached for the menu Katy had already looked over.

"Do you really think so?" Katy asked, as she looked up for the first time from her red Amazon Kindle. She thought about it for a moment, and then added, "Yeah, I guess you are right."

As Clayton flipped through the pages of the badly worn, somewhat laminated menu, his face murmured and his eyes rolled. "More curry, just what I was hoping for," he said sarcastically. It was evident that his sarcasm had years of experience.

"Keep looking, you might find something you like," Katy encouraged him, apparently knowing something he didn't. It was obvious she felt bad for him, but I couldn't tell why.

"Whoa, muesli with curd," he celebrated after he flipped to the last page. "And nutella toast. I guess it's no Grape Nuts with Winder Dairy, but you know what, this place isn't half bad."

"No, not that bad at all. It's also the first place we've stayed that has a hot shower, with a curtain, a toilet I feel safe sitting on, AND toilet paper," Katy hummed, without looking up from her Kindle.

Well that sure is strange, I thought to myself. Where have these foreigners been? As their food was delivered, their moods brightened and I heard them recount in great detail the, in my honest opinion, pathetic but adventurous course of their travels over the past 24 hours. I've seen a lot of foreigners come through the Shahi Guest House in Jodhpur in the last 20 years or so, and well, these two take the cake.

The downward spiral of their trip began a week or so ago in Varanasi. Katy first got sick, then Clayton. A 36-hour train ride didn't help, and two days ago, a 110-kilometer bike ride from Jaisalmer to Pokaran set the stage for " the worst day of their trip," which happened yesterday.

They left their guesthouse at 11am. What they were doing all morning, I'm not sure. But if it were me, and I were riding a bike (of all things) across the desert of Rajasthan, I would start four hours earlier to avoid the midday heat. Anyways, at 11am they set off.

But they set off in the wrong direction. They had to go back into town to get some money out of an ATM. Being from India, I can only say two things, one: why did you leave this for last; and two: good luck. When they arrived at the third and probably last ATM in the small town of Pokaran, Katy celebrated that the ATM actually worked, and Clayton said, "well it's about time."

They were anxious to finally be on the road, but a large crowd had gathered and prevented an easy departure. (I'm sure everywhere they go, we Indians just love to stare at their double cycle. I heard it even has 10 gears). Just as they were about to leave, Clayton spoke, "I'm sure you're all wondering why I called you to this meeting. Business has been a bit slow; we really need to dig in before the Holidays. Now get back to work." It seems Clayton is only able to get through this country one joke or sarcastic remark at a time. Then they were off.

They joked about the dead camel they saw on the side of the road, just past their guesthouse, and they made particular mention of the tearing-ripping-crunching sound engrained in their memories as the stray dogs chewed on the camel's head. I guess that's not common where they're from. Then they argued about their phone not working with Katy reminding Clayton that he is impatient, and Clayton with the look of, well yeah, what do you want me to do about it, before replying, "You could use the camera on your phone, had you not broken it." It was a topic they had argued about before, and as quickly as they argued, they left it alone and moved on with their story.

They rode 30 kilometers before Clayton threw in the towel. He pulled the bike to the side of the road, got off, and declared, "I'm walking." His complaints were legitimate, sort of. Sick for the last couple of days and not eating any Indian food (we only have Indian food in our country), he was most likely exhausted. He said he'd lost ten pounds in the past week. He complained of a headache, which could be true. But then he revealed his greater problem: "Where are we going? Why are we out here? What am I doing, sick and tired, and this damn headache, cycling across this hellish desert?" Clayton's body was weak, but his mind was broken.

"We're going to Rishikesh, like we planned," Katy answered, cautiously. She knew that when Clayton was in a bad mood, Clayton was in a bad mood.

"Well, then why didn't we take the train to Rishikesh? If we're going to Rishikesh, why did we take the train to Jaisalmer?"

"What do you mean? We're bike touring. This is what we do. We've been riding our bike for the past five and a half months, how is today any different?" Katy challenged him.

"This is how I see it. When we were riding across Europe, we had a destination: Istanbul. Every time we got tired, or there were mountains, or whatever else happened, we just kept going because we had a goal: Istanbul. But now we have no goal. It feels like we're just wandering around. Every time we get on a train, or in a jeep or any other non-cycling mechanism, it breaks down my mental fortitude to keep going. If we took a train all the way here, why don't we just take a train back?"

"What do you want me to do?" Katy asked.

"Let me put it this way," Clayton continued. He didn't want answers, he just wanted to vent. "Let's say you're in the LOTOJA and you're 130 miles into the race. You get sick, your mind starts to wander, and your butt and neck hurt. What do you do? You finish the race. But now let's say they remove the finish line and now there is no race. Do you ride the next 70 miles? Of course not. You throw in the towel."

Clayton's argument had some logic. Their 6,000+ kilometers across Europe had been relatively pain free. They never got sick and they had a large finish line – Istanbul – looming at the end of four months of cycling. But things were different now. Sick in India, with no set destination, and surrounded by people who Clayton claims are the "friendliest most obnoxious people on Earth," I could see the reason behind his argument. Life is tough if you don't have a destination.

Katy was quiet for a moment and it seemed she wasn't disagreeing with him, but didn't have an answer for his problem either. After walking a mile or so down the road she finally replied, "So what do you want to do?"

Without hesitation, Clayton answered "All I want . . . is to sit at home in my basement . . . where it is nice and quiet . . . and have a large bowl of Grape Nuts with cold Winder Dairy milk . . . and do nothing. That's all I want. No more. No less." It sounded like he was quoting a movie, but I didn't know which one. And neither did Katy.

Had this been the extent of their day, I'd be the first to say they had hit a low point. But it continued. With this mindset, and no apparent solution, they walked down the highway. Katy pushed the bike, about 15 meters ahead of Clayton and he stopped every once in a while to cough, stretch and stare at the camels, goats and cows. After a silent standstill, Clayton finally caught up and the two resumed their conversation.

"Maybe we should go somewhere for Christmas," Clayton suggested.

"Yeah, like where?"

"I don't know, Switzerland, the South of France, Australia, Italy." Clayton tossed out a handful of suggestions. "Where do you want to go?"

"We could go to Utah to see our families and stay at my cabin, or go to Portland and see my Aunt," Katy answered. Clayton wanted out of India, but Katy wanted away from Clayton.

"There's no way I'm going home for Christmas," Clayton answered.

Of course, his previous desire to be back home in his basement eating Grape Nuts conflicted with his refusal to go home for Christmas. I was confused. I can only imagine that his wife was also confused. The conversation died and they continued walking through the vast, arid desert. After a while, I suppose they realized they'd never reach their destination on foot so they climbed on their bike and continued cycling. Thirty more kilometers down the road they were back off the bike and walking. Their argument continued.

"Where is this place of yours?" Clayton demanded.

"The map says it's in 25 kilometers," Katy quickly answered.

"I can't do another 25 kilometers. I feel terrible. Let's just stop at the next guesthouse. What are we racing through this desert for anyways? We've got nowhere to be."

"But what about our reservation at the Desert Haveli?" Katy

asked. "I called and made a reservation."

Katy was pretty set on her reservation, but Clayton didn't really care. Clayton argued that since they didn't leave a credit card number they could just blow off the reservation but then Katy got emotional, and with tears in her eyes yelled, "But that's the only thing I wanted to do out here. Stay in a nice place in the desert."

"Why do you always have to get so emotional? If you want to stay there, fine. But don't cry about it."

They got back on their bike, again. By now, Clayton really wasn't looking so great, but they continued the 25 kilometers to the Desert Haveli. They passed many other guesthouses, some even looked very nice. At one point they passed Manvar Haveli, a very nice resort where an elderly gentleman in white robes and an orange turban enthusiastically jumped out of his chair, ran to the side of the road, and motioned for them to stop, but Katy's orders were to continue. Clayton dared not say a word because Katy had "made a reservation."

They arrived at the Desert Haveli just as the sun began to set and Clayton collapsed to the ground (the resort happened to have grass) as Katy went inside to check in. Katy returned a moment later and declared, "This place is gross, and expensive. We can't stay here." Clayton rolled his eyes in disbelief.

"Okay, well what do you want to do?" he asked.

"I guess we should keep on going."

"You've got to be kidding."

They got back on their bike and when they reached the road Clayton stopped and asked, "What way?"

In this manner (letting Katy make the decision), if things turned from bad to worse, Clayton could blame Katy for having made the final decision. Katy suggested going backwards to Manvar Haveli, but that was half an hour or so in the wrong direction and Clayton refused: "I'm not going backwards." He refused to go "backwards," but after hearing their prior conversation, I'm not quite sure there was any forwards or backwards to their journey. In any event, they continued down the road.

After 15 minutes, they reached Manowar Resort, pulled off the road and entered the outdoor courtyard area. A friendly man greeted them, offered them chairs (there was a single table with four chairs in a courtyard that could easily seat a hundred people) and asked if they wanted some tea. Clayton declined, first asking to see a room.

"Oh yes, yes. We show you room. Very nice room."

Minutes passed, and Clayton again asked to see a room. Still nothing. With some pushing Clayton convinced someone to show him a room, while Katy got online to send an email home. Clayton was led outside of the courtyard, around the side of the property, to a rusty, old shed. The gentleman yanked on the door until it opened, and said, "Here is nice. You like?"

"Oh no, I don't think so," Clayton laughed.

And knowing tourists, I wasn't surprised. An Indian might be willing to sleep anywhere, but the old tool shed covered in dirt, with broken stuff everywhere, no lights, rodents, and half a bed is somewhere that foreigners never agree to sleep, even if they can choose their own price. Clayton and Katy got back on their bike and were just about to leave when the owner ran across the road. "Next town is 20 kilometers, they have hotel there."

The journey continued. Clayton wished they had called it quits a couple of hours ago. Katy wished the Desert Haveli was cleaner or that they had stopped back at one of those other places.

Twenty kilometers came and went. The air was nice and cool and the scenery was beautiful. India is beautiful in the late evening in the winter. The last light slowly faded and they entered the small town of Balesar in the dark. The lights from motorbikes, tuk-tuks and overloaded trucks illuminated the city's dust and pollution in the air. You eventually get used to the dust and pollution of India; it just takes a couple of years, and ruins your lungs in the process.

As they pulled to the side of the road, just past the central market area, neither of them were in a good mood. With a crowd of onlookers to battle, and needing to find someone who spoke English to direct them to a place to stay, they still had their work cut out for them.

They talked to one guy on a motorcycle, who they followed to another guy's shop, who pointed them to his friend's place, who they then followed down an alleyway across a nasty gutter and to a small room at the back end of an unlit street. No markings designated the place as a guesthouse, but they were out of options. Clayton stayed outside with the bike and entered a staring contest with the group of kids who had followed from the main road as Katy went in to check out the place. Katy and the man argued for a moment over the price, negotiating 600 rupees instead of 800 rupees, and then they carried the bike into the room. Katy grabbed the passports for the official checking-in process, while Clayton stared at the room in disbelief.

The beds looked as though they had offered their last comfortable night sleep about a century ago, and hadn't been cleaned in as many years. It was the sort of filthiness that only rampant overuse and dedicated neglect can generate. At first glance, Clayton wondered if he'd sleep on the floor or standing up because he dared not touch the bed. The walls were filthy, covered in the red stains of masala-flavored chewing tobacco, the spit from countless previous tenants. A claustrophobic bathroom instantly elicited the gag reflex. It was a vile room, diagnosed with cancer and succumbing to a slow, inevitable death. Then Katy returned.

"What . . . the . . . hell." Clayton spoke slow. And he was furious.

"What?"

"What do you mean, what?" Clayton yelled. "Are you meaning to tell me that I rode that bike, all day, feeling like shit, across that desert, to wind up here. Here? Honestly, in what world did you walk into this place and say, yeah, this is okay. I don't even want to talk to you."

Katy crumbled. Clayton had pushed her over the edge. She was an emotional wreck and it showed. She felt bad for making Clayton ride all day and she wished she could return to the friendly gentleman at Manvar Haveli. But that option had passed a long time ago. Without other guesthouses in this dark, unfamiliar town, Katy reluctantly agreed to stay. As the tears began flowing she fought back, "Well where else are we going to stay? It's dark. I'm tired. I didn't see any bright lights and signs that said Clean Hotel, Stay Here, did you? At least I got the place down to 600 rupees."

"Oh wow. You saved us $3. Congratulations." They were doing what stretched-to-the-limit married couples do best: arguing.

"I didn't see you offer to come in and look at this place."

"You are actually going to sleep here, on that bed. I dare you,"

Clayton yelled.

The bickering continued until Clayton lost it, "Enjoy your shit hole. I'm leaving." The man who had rented the place was standing just outside on the street but they didn't care. They packed up their bike and Katy argued for her 600 rupees back to which Clayton added, "Just forget it, he's never going to give it to you." The two of them walked back down the small road towards the bustle of traffic. Their crowning mistake was not taking pictures of that priceless room, something I'm sure they'll regret.

"Before we're back in that mess, what's our plan?" Clayton asked. "Are we looking for another place or should we just hire a jeep to take us to the next town?"

Neither of them answered the question aloud, but the look in their eyes was enough. They were only in Balesar for an hour or two, but that is a town they will always remember.

An hour and a half and three trucks that were all-too-short later, the two finally secured their bike in the back of a pickup truck, agreed on a much-too-high price (we love foreigners, they don't know how much anything costs in our country) and they were on the road to Jodhpur. Amidst the frustration of packing their bike into the truck, Clayton unclipped their helmets and, in a fit of rage, hurled them into the crowd.

As the truck buzzed down the empty road, Clayton stuck his head out the window and stared up at the stars. It was a beautiful night. After some deep breaths Clayton put his arm around Katy and gave her a hug. They exchanged smiles as Katy placed her head on Clayton's shoulder, and just like that, the anger and frustration of a terrible day on the road melted away, as hopes of a warm shower and clean bed filled their tired, confused minds.

GAYA, GAYA, BAKARA

The crowning jewel of the city of Jodhpur is the Mehrangarh Fort. Built in the 15th century, it stands on a 400-foot hill in the middle of the city, surrounded by seven gates and impenetrable walls. It's been attacked by numerous armies, but never conquered.

Looking from atop the Mehrangarh Fort, a sea of lego-like homes sprawls in every direction, with clumps of blue legos scattered in the mix. These homes are painted indigo, a natural sun reflector that keeps homes cool throughout the year long summer, and also repels insects. But most importantly, it signifies the homes owned by the Brahman caste, India's elite. These blue homes give Jodhpur it's nickname, "the blue city."

After the "worst day of our trip", we hunkered down in a nice, but affordable, guesthouse – one with a western style toilet *and* toilet paper. It was a luxury to sleep under sheets and to sit comfortably on The John without having my quads burn while I squat and pull leftover squares of TP out of my back pocket. To further aid our recovery, Katy and I searched high and low for other Western comforts hidden in India. Around 3pm each day, after an adequate dose of rest and relaxation, we hit the streets in search of wealthy, luxurious India. With a bit of hard work and an auto-rickshaw ride across town, we found our first grocery store. Not our first grocery store in Jodhpur, our first grocery store in India. It had two aisles, and a single checkout counter. We were in awe.

"They do exist," Katy whispered, as we reverently tiptoed through the unusually quiet store. The shelves were meticulous and the floors were spotless.

"Should we get one or three?" I asked, as I held up a jar of peanut butter, jam and nutella.

"One of each, or three of each?" Katy asked. We weren't sure when we would next cross paths with these life-saving comfort foods, so we stocked up and were on our way.

Our next stop was the Glitz Cinema, to see *Action Jackson*. At the ticket counter, a dirty sheet of paper with Hindi words but English numbers was taped to the window, listing four different prices. I assumed the different prices were for matinees or evening shows, and adults or children. I was wrong. Seats closest to the screen were the most expensive, while seats in the back of the theater were the cheapest. If you have a little disposable income – and don't mind a strained neck – you can sit up front and not worry about the commotion behind you. We bought midrange seats. After the previews, a number of bizarre advertisements played: a little girl cried hysterically when her dad lit a cigarette; four commercials in a row recruited people to join the Indian Navy: "The Indian Navy, an ocean of opportunity"; and last but not least, an advertisement reminded and encouraged people to pay their taxes.

Five minutes into the movie, a waiter appeared out of the darkness and asked, "Would you like something?"

"What?" I asked, a bit confused at the interruption.

"Something to eat, sir?"

Unsure of our options, I declined. Just as the movie was picking up (Katy and I had a loose grasp on the plot since it was all in Hindi), the film stopped, the lights turned on, and everyone jumped out of their seats and headed to the exit.

"It's over?" I questioned.

Katy was equally confused, "I don't know. I thought it was just starting to get good."

Reluctantly, we also got up and started towards the exit when the words INTERVAL flashed on the screen. I joined the others in the lobby and bought some popcorn, which we both agreed was pretty bad, however, we were careful to not set the leftovers under my seat. A week earlier in Varanasi I had seen *Ungli,* a Hindi comedy, and left a bad snack on the ground. Throughout the show, I heard a rustling, chewing sound under my seat and when the movie was over the food was gone. Rats! I mean literally. I think rats ate my snack.

The night's final highlight came twenty minutes before the movie ended. The main actor lit a cigarette, and immediately the words SMOKING KILLS flashed in large block letters across the screen. India has quite the anti-tobacco campaign.

On our fourth morning in Jodhpur, my recovering body finally had the strength to force deep, productive coughs, so I decided I was strong enough to get back on our bike and brave the noisy road. We rode a casual 40 kilometers east and stopped in the small village of Chadelao Garh.

Before dinner, a walk through town revealed narrow village streets, just wide enough for an oxcart, lined by clay homes with thatched roofs and immaculately swept dirt yards. At the first street corner, two middle aged men with white robes around their waists and orange turbans over their heads sat on a cement wall and discussed the day's events. They smiled as we passed and asked for a photograph. We took some photos on our iPhone and the men meticulously scrutinized their own photos, occasionally erupting into howls of laughter. I can understand if they haven't seen a recent photo of themselves, but don't they have mirrors in town?

Further down the street two girls assembled firewood. One crumbled a dried plant into pieces, while the other combined these pieces with ox dung gathered from throughout the village. She mashed the two together, until she had a Frisbee sized piece of fire-poop, and then she spread them out on the ground so they would bake in the sun. Fire-poop construction: not your typical afterschool activity for a pre-teen.

News quickly spread that foreigners were in the village, and by the time we reached the main street, a small entourage followed. We didn't want to take selfies all evening, so we decided to try our luck with some children's games. It was difficult to explain the rules of Kick-the-

Can, Duck-Duck-Goose or Red Light Green Light to kids who don't speak English – especially when they've never seen a red light – but we did our best.

"All the children," I put my hand at my waist to signify little people, "need to sit in a big round." I said round, instead of circle because that's the word one of them used. Verbal instructions failed, so I drew a large circle in the dirt in the middle of the road, sat down at the edge and motioned for the kids to follow. After most of the kids were seated, and a third of the village was watching, we started.

Gāya . . . I touched the first child on the head, Gāya . . . Gāya . . . Gāya . . . Gāya . . . and when I reached Katy . . . Bakarā. We used the Hindi words for cow and goat because we assumed these kids were less familiar with ducks or geese. Katy chased me around the circle and the kids erupted. They learned fast. Except for a few instances of running the wrong direction or not sitting down after a single loop, they were in heaven. We played for almost an hour and Katy was chosen as the Bakarā almost every time. When Katy couldn't run any more, a giant rope was brought out for a game of tug-of-war and we finished with some foot races. I was holding my own until an 18 year old recruit, fresh out of the army's basic training, showed up. He was fast. We then tried to explain the rules of Kick-the-Can, but the idea of being "in jail" just didn't stick. We would have played games all night, but invitations for tea eventually prevailed and the kids skipped home barefoot in the dark.

Four days of rest, and a memorable evening of night games in Chandelao Garh, buoyed our spirits. So Katy and I gritted our teeth and put on our cycling clothes. The first day back in the saddle after a couple days of rest is always difficult, but when we ventured back onto the road, we quickly got back into our groove.

We stopped for lunch at a dhaba, a roadside restaurant, and ordered our regular lunch of roti, a salad of tomatoes, white radishes, purple onions, and green peppers and a side of curd. To celebrate feeling healthy, we treated ourselves to Orange Fanta, the absolutely terrible beverage you are probably familiar with, and some Cracker Jacks. It's the best lunch available if you're not yet in the mood for curry.

That evening we pulled up in front of the Hotel Jyoti Palace and I turned around to ask Katy the question of the day, "Do you want to check us in or should I?"

Without listening to me, she answered, "100 kilometers is too much."

"I agree," I answered.

It's not the distance that will kill you; it was the exposure. And not to the sun. It's tough to be "in" India for six straight hours. Everyone waves. Everyone says hello. Six hours on the bike exceeds the mortal ability to respond to such incessant attention.

We took some deep breaths, reflected on the day and then I broke the silence, "They're the friendliest people we've ever met. There's a billion of them. And they aren't going anywhere." It was enough humor to shake off the past few hours.

The Hotel Jyoti Palace was full, so we continued down the road to Hotel Manoj. Katy went in and from across the street I heard the echo of a voice, "Hello, hello, hellllooo." A frail old lady appeared, pulled a kid off the street to help with translation and a phone call or two later a man appeared on his motorbike. He had a presence about him. He wore dark blue jeans, shiny leather shoes, a button-up dress shirt and a dark brown tweed jacket. He wore gold and diamond rings, and carried a noticeable paunch (India's telltale sign of wealth) above his black leather belt. He personally checked us in to his hotel, and then invited us to come across town to have tea in his home.

"Thank you for the offer," I replied. "I'm going to take a shower and talk to my wife and then we'll come over."

"Tea first," he politely demanded. "Then you can have a shower."

I went upstairs and broke the news to Katy. Her shower and solace would have to wait. We hopped onto his motorcycle and rode off. It was the first time in five months I wished I was wearing a helmet.

He invited us into his living room and asked his daughter-in-law, Priyanka, to prepare us some tea. We sipped some chai and listened to his stories. After numerous stories of his life, Katy started talking to Priyanka about her recent marriage.

"In Gorakhpur, someone asked us if we had a love marriage," Katy began.

"I hope you weren't offended," Priyanka quickly interrupted. "Indian marriages are quite different than what you might be used to."

"Not at all, but what is a love marriage?" Katy asked.

"We have two types of marriages in India, love marriages and arranged marriages. Most Indians have traditional marriages, or arranged marriages. Parents decide who their children will marry. I know this sounds strange to a foreigner, but this is how marriages have been in India for thousands of years. Recently, however, some people, mostly the educated or wealthy who live in larger cities, will choose for themselves who they'll marry. We call this a love marriage."

"That's what I thought," Katy replied. "But I wasn't sure. Can I ask you another question? A personal one?"

"Of course."

"Did you have an arranged marriage?"

"Kind of. We actually had what we call a love-arranged marriage," Priyanka answered. "I met my husband at college and we fell in love. Before we got married though, our parents were introduced and they decided our marriage was acceptable. Love first, but then arranged."

"How did they decide it was acceptable?" I asked, rather intrigued.

"There are many criteria for a marriage, and not just good looks and lots of money. The big criteria are caste, religion, profession, language and finances, but there are many others. The one that always surprises foreigners is horoscope."

"Horoscope?"

"Yes, the horoscope is very important in predicting a successful marriage. I have a software program on my computer that predicts marriage success in 36 categories, based on time and location of birth. We matched in 28 categories. A very high match."

"Hmm, what is a bad match?"

"Any match less than 16 out of 32 is unacceptable."

Katy and I stared at each other and tried to process this information. Priyanka must have seen the confusion on our faces, so she broke the silence and changed the conversation, "Would you like some cheese bread?"

"I'd love some," we answered.

Cheese bread turned out to be grilled cheese sandwiches with Sriracha Hot Chili Sauce, and Katy and I realized we'd found the Indian high life. After my fourth sandwich, a personal driver arrived and took us to visit the temple, dropped us off at the family's favorite restaurant (where the driver came inside and ordered for us), and then returned after our meal and dropped us off at our hotel room. I could get used to having a driver.

In the morning we were almost on the road when the man with the golden rings showed up. Local street boys came running and kissed his jeweled fingers, so when he requested that we visit the nearby preschool before leaving town, we assumed turning him down was not an option.

The walls of the preschool were painted with images of Snap, Crackle and Pop in one room, and Winnie-the-Pooh, Piglet, Eyeore and Tigger in another. The three and four year old students, wearing matching purple and red sweat suits, sat quietly on top of their backpacks in small plastic chairs behind shared desks. In each room, students recited memorized English phrases, smiled and waved. Their teachers requested countless photos. *No wonder everyone in this country takes pictures of us; they're taught to do it in preschool.* Before we left, the supervising teacher gave Katy a five pound, awkward sized pencil holder – just the thing we were hoping to cram into our already full panniers. We said thank you, and with permission of the man with the gold rings, got back on the road.

About an hour or so out of town, in front of a row of tollbooths, we approached an enormous highway sign that obstructed most of the horizon, which read: National Highways Authority of India – Exemption From Payment of Fee. No fee shall be levied and collected from a mechanical vehicle transporting and accompanying:

1. The President of India
2. The Vice President of India
3. The Prime Minister of India
4. The Chief Justice of India
5. The Governor
6. The Lieutenant Governor

7. The Union Minister
8. The Chief Minister
9. The Judge of the Supreme Court
10. The Chairman of the Council of State
11. The Speaker of the House of People
12. The Chairman of the Legislative Council of the State
13. The Speaker of the Legislative Assembly of the State
14. The Chief Justice of the High Court
15. The Judge of the High Court
16. Ministers of State, and
17. Foreign Dignitaries on State Visit

"Could we pass as foreign dignitaries?" Katy joked.

"I would think so," I answered. "But joking aside, I just hope they let us through. Back home you can't ride a bike on a highway."

We cautiously approached the tollbooth when a motorcycle flew by and the passenger motioned for us to follow. We followed the motorbike onto the shoulder, and then off the road onto a well traveled dirt trail. We cycled right past the tollbooth and then back onto the road. The motorcyclist gave us a thumbs up and some pedestrians smiled. It was an accepting smile, as if to say *that's the way we do it.*

"I guess they need to add a number 18 to that list," Katy laughed as we continued on the other side of the row of tollbooths.

"Correct. Anyone capable of going around the tollbooth doesn't need to pay the fee."

That afternoon we arrived in Pushkar, home of the world's largest camel fair, and the front tire on our bike started going soft.

"Not this again," I complained.

"Last time, your own patch job failed. Maybe you should just find a bike shop instead of trying to fix it yourself," Katy suggested, as I fumbled through our repair equipment.

"You're right. Should we go for a walk?"

"There's one," Katy chimed, pointing across the busy road. She wasn't pointing at a person or a shop or even a bicycle, but at a large bowl of dirty water.

"Good eye," I answered.

"It's so strange. I can't believe the way we find a good bike shop is by looking for a bowl of dirty water out front. Can you imagine this happening in the States?" Katy asked.

The routine with this mechanic was identical to our previous experience in Nepal. After I submerged my punctured tube in the bowl of dirty water, and mimed little bubbles floating to the surface, the mechanic went to work. He worked feverishly and sanded and patched our flat tubes and then banged the patches on with a metal rod.

"How much?" I asked, as I rubbed my thumb and fingers together to ask for the price.

"200 rupees," he mumbled.

I handed the man the money, but he shook his head, "No. No. 20 rupees."

I swapped out two 10 rupee notes for the two 100 rupee notes, offered another thank you, and we started back into town.

A couple minutes later, Katy exclaimed, "That's crazy."

"Where? What's crazy?" I asked.

"For $0.33 we just got two tubes repaired. Back home we would have spent $14 on new tubes. If we needed those tubes shipped to India we'd be talking $50 for shipping and two or three weeks of waiting."

"It's a good thing India has lots of camel carts and bicycles and motorbikes and all sorts of push carts that frequently get flat tires."

"Yep. Or else our trip would have ended a while ago."

The next day we rode to Jaipur, and found nothing out of India's ordinary: a man pushed a cart down the highway while thirty feet of rebar hanging out the back dragged and screeched on the road; another man on a bicycle carried 40 buckets stacked taller than himself down the highway; and someone cut up expired (but recycled) car tires and used the rubber to re-sole worn shoes. The road was flowing with pedestrians. Garbage was everywhere. It was a beautiful day. Oh, and we stopped at our first McDonald's since Italy, and admired the McAloo Tikki, McPaneer Royale, McSpicy Paneer and Chicken Maharaja on the menu.

Later that day we reached Jaipur, which is home to the Amber Fort, one of India's top tourist attraction. Tourists mean money, and touts show up in large numbers on their A-game, intent on getting their hands on some of that money. A tout has two objectives: convince you that you *truly* need what they have and that you're getting a really, really good deal. The hard part of their job, of course, is that they're both lies: you don't need what they have, and it's a terrible deal. A tout approaches his work with energy proportional to the magnitude of that lie.

Papu knew this, so as I exited the fort, he threw all his energy into his tiresome, competitive job.

"Five for twenty," he shouted, showing me some cheap fabric with paintings of holy people and elephants.

I took a quick look. Five little paintings for twenty rupees (less than $0.50) seemed like a pretty good offer. Papu saw me look and he moved quickly. I tried to brush him off, but he followed in front of me and flipped through an arsenal of more elephant and Hindu deity fabrics, and his prices started dropping. We walked for a few minutes and when he finally got to ten for twenty rupees, I stopped and looked again.

"Ten for $20," he shouted once I stopped. "A very good price. Just for you."

Ah hell. I realized I'd been fooled. He meant $20, not 20 rupees. It was the first time in India anyone had quoted prices in US dollars.

"No thanks," I said.

"1000 rupees," he shouted, moving the negotiation to local, barterable, currency.

"No thanks. But go ask her, she loves shopping." I pointed at Katy to divert the frenzied tout, so I could get a breath of fresh air. "And she needs Christmas gifts," I added.

"Oh, I have a nice gift for friends, and mother, and father, and sister, and brother."

When we reached the fort's outer walls, Papu doubled his efforts. He knew that he had less than sixty seconds to make a deal or he'd be making the long walk back up to the fort with empty pockets.

"900. 800. 600. My best offer, 10 for 500. And one extra as a Christmas gift from Papu."

I caved. I paid too much for something I didn't need because

Papu convinced me that cheap prints of elephants and Hindu Deities were something I truly needed. And that I was getting a really, really good deal.

In Jaipur, we stayed in the Krishna room at the Hotel Pearl Palace and feasted on dal makhani, chicken biryani, paneer butter masala and copious servings of roti and naan, with endless refills of fresh lime soda. Dessert was always gulab jamun and vanilla ice cream at their Peacock Rooftop Restaurant. It was a spicy, luxurious weekend.

Three days later, on Christmas Eve, we arrived in Agra. On Christmas morning, we woke to frigid temperatures and I ate breakfast inside my sleeping bag before we set off for the Taj Mahal.

The Taj Mahal sits in the middle of a great love story. In 1592, Shah Jahan became the fifth Emperor of the Mughal Empire, a Persian empire that ruled most of present day Bangladesh, Afghanistan, Pakistan and India. The Empire was doing well until 1631, when Shah Jahan's third wife, Mumtaz Mahal – the most loved and beautiful of his seven wives – died during childbirth. Shah Jahan was stricken with grief and his never dying love led him to build the Taj Mahal, as a monument to that love and a final resting place for her body.

Unfortunately, their son, Aurangzeb, later took control of the Empire and placed Shah Jahan on house arrest in the nearby Agra Fort, where Emperor Jahan spent the last 8 years of his life confined to an upper room, admiring his Taj from afar, waiting to be reunited with his Mumtaz. (Shah Jahan also founded Shahjahanabad, now known as "Old Delhi," and left behind famous cuisine at Karim's Restaurant – I recommend the Badaam Pasanda and Chicken Mughlai, two dishes that were staples of the Mughal Empire's cuisine of Northern India and Pakistan. They are to die for. Whereas most Hindus are vegetarian, the earlier Muslim cultures were definitely not, and their chicken and lamb curries are unparalleled.)

Photographs of the Taj Mahal, a perfectly built, white marble structure with inlaid precious stones and Arabic calligraphy, on the banks of the Yamuna River, are impressive. Standing at the foot of this Wonder of the World, however, felt surreal and unlike anything I had ever seen. We could have admired it for days.

North of Agra, we visited Vrindavan, the childhood home of Lord

Krishna and the center of the International Society for Krishna Consciousness (ISKCON), more commonly known as the Hare Krishna movement. We arrived at the MVT Guesthouse and I collapsed onto the toilet (food poisoning) and then into bed, while Katy headed to the temple in search of a spiritual guru.

Katy returned after my nap with prayer beads in hand, talking about some guy named Abhay Charanaravinda Bhaktivedanta Swami Prabhupada (but everyone calls him Pra-bu-pod), and the Bhagavad Gita (known as the Gita). Then she started chanting: "Hare Krishna Hare Krishna, Krishna Krishna Hare Hare, Hare Rama Hare Rama, Rama Rama Hare Hare."

"What happened to you?' I asked, concerned she may have fallen upon some LSD.

I tried to make sense of what she was saying, but then she said something I just couldn't figure out. "Did you just say we need to go to the temple to join the Kirtan, after Krishna and Radha take their nap," I asked.

"Yeah, why?"

"What do you mean, take their nap?" I asked.

"In the temple are two deity statues, but they don't call them statues, they call them Krishna and Radha. Each afternoon the deities are taken down. They have a nap and then they're changed into evening clothes and brought back out for evening worship," Katy answered.

"Someone changes these deities clothes every single day?"

"Well, yeah. It's Krishna and Radha."

"And in the morning?"

"They wear daytime clothes. It sounds a bit strange, but let's go over there. You'll like it."

"And what was all that Hare Krishna Rama stuff you were saying?" I asked, as I chased Katy out of the guesthouse.

The Hare Krishnas are sometimes confused with America's hippie culture of the 60s and 70s. I suppose this is because of their super groovy orange robes and bare feet. Maybe George Harrison's *My Sweet Lord* blended the two together. But the similarities end there. Krishna devotees follow a strict moral code – no meat, no illicit sex (sex is only between a husband and wife for procreation), no gambling, no alcohol, no caffeine and no tobacco or other drugs.

We entered the ISKCON temple that night, and Krishna devotees danced with religious fervor and chanted their mahamantra over and over and over. Spiritual energy emanated from the crowd. There were no teachers, no meetings, no announcements. Just chanting. They chant Hare Krishna to remember and worship God, and someone has been chanting the mahamantra in Vrindavan nonstop, around the clock, twenty-four hours a day since the late 1980s. They always remember Him.

The next day we got back on the road. We had two days left to reach Delhi. It was a tough ride. The road was flat and there wasn't a headwind, but as we approached the urban sprawl of the city, larger and larger crowds wouldn't leave us alone. Traffic slowed down and for hours people talked to us non-stop from their passing vehicles. I suppose we hit our low point when we started yelling at passing motorcyclists to leave us alone. We even occasionally tried to kick them and their motorbikes out of our way. To avoid the storm, I put in some headphones, and listened to Phish's *A Live One,* and did my best to pretend I was in a far away place with some peace and quiet.

Forty eight hours later, we reached Phase III, Sector 24 in Gurgaon, a suburb of Delhi, and went in search of our WS host, Shailja Sridhar. Gurgaon is in India, but it sure didn't feel like it. It is the uber-modern, leading edge of India's booming economy, quickly catching up with, and in some ways outpacing, the rest of the world. Shailja arrived home just after we did, riding her carbon fiber Pinarello road bike, and wearing pink Pearl Izumi spandex. She never cooked dinner or cleaned; that was work for her servants. Her six year old son, Airhan, spoke fluent English and repeatedly proclaimed that he would break his friend's nose if his friend took his iPad. At the grocery store, we saw Belgian chocolates, salsa, blueberry muffins and Dannon Yogurt.

We had made it. We had cycled through India and had come out alive on the other side. In the quiet coolness of the air conditioned grocery store, I thought about the hectic chaos of the roads. We celebrated our accomplishment, but were sad it was over. It was the most bitter-sweet moment of our trip.

* * *

We spent a week in Rishikesh, India – the yoga capital of the world – to stretch our bodies and unwind our minds, before flying to Laos to start the beginning of the Southeast Asia part of our trip. Our first yoga class was Dharana Yoga, taught in a local ashram. In ninety minutes, we did five poses while listening to the yogi repeat the phrase, "Your body is a block. You are not your body. Your body will only cause you suffering. You are not your body. Your body is a block." It wasn't exactly the athletic, sweaty yoga I had in mind, but I liked it.

We made quick friends with Ruaridh and Susie, a Scot and a Brit about our age, who were staying at our hotel. Their "base" back in the UK is a van parked somewhere on the west coast of Scotland, where they bathe in rivers and lakes, use eco friendly soap and float between gardening, construction and working at summer camps on "wee little islands" to make ends meet. Two summers ago, they spent a month in France working on a vineyard and the following year returned to drink the sweet (and fermented) fruit of their labor. Susie asked if we liked Yorkshire tea, because it's a "hug in a mug," and Ruaridh wondered if the sadhus knew he "didn't believe in begging." They had traveled through Nepal and India for four months, and were anxiously awaiting their fifty-hour, across India, sleeper class train ride for $20. Life on a budget is a good life. Life on the move is also a good life.

One morning, we met an Australian named Simon at a German bakery overlooking the Ganga River. He had recently completed a five year law degree before realizing the law wasn't for him. He's now "floating through Asia." His Instagram name is *drifterphotos*, which he says "pretty much sums up my life." On the topic of arranged marriage, he said he wished his mother was working on that for him. After India, he was headed to Thailand to do some surfing before heading to Nepal to "get into the mountains."

At Ashtanga yoga, we met a smiley redhead with freckles who introduced herself as Marley. You can tell a lot about a girl named Marley, with an American accent, doing yoga in Rishikesh.

"Where are you from?" Katy asked.

"Colorado."

"Oh really? What part?"

"Boulder. Just like everyone else."

Just like everyone else? She wasn't ignorant of the other cities throughout the state of Colorado, she was referring to the near 100% certainty that if you met someone in India that was from Colorado, they were from Boulder. She'd been on the road for 6 months or so, and was in Rishikesh doing a 40 day yoga training because it's "a nice place to unpack my bag for a while." I suppose it's also a rite of passage in her very cool Boulder community.

On our train ride back to Delhi, I tried to make sense of the past two months. I'm still trying to make sense of what we saw and heard over there. People live very different lives. Ruaridh and Susie are content to live in a van, work at a garden and go where the wind blows. Simon had been motivated to work hard and study harder, but he graduated from law school and still doesn't know what he wants to do with his life. (Although he has found something he doesn't want to do.) Marley has the opportunity to do anything she wants in life, but presented with so many options she's afraid to make the wrong decision, so she's in India biding her time before responsibility sets in. Some Indians wear pink spandex and spend their time on carbon fiber road bikes that cost more than what most Indians will make during ten long years of serving chai, herding goats or repairing shoes with used car tires.

From my seat on the early morning train, I watched fog settle over green fields, and men wrapped in blankets cycle down dirt roads. Pigs and dogs rummaged through piles of rainbow-colored garbage, while water buffalo yoked to carts pulled rice and vegetables into town. At each train station, cement floors covered in blankets were the beds for sleeping families, who carefully listened to the loudspeaker for the announcement of their departure. Barefoot children and women huddled around small fires to stay warm in the cold, early morning air.

Inside the train, Katy played a game of tic-tac-toe with an Indian girl, while her younger sister practiced counting in English, "37, 38, 39, 30-10" before her father would correct her. At one stop, a twelve year old chai-wallah came walking down the train shouting, "chai, chai." His life is so different than mine. He sells chai, probably every day of his life. He walks up and down these trains with a hot kettle of tea, a couple dozen paper cups and lots and lots of sugar. A cup of chai costs 10 rupees, or $0.16. If he sells all his cups he might make $5 today. To me it seems like an unfortunate life. But the contagious smile on his face radiates energy and optimism. It forces me to look up from my laptop and I can't help but return the smile.

"I'M SO BLESSED."

"India is about six times the size of France but it has almost twenty times the population. Twenty times! Believe me, if there were a billion Frenchmen living in such a crowded space there would be rivers of blood. Rivers of blood! And, as everyone knows, the French are the most civilized people on Earth. Indeed, in the whole world. No, no, without love, India would be impossible."

– Shantaram

More than any other country, India evoked deep, often contradictory feelings that have been difficult to assimilate. It was the country that I was the most excited for, the country I enjoyed the most, the country that drove me the craziest, and the country I can't wait to return to. India is a rollercoaster.

On our early morning drive to the Indira Gandhi Airport in New Delhi, I was sad to leave a country and a people I so loved. Our taxi driver passed a giant sign that said Lane Driving is Sane Driving, but he still managed to drive in two lanes all the way to the airport. Maybe he can't read English. Or maybe he's content with the old India and resists its modernization. It wasn't until our plane lifted off the tarmac, headed for the quaint village-capital of Vientiane, Laos, that I realized how much I would miss a country that had caused me so much misery. India was difficult, but difficult times are memorable times.

On our flight to Laos, I thought about our last night in India with two of Katy's work friends from Google. They had taken us on a quick tour of the Google office (complete with gym, fitness room, room with bunk beds, massage room, micro kitchen, cafeteria) and then we went to dinner in Cyber City, Gurgaon. Gurgaon is one of the fastest grow- ing, and prosperous, neighborsomehoods in India. Ten years ago it was farmland, but today, it's a landscape of high rise residential build- ings, international offices and a slew of modern fast-food cuisine: KFC, Burger King, Pizza Hut, Dominos, Starbucks, Krispy Kreme, Red Mango, Dunkin Donuts. It's clean and predictable.

Most people view Gurgaon as a mark of tremendous growth and development. But I was less impressed. To me, it's unfortunate that economic progress seems to be synonymous with an infiltration of America's flavorless, cultureless fast food chains. I didn't travel halfway around the world to stop at Starbucks in the morning, get KFC for lunch, and have Domino's deliver dinner.

The best part of India is that part of India which will never change. And for better or worse, most of the 1.2 billion people in that country will never change. There will always be chai-wallahs and sa- mosa chaat served up fresh on the dirty streets of Old Delhi. The cycle rickshaws will never be entirely replaced by public buses or subways. Lives will continue to be defined by the caste system, and parents will still arrange their children's marriages. It's a different reality, and one that can be hard to swallow, but that is India.

After dinner on our last night in India, we walked back to our hotel and passed a guy on the street, about my age, asleep on a piece of cardboard on the sidewalk. His cycle rickshaw leaned against a nearby wall near half a bag of some odds and ends – all of his worldly posses- sions were right there with him. I'd been "roughing it" for the past 6 months, but my panniers carried more possessions than he'll ever own. My bike cost the same as what he'll earn in five or ten years. Let's not talk about my townhouse in Ann Arbor, the closets full of clothes, the car in the garage, sailboat in storage, bank accounts, credit cards and the list goes on. If this man works all day, he'll make two or three dollars – enough to have chai with his friends, eat a meal or two, chew some paan and find a nice spot of ground to sleep on. The next day it will be the same. He'll never get ahead in life. As I walked past him, I felt that I should take $20 out of my pocket and tuck it into his shirt pocket. Generosity is an easy way for me to deal with conflicting thoughts I have on poverty. I don't like beggars, but I felt compassion for this individual. And he was sleeping, not begging.

India is poor, very poor. It's difficult for me to see people live a life so different from my own. It's easy to leave India with an overwhelming sense of gratitude that "I'm so blessed," and that "I have so much" and that my life "isn't as bad as theirs."

But gratitude is a tricky thing. I have been blessed, but what exactly am I grateful for? A car? A microwave? A comfortable couch? Air conditioning? A closet full of shoes and a basement full of bikes? A sailboat in the garage and three or four pairs of skis? Or the 24 hour weekend shifts I work in the hospital? Or all the emails? Or student loans and a mortgage payment? Or enrollment in medical school? Family and friends?

Money solves many of life's problems. It provides food, shelter, education and access to health care. But the glamour of money stops there, and after those needs are met it may even begin to create problems. After the basic necessities of life, money becomes irrelevant in the quest for things that truly matter in life – meaningful relationships, fulfillment from work, devotion to God, a sense of well being and an optimistic approach to life.

Is my gratitude truly an expression of humility? Or do I project my own uncomfortable feelings onto this homeless man, and then express gratitude that I'm not like him? It's easy to assume this rickshaw driver sleeping on the street is miserable, because I believe I would be miserable if I were in his situation. I assume a man that herds goats in the hot desert doesn't enjoy his job because I don't think I would enjoy it, but he might be grateful to own a large enough herd to send his children to the local school. I assume selling chai on the trains of India would be horrendously boring, but the twelve year old chai-wallah might be proud to have a job and help support his family. It's dangerous to project feelings onto others and difficult to understand life in a different culture. Goat herders and farmers may have similar thoughts about working in a cubicle for 12 hours a day, being unable to go home for lunch with family. Why would I want to work inside and stare at a computer for the rest of my life? they might reasonably ask. They might prefer the warm sun and regularly scheduled naps under a shady tree. We love our microwaves and toasters and air conditioning because they save time as we rush out the door to all our appointments, but Indians love real food cooked from local ingredients and a morning chat with the chai-wallah at the end of the street. We like quiet, safe neighborhoods where children can kick a ball in the grass or play on artificial plastic playgrounds, but Indian kids love to play in the dirt, chase goats in the street and roam the village.

There isn't a right or a wrong way to do things in this world. India taught me that. India made me think about what is important in life and what makes people happy. The streets of Delhi, I will tell you, are filled with many more smiles than the streets of New York City, so what does India have that we don't? I'm not sure. But it isn't something you can buy with money and it doesn't require a college education. And it certainly doesn't come from scheduling another something or other into our already busy days. It's something much less tangible than all of that.

Tomorrow morning, when the guy sleeping on the cardboard box wakes up he may not have a lot of the worldly conveniences I take for granted, but I bet that when he climbs on his cycle rickshaw and goes for his morning chai, and then to work, he'll have a smile on his face. And when our time on Earth ends and all of my worldly possessions remain in this world, he will take his smile with him.

Another suspension bridge, west of Kathmandu, Nepal

The Nepal-India border, Siddharthnagar, Nepal

Katy fills a water bottle, the Terai, Nepal

Rough Roads, Uttar Pradesh, India

The Ganges River, Varanasi, India

The Thar Desert, Rajasthan, India

**Right:
Snake
Charming,
Amber Fort,
Jaipur**

**Below:
Women in a
Truck,
Rajasthan**

Left:
Samosa Chat,
Streets of
Old Delhi

Below: Curry,
paneer, and naan,
Hotel Vivek,
Gorakhpur

India serves
up our planet's
best food.

Nam Song River, Vang Vieng, Laos

The Mighty Mekong, Luang Prabang, Laos

Left:
Katy celebrates
our arrival in
Thailand

Below:
Clayton enjoys
another
swimming
break,
Luang
Namtha, Laos

**Right:
The Burr Trail
Utah**

**Below:
Highway 12
Utah**

PART FOUR

"Thank you for bikes, and the freedom they bring."

Chad Harris, Warmshowers Host

MYANMAR

HANOI

CHIANG RAI

LUANG PRABANG

CHIANG MAI

L A O S

VIENTIANE

PHITSANULOK

SOUTH CHINA SEA

THAILAND

BICYCLE
TRAIN

BANGKOK

SIEM REAP

CAMBODIA

ANDAMAN SEA

PHNOM PENH

HO CHI MINH CITY

GULF OF THAILAND

PHUKET

KRABI

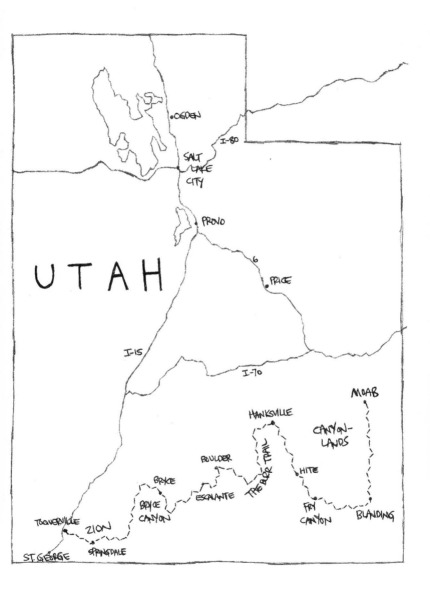

HIGHWAY 13

After our Thai Airways flight landed in Bangkok, we entered the airport terminal and a wall of cold air smacked us in the face. On a moving walkway, my iPhone connected to free public WiFi. Public restrooms were stocked with complimentary toilet paper. At a Dairy Queen, a girl named Mook served us a salted caramel Blizzard. Welcome to Southeast Asia.

During our connecting flight to Vientiane, Laos, we planned the final third of our trip: two days in Vientiane, meet my parents for a two week vacation from our vacation in Cambodia and Laos, and then a month of cycling from Vientiane through northern Laos to Chiang Mai, Thailand before another vacation with Katy's family. After that, it would be March 1st and we'd only have six more weeks left to see more of Southeast Asia, or maybe Australia, or to visit Southern Utah's National Parks or maybe just sit on a beach somewhere and sip mango smoothies. So much to do, so little time.

Our first day in Vientiane was an out-of-body – or at least an out-of-India – experience. At the airport, we obtained a visa without any hassle or headache. The baggage claim area was quiet, and except for our cardboard boxes and gigantic, disposable plastic nylon bags, completely empty. We grabbed our bags and a taxi driver helped us fit our belongings into the cab – which felt like teamwork instead of war.

We were in the taxi for less than a minute before Katy and I exchanged identical glances: *Where are we?*

"Shhhh," I whispered.

"I know. It's so quiet".

"And so clean. And there's so much space everywhere."

Streets were clean, and lanes were marked with stripes of white paint. People walked on the sidewalks. There was a paucity of camels or cows. Our driver stayed in his own lane – as if some unwritten rule required him to do so – and he stopped at a red light. He *actually* stopped. The road was empty, but he waited many long seconds for the light to turn green. It was entirely unnecessary.

The sudden return of driving rules and general law and order was very uncomfortable, and that discomfort was not something I was expecting. What surprised me was not how "normal" everything felt, but that normal felt so abnormal. As we sat at the red light, impatience bottled up inside me like a geyser about to erupt, and the clean, pristine streets made my body cringe. *What type of people live such meticulous lives?* For the first time I realized how far from home we had come.

On that taxi ride, I also realized that one day we would return to Ann Arbor, where streets are clean, people walk on the sidewalks and drivers stop at red lights (even when no one else is around). And where I'm a student at the University of Michigan and Katy is a Googler. Our great adventure would someday come to a crashing halt.

"Where are all the people?" Katy whispered. "The traffic jams? The commotion? The kids in the street?"

"I don't know. This place is so strange."

* * *

Good hostels must be three things: cheap, clean and quiet. Cheap is easy to find. A quick glance at Lonely Planet, booking.com or asking the hostel receptionist sorts this out. If the price is right, we always, always, always ask to see the room. Is it clean? Does the hot water work? Can you hear mice in the walls? I typically lay down on the bed to check for mattress integrity.

Last, but not least, is quiet. Is the TV blaring in nearby rooms? Are drunk college kids in the lobby? How many roosters live within a two mile radius? Where is the nearest railroad track? Are the other guests obese, raising the risk of obstructive sleep apnea and an evening of apneic snorting? These are questions that demand answers, because there's nothing worse than listening to the near suffocation of the fat dude on the bunk above you. We had checked-in to too many guest-houses, and knew exactly what to look for. We left nothing to chance.

The Vientiane Backpackers Hostel met all our requirements: $2 per night, immaculate (to be fair, everyone in Laos removes their shoes before entering a building, and places are kept rather tidy), and much quieter than the raucous place down the street. After a superb night's sleep I tiptoed down the slippery white tile stairway, toward the common area for breakfast. I took a deep breath. My main gripe with hostels is the over-inflated stories told by soul-searching travelers. Too often hostel life is a listen-to-how-cool-my-story-is situation, a constant barrage of one-uppers that goes nowhere. For six weeks in India, we never saw more than a handful of international travelers. But now we were in backpacking central.

I sat down to breakfast on a long wooden bench, fortunate to be carrying the ultimate one-upper in my back pocket: "My wife and I rode a tandem here from London." It's not exactly true, but if used correctly, it's often enough to end a conversation entirely. I reserve it for only the most desperate situations. Fortunately, the seven others at breakfast that morning were so utterly consumed by free WiFi, they never once looked up from their smartphones. Thank goodness.

Adjacent to our hotel was Le Banneton, a French boulangerie. What is a French bakery doing in Asia? Well, from 1887-1954 France ruled Indochina, and part of their surviving legacy is a smattering of bakeries throughout Laos. We entered cautiously, unsure if Asians could adequately recreate French cuisine. I was skeptical, but when I sunk my teeth into that warm and flakey pain-au-chocolat memories of the Loire River Valley immediately bubbled up inside me. Not only is Laos very clean, but it also has top-notch French bakeries.

After a second breakfast, we walked along the banks of the mighty Mekong until we stumbled upon a row of thatched roof stalls at an outdoor food market. Dangling from each roof, small motors spun metal wires attached to plastic bags in circles over piles of chicken legs, pork products, hot dogs, grilled fish and other skewers of meaty delicacies, which sat in perfect rows on top of neatly folded banana leaves. The spinning motor contraptions tried to keep the flies away. After India's relative vegetarianism, it was a lot of meat to look at, but we pointed to a fish, a chicken skewer and pig heart (mimed to us by an oinking sound with a fist pounding over the heart) and a teenage girl used my pen to write the price on my hand, 37,000 kip (or about $4.50).

* * *

Three days later, we flew to Phnom Penh, the capital of Cambodia, and spent a day at the Killing Fields and the Tuol Sleng S-21 Genocide Museum. April 17, 1975 changed Cambodia forever. On that day, Pol Pot and the Khmer Rouge marched into Phnom Penh to the cheers of thousands of civilians who assumed their ongoing civil war had come to an end. But they were wrong. The worst was yet to come. For Pol Pot, April 17, 1975 was day zero, the day he would begin to build an agrarian, communist civilization. Within three days, he forced 90% of the city from their homes . . . to grow rice. In the next three years, the Khmer Rouge killed one out of every four Cambodians, approximately 1.7 million people.

Tuol Sleng used to be a high school. The Khmer Rouge turned it into a torture chamber. Seventeen kilometers south of Tuol Sleng is Choeung Ek, one of the many mass graves scattered throughout the country. During his reign of tyranny, Pol Pot killed professional workers, anyone with an education, those who wore reading glasses, and anyone else in his way. He sent individuals he suspected were in league with the CIA or KGB to Tuol Sleng and tortured them until they confessed to wrongs they hadn't committed.

A couple of times each month, around 6:30pm, prisoners were loaded into a truck and taken down the road to Choeung Ek. Under the loud drone of a diesel engine, with Khmer Rouge party music blaring on a loudspeaker, mass graves were filled with innocent bodies. The Khmer Rouge used pickaxes and metal rods to murder the prisoners because bullets were too expensive. Corpses were buried by morning.

We walked through the Killing Fields and felt a tragic, but peaceful, calm. Many lives were ruined, but their torture is now over. A small sign on the trail reads, *Don't Step on Bones,* next to bone fragments that had risen to the surface during the monsoon floods. Next to the sign, I saw a couple of teeth on the trail.

During our visit, we listened to an audio guide narrated by a Tuol Sleng and Choeung Ek survivor. At the conclusion of our visit, he said, "I'm physically well now. I have food to eat. I have air conditioning. I live in a good house and I have a car. But, emotionally I'm broken. Genocide destroys the strings of humanity."

* * *

We spent the next two weeks with my parents, first at Siem Reap visiting Angkor Wat and then in Luang Prabang and Vientiane, Laos. The entire two weeks were great, but the highlight was our week in Luang Prabang. It's an incredible place (and also has a Le Banneton). In our blog my mother wrote:

"Two months ago I left Clayton and Katy on a dirty side street in Kathmandu. For the last two months I've woken up with the thought, "I can't believe those two are *still* on their bike."

In Luang Prabang we rented some mountain bikes and rode a 25-mile loop into the Chompett District, northwest of Luang Prabang. We first put our bikes on a giant canoe to cross the Mekong River, but as soon as our boat driver pushed off from shore the engine wouldn't start. Lucky for us, the current wasn't too brisk and we were rescued a quarter mile down river. Transferring bikes and bodies from a 25 foot by 3 foot boat to another boat of similar dimensions can be very comical! George's weight distribution almost sent us all swimming.

At last we were on our way, cycling a bumpy mountainous road with rutted tire tracks, and hills after hills that tested my legs. But not Katy's. She powered up those hills like nobody's business. The country was extremely rural with small villages of just three or four homes here and there. No one spoke English. No signage. Just the four of us, and Clayton's GPS (which is asking locals for directions followed by lots and lots of pointing).

Around noon I started getting hungry and didn't think the single can of Pringles Clayton put in his pack that morning would feed the four of us. "Don't worry Mom, we'll find a meal," Clayton reassured me. After a robust game of duck duck goose at a Primary School we rode to the next village of maybe a dozen homes. Thirty or forty adult men were sitting up to tables on plastic white chairs and looked like they were having lunch alongside a game of gambling. They used sunflower seeds as poker chips. Clayton didn't hesitate to jump off his bike and investigate what they were up to, and how to get a meal. Clayton is very good at this.

As you might expect, a dozen women were busy chopping indistinguishable plants and cooking over the most enormous kettles on an open fire. A table was prepared for us and we were served four large plates of fantastic looking food. It tasted better than it looked. After sticky rice, chili paste, greens and chicken, George was motioned to enter the village temple to see the coffin of a deceased wife and make an offering. Two dollars per person, donated to the town during what might have been a funeral luncheon, covered the price of lunch.

We continued cycling past rice fields, water buffalo, poinsettia trees in bloom and bamboo houses with thatched roofs. Young children carried their younger siblings to school on the back of their bike or back and shouted *Sabaidee* as we passed. Laos is a beautiful country with beautiful people. I wish days like this could be relived over and over."

Later that week we went on an overnight trek to a Khmu village north of Luang Prabang, which my father wrote about:

"We got into a tuk tuk first thing in the morning and were escorted by our guide Nong for an overnight trek to a Khmu village. We drove about an hour north and then headed on foot across some rivers and up into the mountains. Lunch was served on a couple of banana leaves in a little outdoor hut, consisting of sticky rice and an assortment of vegetables, and was delicious.

Just before we stopped for the evening we walked through a Hmong village. There were perhaps 80 dwellings, and people there living a very basic life. Weaving bamboo, taking care of farm animals, that sort of thing. Speaking Hmong.

Then we climbed over the brow of the next hill and below us lay a Khmu village, roughly the same size. We wandered into town just before sunset. It was amazing. This little town is completely self-sustaining, with many pigs and chickens and ducks, wandering everywhere between the various wood and bamboo dwellings. The people were living about the same as say a thousand years ago, with a few notable differences: many corrugated metal roofs, a couple of little stores where you could buy a soft drink (warm), several motorcycles and some electric generators.

Otherwise this could have been an ancient village. We had sticky rice (of course) for dinner, we watched them kill the chicken we ate and also had a good assortment of greens. Among his many other roles, Nong was an excellent cook. The kids were everywhere, playing, playing, playing, and laughing. There were a couple of central bathing areas where you could clean up.

After it got dark we crawled into bed. We slept on mats placed on wood platforms inside a home with a dirt floor. The home next door had just been completed, and the local custom is to inaugurate a new building by partying all night. A generator was used to power music that went well past midnight. Bad timing for us sleep-wise, but now and again these things just got to be done! The music was really great: a little disco-ey, and some reminded me of Pink Floyd, but all the singing was Asian (maybe Lao, how would I know)? It was most triumphant.

Morning came and we didn't want anyone to think we were just a bunch of stiffs. So when they stoked up the music again at breakfast time first Katy, then Clayton, then Charlotte and I started dancing out in front of our place. And attracted quite an audience. They were all very amused – by Katy's dance moves, Clayton's celebratory hairstyle (ponytail on the side, reserved for special occasions), and somehow, although this is one of the most surreal things I have ever done, it all seemed to fit. The little kids joined in and it turned into a nice morning dance party with the Khmu hill people in northern Laos. Little did we know at the time that the women had resumed the inauguration ceremony inside the new building by drinking rice wine from long straws."

Two weeks after my parents arrived, we took them back to the airport and returned to our tandem. People come and go, but life in the saddle must continue. It had been three weeks since we'd done any cycling and I was more than ready to get back onto my Brooks B-17 and explore the back roads of Laos.

For the next 700 kilometers, our new home was Highway 13, the largest highway in Laos, which runs north-south throughout the country. Although it's the largest highway in the country, it doesn't feel like I-80, or the Long Island Expressway at 5:30. It's more like an abandoned road in northern Montana on a Sunday afternoon. Five and ten minutes often passed with no other traffic. It's peaceful and it's quiet. There are no lanes, no paint in the road, no shoulders, no medians and very few signs. It's just a swath of pavement, smooth at best, bumpy on average, and riddled with potholes and nearly impassable at worst.

On Highway 13, children rule the road. Little kids march up and down the highway each day on their way to school, often giving piggyback rides to their younger siblings. Five year old girls are always on the lookout. They shout *Sabaidee!* and race to the roadside when they see us approaching. We feed off their energetic curiosity and veer to their side of the road for moving high-fives. Sometimes we make a game out of it and see how many continuous high-fives we could get before missing a child's outstretched hands. Ten high-fives in a row would give us a Power Up. While girls warned the town of our imminent arrival, boys would race old bike tires down the road, carefully navigating the tires' every turn with a wooden stick.

Older children traversed the highway in search of firewood, bananas and rice, as they accomplished their daily chores. Compared to growing up in Laos, childhood in the good ole' USA comes with some restrictions. My nephew, Charlie, can't walk half a block down the street to his friend Max's house without some lady pulling up in her SUV, assuming he must be lost, and wondering where on Earth his deadbeat parents are. "You gotta be kidding me," Charlie often complains while rehashing yet another incident. Parents nowadays prearrange "play dates" for their children, not leaving it to chance who their child might walk home from school with. But kids in Laos roam the highways and hills with their buddies, play in the dirt, and chase chickens through the fields. If you were a kid, which life would you prefer? Life in Laos is quite the life.

After the kids, animals take the next priority on the highway. Baby chicks squeak and chirp as they follow their mother hen carelessly across the road. Bamboo chimes hang from the necks of cattle; they wander aimlessly because they don't know where they're going and are unsure when they'll get there. Unlike the cows of India, these cows quickly move out of the way if we head right at them. The cow's demeanor reflects local behavior, Indians are persistent and in-your-face, but the Lao avoid confrontation at all costs.

Highway 13 is a snake. It climbs up and around and over the never-ending mountainside. At best, the road is straight for 70 meters before it twists around another corner. Each day we cycled over countless false summits, never sure when we would reach the top. When we finally came to an opening and spotted the summit in the distance, we'd drag our tired bodies to that spot and ride around another corner

. . . just to see more mountains. I watched my quads grow as we climbed those mountains.

Two days north of Vientiane we reached Vang Vieng, a stop on the Banana Pancake Trail for wandering college kids to unwind and enjoy a beer while they float down the Nam Song river. The Banana Pancake Trail is a string of tourist towns throughout Southeast Asia that cater to Western tourists and serve banana pancakes. In the middle of town, a single intersection was jam-packed with tattooed, shirtless white dudes with their bikini clad girlfriends in tow. Against the backdrop of Communist Laos, all I can say is *awkward*.

The street was lined with menus painted on white plywood boards, with a weathered, middle aged woman standing at each board. The board either proclaimed Pancakes, Sandwiches, Burgers or Fruit Shakes, and then contained a long list of other, optional menu items. Pancake options included Banana Nutella, Banana Peanut Butter, Banana Eggs Milk, Banana Honey Milk, Lemon Honey Sugar, Coconut Chocolate Milk, Peanut Chocolate Milk, Onion Tomato Cheese, Chicken Bacon Cheese, Ham Bacon Cheese, Chicken Cheese, Bacon Cheese, Ham Cheese, Omelet Cheese, Tuna Cheese, Hot Dog Cheese. I wonder if that last option gets cooked up much? I don't know anyone who likes Hot Dog Cheese pancakes.

We put in our order, and stepped back and spun our heads at the peculiarity of the situation. We rode thousands of miles across the globe intent on "getting away from it all," but ended up with an inebriated, half-dressed college crowd that had Ann Arbor on a football game day written all over it. Then a college kid started bartering with a little old lady because he wanted a sandwich for $1 instead of $1.25, and I knew it was time to get back on the road.

Lucky for us, the stench of tourism's malodorous winds don't blow far. Only two kilometers out of town, tourism disappeared and Laos returned. Half an hour north of Vang Vieng, Highway 13 crosses the Nam Song River and creates the best swimming hole east of the Rhone River in Geneva. The sun was hot, the river refreshing, and a Dr. Seuss-inspired, jungle-infested mountain range surrounded us on all sides. We jumped off the bridge's cement footings and into the river again and again. Secluded and picturesque Laos was just a short ride from what felt like South University Avenue on a Friday night. Travel outside the box. Go where others are not. Get there on a bicycle.

But if you can't go by bicycle, I suppose the next best option is a souped-up Land Rover Defender 90, which we passed on a long uphill climb later that afternoon. A family of six from Lyon, France had left home 18 months earlier in their Defender, and traveled all over the world, homeschooling their four children along the way. They couldn't wait to get to Vientiane to enjoy some of Le Banneton's baguettes and pain au chocolat.

Outside of larger cities, however, cuisine options in Laos are a bit limited. For lunch we typically had one option: feu. The Vietnamese call it pho, but the Lao call it feu. The words are pronounced similarly, but not identically – unless you are Katy, because after ordering the exact same meal every single day for two weeks she still could not pronounce it. Pho sounds like the beginning of the word fun and feu sounds like the beginning of the word foot. It's not that difficult.

What is feu? Feu is various amounts of white rice noodles and some sort of meat ensemble, typically beef and mystery meatballs, in a dark broth served in a giant bowl. The giant bowl is accompanied by a larger dish of green and white onions, basil, chili peppers, lime wedges, cilantro, lemongrass and bean sprouts. Bean sprouts are crunchy and delicious; lemongrass adds flavor, but is inedible. Every restaurant or roadside food stand serves four condiments with feu: chili paste, sugar, fish sauce and soy sauce. This is where the meal is won or lost. Each day, we upped the ante with an extra dribble of chili paste, until by the end of our two weeks, our lips were permanently ablaze, barely returning to normal before our next bowl of feu.

Since we're talking about food, I'll throw in the last (and most famous) of Laos cuisine: khao niao (sticky rice) and jeow bong (sweet chili paste with buffalo skin). The gelatinous rice is steamed over boiling water in a bamboo basket. I love pulling the cover off of a bamboo basket, wadding up a ball of sticky rice in my fingers, and dabbing it in just the right amount of jeow bong before popping it in my mouth. It's the perfect go anywhere snack, and a cyclist's dream.

North of Luang Prabang, the entire countryside was involved in the most peculiar activity – roadside broom construction. It goes like this: kids are sent to scramble through the hills and chop down a specific green plant that's thinner than my pinky finger, 3 feet long and has a long tail of dozens of wispy thin leaves. We saw a hundred kilometers worth of these plants drying on the side of the road. Once they are sufficiently dry, and the rich green color starts to turn yellow, they get smacked on the road over and over again to remove a fine green dust from the wispy leaves. This appeared to be a child's or woman's job, and we passed thousands of mothers and daughters, standing in the hot sun, smacking away at the pavement. Once dried and sufficiently smacked, they get tied onto the end of a bamboo handle, all at different lengths, to create the perfect fanned out broom, which is then exported throughout Southeast Asia. For several weeks, when this great plant is in season, all of rural Laos stops what they are doing and focuses on nothing but brooms. Shouldn't someone import brooms to these people? Wouldn't this free up thousands of Lao hands that could be put to better work? Or, would this just put all of those hands out of work and out of business? It's always difficult to determine how to aid a country that appears to be a bit behind.

In the midst of broom wonderland, Katy and I stumbled upon the most arduous day of our trip. I frequently told Katy the most painful days would be the most memorable days. I was right.

Let's start at the beginning. My alarm was set for 6:30am, but a distant commotion woke me before that. I stumbled over to the window and heard the town's loudspeaker radio blaring. Just like every other morning in Laos, *Communist Radio* - as Katy and I liked to call it – broadcasted advertisements and propaganda for everyone to hear. At 7am, a couple of hymns reminiscent of marching into battle were sung, which signaled that the indoctrination was over and we could proceed with our day. We were on the road at 9:30 and, around 11am, our bellies started rumblin' so we hunkered down for some feu and khao niao.

Usually a road *has* potholes, but our road that afternoon *was* a pothole. The road was paved maybe 40 years ago, but had not had any maintenance since, which left giant patches of crumbling cement on a washed out, rutted dirt road. Oh, and this was still Highway 13, the country's largest highway. Things like this are comical at first. *Holy balls Batman! It feels like we're riding on the moon.* But the awfulness didn't go away, and the day spiraled into a rollercoaster of emotions, with lots of laughter at the plight of our situation and lots of downright anger.

Then the climbing started. We hammered away at the pedals and climbed and descended over multiple false summits. Sweat poured out of our shins and we consumed entire water bottles in single gulps, the telltale sign of a good workout. Three hours later, we reached *the* summit, asked some Koreans to stop taking our photograph, chugged a Vita Milk, a couple of bottles of water, and took a couple shots of soy sauce. Soy sauce is the cheapest and tastiest antidote I've found for exercise-induced hyponatremia.

The descent was worse than the climb. On a smooth road, the hard work of climbing is rewarded by a relatively effortless descent. The windy roads and minimal traffic of Laos makes for great slalom ski turn practice, often at speeds over 40mph. But not today. I clung to the brake levers with my life, and we crawled down the bumpy mountain road as slowly as we had come up. (We did see a mother pig getting ravaged by her piglets, so that was nice.)

The tandem fares awfully on bumpy roads. The longer wheelbase is perfect for avoiding rocks and holes with the front wheel, but hits them dead on with the rear wheel. Towards the bottom of the climb we passed some construction workers and I almost celebrated their attempt to repair the road, but then I noticed they were working with shovels, rakes and bags of dirt. Frustration mixed with amusement.

"Hey, I rode my bike half way around the world and your road is the worst," I shouted as loudly as I could, but in a high-pitched, friendly tone hoping no harm would be done as none of the workers spoke any English.

At other groups, I vented similar frustration: "It looks like y'all are working hard, but that dirt is just gonna wash away when the rain comes." I mean honestly, how can you fix the national highway with a rake and a bag of dirt?

I'd get halfway through one of these rants when half a dozen men with smiles stretched across their faces would turn and shout *Sabaidee!* So much for trying to vent.

When it couldn't possibly get any worse, it got worse. The road disappeared entirely under two or three inches of fine dust. Every truck that rolled by engulfed us in a brown cloud of dust. Lung damage, vision problems, gritty teeth, fingernail sensitivity. Dust gets everywhere. Dust also hides stuff, like giant rocks. I pointed the tire towards the smoothest section of road, but that smoothness was only dust, dust that hid . . . SMACK! Our rear wheel collided with a small boulder and left us with a flat tire . . . and a broken spoke. It was our first broken spoke of our trip, and I was beginning to lose my patience with this road. I let Katy fix the flat tire because it's good practice, and I decided to fix the spoke later.

Then it got dark. The glare of headlights illuminated the dust clouds, which was pretty cool, because now we couldn't see *anything*. Each time a truck approached, we were forced to pull off the road and wait for the dust to settle. Then we smashed into another rock. This time I fixed the flat while Katy attempted hitchhiking. A truck stopped, and Katy was halfway into the passenger seat, before I reminded her that Pratts aren't sissies. "Get out Katy. We finish what we start. Don't ever give up. Ever."

We rode through the dark and finished our 90 kilometer, 9 hour bike ride with a new personal record for slowest average speed of our trip – just over 6mph. I suppose we could have walked.

After a giant bowl of feu, we sat down at a small fire in our hotel's parking lot with two middle-aged security guards, one with a machete and the other with a pack of cigarettes. I munched on my bag of sunflower seeds. Mr. Machete pulled some smoking hot yams out of the coals. I traded seeds for yams.

While we ate, Mr. Smoker placed a two foot piece of bamboo in the fire. He methodically rotated it and watched water bubble out of the top until, twenty minutes later, he decided it was done. So he handed the bamboo to Mr. Machete. Mr. Machete wacked it a couple of times and then pulled out some coconut-milk sweetened sticky rice, khao lam, for all of us to share. I always appreciate a second dinner. My tandem-bike-handling-on-dark-roads skills are improving, but I definitely need to work on my cooking-rice-inside-bamboo-over-a-small-fire-in-a-parking-lot skills. I mean honestly, I don't think there is a security guard in the United States that can cook rice inside bamboo over a makeshift fire while he's on the job.

The following afternoon, we rode upon a house in full swing. It was another house warming party. Three men jumped into the road and obstructed our path, so I slammed on the brakes, hopped off the bike and clambered up some wooden stairs into a one-room bamboo house on stilts. Sticky rice, noodles and greens were spread out on a giant banana leaf on the floor, and the Beerlao was flowing. Half the village was packed into that small room on that hot afternoon; most of them were drunk. Someone's drunk grandpa hit the floor hard and got carried outside. (If I knew then what I know now, I would have suggested he go to the local ER to get a CT scan of his head to rule out a possible intracranial bleed.)

Katy soon left the party. She didn't care for the claustrophobia or the oppressive temperatures. But I raised my glasses of Beerlao high into the air and danced to the music. Instant celebrity status. Then Maroon 5's *Moves Like Jagger* came on and, being the only English speaker in the house, I felt it was my responsibility to sing the English lyrics at the top of my lungs.

And it goes like this
Take me by the tongue and I'll know you
Kiss me 'til you're drunk and I'll show you
all the moves like Jagger
I've got the moves like Jagger
I've got the moves like Jagger

It was a riot. With each beat of the music, the collective weight of the party-goers rose and fell, seriously stressing the wooden planks and bamboo supports of the new house. If the bamboo home survives the inaugural dance party, it will likely stand forever.

North of the housewarming party, we reached Luang Namtha where we spent the weekend with René Rosler, a German expat about our age, who helps set up community banking and loans in rural villages. He promised a good weekend, and he did not disappoint. Crispy, thin crust pizza, a sweltering local sauna loaded with lemongrass, trekking through the jungle, swimming in rivers, lunches of khao niao, pork larp, and joew bong, 2-for-1 soft-serve ice cream cones, a bonfire overlooking the Nam Nga River, and a leisurely Sunday afternoon bike ride to sunbathe at the local waterfall. It was heavenly, maybe even Nirvana. Our bodies were restored and rested, our souls rejuvenated. It's what every weekend should entail. Some might think working in rural Northern Laos might be a bit lonely, but René makes every day count and lives life to the fullest. He's an eternal optimist.

Two days later, we left a quaint riverside bungalow in the small village of Vieng Phouka at 8am, and headed towards Huay Xai and the Laos-Thailand border. The day was hot and long. Katy documented our travels that day:

> "To add to the tough day, our timing chain kept coming off (I think because our pedals hit some rocks the other day which loosened our chain) which completes the short recipe for Clayton's anger. After the third incident he screamed, "Worthless dipshit bastard son of a bitch." He jumped off the bike and tried to throw it to the ground, but I steadied it—as I was still on it. He kicked the front pannier and I told him to cool off. He's tightened that chain many times, but somehow it continues to loosen. He walked off down the road and I put the chain back on and caught up to him down the road.
>
> After five hours, and too many hills, we reached our final opponent: a 12% grade for three kilometers. It was too steep. And our bodies were empty, empty of carbs and energy. We also rode those five hours on only two water bottles and a handful of sticky rice. Each turn of the pedals was painful. We stopped. We were beat. I got off and walked and Clayton kept cycling. Even walking was hard; I'm not sure how Clayton cycled our stuff up that hill. Around the corner Clayton left a water bottle on the side of the road for me. I like mountains, but I also like knowing where the top is. Those mountains in Laos, however, they were never-ending.
>
> That night, after my shower, I sat down to a mango smoothie on the banks of the Mekong River at the Laos-Thailand border and Clayton informed me we had climbed

52,000 vertical feet – a little under two Mt. Everests – in the past two weeks. I'm going to miss Laos."

7-ELEVEN

I woke up early the next morning, and although tired and achy from all the climbing over the past two weeks, I put on a tank top and a pair of shorts and wandered outside into the guesthouse's open common area. The sun's morning rays were just beginning to appear in the sky and an array of oranges and yellows lit up the horizon. Down a steep hill from our guesthouse, the giant Mekong River separated Laos from Thailand and it's banks were lined with fishing boats of every kind. The river was teaming with fishermen coming from or going to their favorite fishing spot. I waited until the sun was well above the river before returning to my room to get started on my morning routine.

Just as breakfast is the most important meal of the day, morning is the most important time of day. The first half hour of the day often dictates how the next twenty three and a half will go. Because of this, morning needs a routine. For our year of cycling, our routine went like this:

After I brush my teeth, I flick the excess drops of water off the last bristle and put my toothbrush in the little blue and white bag, the one with the zipper that can't quite close because the toothbrushes are longer than the bag. From then on it's Katy's responsibility. "Katy's responsibility" means she can pack that little blue bag wherever she wants and, as long as my toothbrush resurfaces twelve hours later when I'm ready to brush again, I'm happy.

Then I take off my shorts, boxers and t-shirt and roll them up into a nice little "outfit to-go." The roll-up method turns three items to keep track of into one, cuts down on wrinkles, and allows the shirt to block any incoming or outgoing malodorous scents – a win-win-win situation. My non-cycling clothes can last about two weeks before a wash. They might not smell optimal, but compared to my cycling clothes, they carry a delightful fragrance and Katy doesn't complain. I'm an anosmiac, so odors don't exactly bother me.

I slide my Pearl Izumi spandex shorts on, which are usually a bit slimy and damp to the touch. It takes a minute or two for the clammy upper thigh, wet swimsuit feeling to go away. If, however, that feeling doesn't go away, or the feel of my spandex elicits the gag reflex, then I rotate them out of the lineup, place them in my dirty clothes stuff sack and pull out my other pair of Pearl Izumis. When cycling across the world, two pairs of spandex are a must. I prefer to cycle sans-shirt so after I've got my spandex on and I've located a pair of socks, I'm pretty much dressed. The only additional item would be cycling gloves, which I choose to wear based on the amount of chronic right wrist pain I've been dealing with lately secondary to my dorsal ganglion cyst.

About packing. My panniers go on the left of the bike; Katy's go on the right. My front left pannier contains personal belongings including my REI garment bag (clean clothes), sleeping bag stuff sack (dirty clothes), and a bag of odds and ends: Advair, headlight, small towel, Albuterol inhaler, spare socks and a white sheet we picked up in southern Nepal where the beds became too dirty to touch. The rolled up clothes go in next, and my New Balance 574s last. When evening comes, I can strategically unpack my stuff in the order I'll need it.

The external hard drive, chargers, and cables, along with our headlight and taillight, are usually scattered across the room wherever outlets were haphazardly placed. These items are also Katy's responsibility. She packs them in our little red bag. Color-coding is key.

Panniers come next. Any bike tourer will tell you the quintessential daily ritual of "getting on the road" each morning entails the repetitive action of rolling up their panniers and cinching them tight. We do it over and over. I never have to ask Katy if she's ready to get out the door, I just check whether or not her panniers are cinched tight.

When I'm positive I've packed everything, I place the pannier's mounting hardware facing away from me and scrunch out all the air. Ortlieb recommends at least three rolls to guarantee a watertight seal on the bag, and I comply. Two clips of the buckles later and I snap it on to our Tubus racks. On top of the rear panniers, we pack a Sea to Summit dry bag with most of our camping gear, secured to the rack with two bungee cords. Almost ready to go.

Our 13" Macbook Air fits perfectly into the left side of our custom made Porcelain Rocket frame bag. The frame bag was Katy's idea, and it was a lifesaver. Besides the laptop, the left side of the frame bag belongs to Katy. The right side is my territory, and contains our bike locks (U-bolt and cable), spare tire, extra bike tubes, a pump, Pedro's Wet Chain lubricant, and a filthy dirty grease-covered bandana for chain maintenance.

The most useful bag happens to be the smallest: my Planet Bike top tube bag that attaches right in front of me on our top tube. In it I carry a pen, ChapStick, Carmex, a multi-tool, a Sharpie, some Allen wrenches, keys to the locks, a couple of Glide floss picks, my headphones, a stack of our TouringTandem business cards, a miniature pocket knife and some garbage. After I shove my sweaty handkerchief and iPhone in there, we are ready to roll. We have a place for everything, and we put everything in its place. As bike tourers go, Katy and I run a pretty clean ship. Much different from other bike tourers we came across, who seemed to be carrying a miniature Salvation Army, haphazardly strapped to their bike with fraying bungee cords.

When the bike's ready, there's only one thing left, a double check for any belongings left behind in a guesthouse that we'll never revisit. Katy is very good at double-checking our room, but under my watch I've lost a pair of Gramicci shorts, a swimsuit, a towel, a pair of shoes and a couple of shirts.

* * *

The next morning was our last in Laos. We banged out our morning routine in record breaking time and cycled off towards the International Friendship Bridge IV on the Mekong River. Thailand was in the distance. Border crossing is usually a painless and straightforward process, but when we entered border control and got into the car lane, we were told to take our bike inside with the pedestrians using public transport.

We already had our Thai visas – we had picked them up in Vientiane, and didn't understand why we had to go inside. After some more unnecessary paperwork, we were ushered outside and told to pack our bike onto a bus to be driven three kilometers across the Mekong River to Thailand. Our bike wouldn't fit on the bus without being disassembled. I protested.

We argued a bit with a short uniformed fellow but our requests to return to the car lane and cycle across the border were denied. We got impatient and walked out of the building. The original passport officials looked at our passports, then at our bicycle, back at our passports, and at our bicycle. After too long of a wait another guy came out and the process repeated.

"Should we just go for it?" we asked each other.

People in Laos will avoid confrontation at all costs, and we knew it. We feigned misunderstanding and took off pedaling toward the border. They shouted something at us but we just rode past them. I thought we were home free, but we were stopped at a tollbooth 100 meters down the road. The confusion and negotiations continued (difficult to do in Thai.) Then I heard a siren. I glanced around, curious what was going on, when Katy informed me of the worst. The siren was from a police car, and that car was headed down the road towards us. *Oh shit.*

"Be nice Clayton. Do what they ask," Katy demanded, as the officers approached.

I crafted an apology in my mind, and hastily contemplated my options. But as fate would have it, five minutes later this police car escorted us across the Mekong River into Thailand. A near catastrophe turned into quite an entrance and we entered Thailand in style, with our own police escort.

Differences between Thailand and Laos were immediately noticeable. Rural bamboo villages disappeared, replaced by billboards, concrete, traffic lights and grocery stores. The smiling, barefoot children playing on the side of the road were now safely indoors, because playing in the streets is dangerous. Dogs turned into pets, and there were 7-Elevens EVERYWHERE. I wasn't particularly excited about these changes. I mean honestly, I didn't come to Southeast Asia to stop at a 7-Eleven for a Slurpee. That's what I did in Junior High. Our adventurous third world travels were coming to an end.

At the border, we forgot to exchange our money, and although every town we passed had an ATM, each refused our debit cards. After an hour or two in the hot sun, we ran out of food and water. We slogged through the humidity until we reached a larger town and stopped at the first 7-Eleven. A Visa/Mastercard sticker on the window of the motion-detector sliding door was a relief, so Katy stocked up on a couple liters of water, two panini sandwiches and some momos. By the time she got to the checkout line, she had guzzled a liter of water and chomped through half a panini. She swiped her credit card, but it didn't work. She swiped again. Nothing. She tried all of her credit cards. Still nothing.

She was about to place her half-eaten items back on the shelf and offer an apology, when a four foot tall lady with dirty feet tapped her on the shoulder. She spoke only Thai, so another customer translated, "It's really hot outside. You look tired. I will buy your groceries." Tears started to flow down Katy's cheeks. Katy offered her a couple dollars, but the short lady smiled, shook her head and disappeared down the street.

Katy was in the middle of relating this story when a guy pulled up on a motorcycle and asked us the usual questions. Kong, also a bike tourer, invited us to his home for a cappuccino and a hand of bananas. Twenty minutes after we left his home, he caught up to us on his motorcycle and gave us some bracelets from a local monk.

"These will bring you good luck," he promised.

The rest of the evening was a beautiful ride through brilliantly green rice paddies and a red setting sun. I wasn't thrilled to see some of the changes in Thailand, but the warmth and goodness of these strangers made up for that.

That evening in Chiang Rai, we met up with Edouard Berthier (the son of the French parents who cooked us a plum crumble), and reminisced about life in France and shared stories from the road.

Then, I got a bit restless. The roads were now paved, street signs told us where to go and air conditioned 7-Elevens sold Reese's Peanut Butter Cups, Magnum Ice Cream Bars and Diet Cokes. Katy welcomed our return to civilization with open arms, but I couldn't. I like the unexpected and the atypical, and I wasn't excited to return to the predictable and reproducible. The best part of our trip, in addition to being outside everyday, was forging into the unknown. Katy might try to give you a different answer, but she loves adventure, too. As civilization reared its ugly head in the way of our journey, and I felt our trip coming to an end, I made an executive decision and told Katy we were going on an adventure.

"An adventure?" Katy asked.

"Yeah, we need an adventure."

"Isn't this trip an adventure?"

"Yeah, but . . ."

"But what?"

"I'm not ready for these flat roads and all the tourists we'll see in Chiang Mai. I need another day of getting lost and not having a plan. Let's do some exploring."

Katy took a deep breath and replied, "What do you have in mind?"

"I've been looking at the map and I've got an idea." Katy didn't say anything, so I continued.

"The main road from Chiang Rai to Chiang Mai is pretty straight and pretty flat," I explained, while showing her the map. "I say we try this other road. At first it's paved and follows the river. Then it climbs a bit, and then I'm not really sure what happens for a couple of miles. It looks like we go over a mountain, and we connect up with this road on the other side."

"A mountain?"

"Well maybe a small one."

"Will we make it?"

"I think so. Based on these topographical lines I think we're looking at a 10% grade for 2 or 3 miles. If worst comes to worst, we can just push our bike. Right?"

"If you say so."

"And besides, didn't your dad always tell you that you can do hard things?"

Morning was a blue sky and a warm sun. For the first time since Western Europe, we cycled along secondary roads with minimal traffic, a delightful contrast to the busy roads between most third-world towns. We passed an elephant carrying two overweight white folks down the middle of the road. Awkward. At the river, the road turned into hard pack, and we cycled through rice fields headed towards the hills. We stopped at a small store, in what we guessed was the last village before the mountains, and treated ourselves to a slew of snacks, the best of which was an ice cream sandwich. The Thai had recreated this Western dessert the best they could, and when I unwrapped my package I found a square of ice cream between two slices of white bread. It was, literally, an ice cream sandwich.

After lunch, we lounged by the riverside until a horde of sand flies chased us back onto our bike and further down the road. Then the going got tough. The road pitched up, crossed some small rivers, and then got steep, too steep to pedal. We got off and pushed. I don't like pushing my bike, it just feels wrong. The road flattened out briefly before our single lane dirt road got steep again. We got off again. To cross the next river, we had to pick up enough speed before we reached the river so we could coast through the water with our feet lifted off the pedals, away from the splashing. It's not easier than it sounds, especially on a rutted road with a bunch of rocks hiding in the water. We splashed through. The next hill was probably a 25% grade. We got off and pushed with all our strength but that tandem would barely move. We were almost to the top, when we came around a corner and realized we weren't even halfway. When we couldn't push anymore we rested and admired the beautiful scenery. It felt like we were in Forrest Gump territory, and expected to hear Lieutenant Dan yell out, "Get down. Shut up!"

When Katy got angry about our self-inflicted predicament, she let me push by myself. "Because I want you to have an adventure," she said, when I asked why she wasn't helping. A four-wheel drive vehicle barreled down the mountain towards us and we jumped into the tall grass to let them pass. A truck going in our direction offered us a ride and Katy accepted. I declined. Then Katy also declined. We were going to stick this one out together. We pushed our tandem up and over the never-ending mountain. When we finally reached the main road, and were thoroughly exhausted, we still had a three hour ride to the next town.

It was the road less traveled, and it was an adventure. We rolled in to Tha Ton in the darkness, but the evening street food was still in full swing.

Thai street food is superb, a close second place after India. We hunkered down at a small plastic table and had the best fried chicken since Dodge's Chicken on Highway 82 in Greenville, Mississippi. This stuff was crispy, juicy and done right. As fried chicken disappeared, we started on grilled sausage, spicy pork, pad thai and noodle soup. When we couldn't eat anymore, Katy stumbled upon mango and sticky rice and we ate some more. Katy loves that stuff. She claims it surpasses baklava as the best dessert of our trip. But as my nephew Charlie would say, "You don't know what you're talking about." The following afternoon, to celebrate Valentine's Day, we had three plates of mango and sticky rice for our 10am snack. It's no baklava, but it is pretty tasty.

The next day we arrived in Chiang Mai and spent a week with Katy's family in Bangkok, Phuket and Chiang Mai.

* * *

Katy wrote about our time with the Clarks:

"Clayton and I had a great time when his family came to visit, so I hoped we'd be able to share some of our adventure with my family as well. Back in Europe, I wasn't sure this would be possible because my mom was diagnosed with breast cancer. It was a difficult time for me, and being away only made it harder. I debated going home to be with my mom, but every time I asked her or my dad about it they both insisted I stay out here. They have been so excited and supportive of this crazy idea. Fast-forward six months and my mom is post radiation, in remission, and relaxing with me on a beach in Thailand. Here are a few highlights from our time together.

After a celebratory meeting at the airport, we headed for the Bangkok Airlink Tram. Tickets were 35 Baht (about $1) per person. Clayton walked up to pay and my dad whipped out his new wad of Thai cash and handed Clayton a 20 thinking it was like $20 back home. Clayton and I just laughed. Clayton let everyone in on the joke, and said, "It's nice you want to pay for two-thirds of your ticket Dave, but I got this."

At a Sunday Street market in Chiang Mai, Jen saw a row of chairs and a bunch of Thai women standing around. Her eyes lit up like Christmas morning when she realized these ladies offered wonderful foot massages for only two dollars. "If only I had this on my street back home…" she muttered, before she fell asleep during massage number two.

Before my family arrived, there was a long debate about the ethics of elephant tourism. I did a little homework and found the Elephant Nature Park, an elephant rescue and rehabilitation center in Northern Thailand. It started off as one rescued elephant and one passionate Thai woman, and has grown into dozens of rescued elephants, many other rescued animals, a sanctuary over three square miles and hundreds of volunteers.

On a hazy sunny morning with my family, I slung on a shoulder bag filled with bananas, watermelon, pumpkin, and sugarcane, and walked cautiously into an open meadow with five, two-ton, wrinkly, curious elephants who were awaiting a delicious meal. I hoped not to die by stampede. Despite their massive presence and lumbering gait, these creatures were friendly and playful, pushing you around and tricking you into looking the other direction while they snuck their trunk into your goodie bag.

After feeding, we walked alongside the elephants to the river, where we participated in bath time. One elephant even tried to wrap her trunk around Patrick and nudge him into the river to play. Cleaning the elephants turned into a water fight, while the elephants languished in the water being thrown from both sides. Everyone got soaked. One of the baby elephants walked out to a deep part of the river and rolled around below the surface of the water with his trunk above the water to keep breathing. If only I could do that at the pool. Bath time was pretty magical with these animals.

Every time I talked to my dad on our trip, he was amazed Clayton and I continually ate our way through cities, communities, WS hosts and markets. My family experienced this first hand when they showed up in Thailand. Sweet pork covered in fried dough, fried chicken, spring rolls, coconut milk soups, sticky rice with mango, crepes with fried bananas and sweetened condensed milk, pad thai, pork skewers, corn on the cob, rice and beans cooked in bamboo stock and smoothie drinks – banana, strawberry, pineapple, papaya, watermelon and of course mango.

The food was so good. We even signed up for a cooking class, which has paid off, since a few dishes have been recreated back home by my mother and sister. Our markets in the U.S. unfortunately lack the necessary variety of chilies and fresh ingredients, but my resourceful mom started growing her own. Food was a big part of our time together and kudos to my family, because they tried anything Clayton and I ordered—well almost everything. Not everyone needs to eat beetles and ants.

Later that week, on the beaches in Phuket, we set sail in a catamaran with Clayton at the helm. I wanted the moment to last forever. It was perfect. The turquoise water glistened, the sand sparkled, the wind pushed us forward, the glowing sun sat on the horizon and the company was fantastic. It was idyllic. I couldn't believe Clayton and I had actually achieved our goal of biking across the world. A year ago, this was just a crazy idea. But we made it happen. Clayton made it happen. He dreams big and achieves those dreams. It is absolutely why I am lucky and grateful to be with him and share in these dreams. I shed a few tears that night thinking about our trip coming to an end. I asked myself how did it go so quickly and did I enjoy every moment. You have to enjoy it while you can because moments don't last forever, because if they did, I would still be sitting on a sailboat in the Andaman Sea."

* * *

After Chiang Mai, we were optimistic about the last six weeks of our trip. Our plan was to ride southwest into Myanmar and then along the Andaman Sea before crossing back into Thailand and heading towards Singapore. It was a good plan, but it didn't go so well. I blame the heat.

We left Chiang Mai early in the morning, but not early enough. By 9am the sun was out and about. Maybe scorching would be a better word. When we stopped for khao soi, Northern Thailand's best $1 lunch option, we were parched and exhausted. I struggled to consume fluids at the same rate I was sweating. That afternoon we arrived at a small town aptly called Hot. We took it as an omen to not go any further. We raced to the nearest 7-Eleven, sat down on the tile floor and enjoyed a cold Slurpee. Later we found a guesthouse, cranked up the air conditioning, and checked the weather forecast. It called for highs over 100F for the next seven days – plus the dreadful humidity. The next day at 11am, I wanted to keel over and die. It was just too hot.

So we changed our schedule. The days of staying up past midnight watching Tour de France reruns and getting on the road whenever were over. We adopted a strict policy of lights out at 9pm, arise and shine at 5am, and then move at a frantic pace until the late morning heat melted us into submission.

The next day things went according to plan and my afternoon nap began at 10:30am. Katy read her Kindle, and we sat around until 8pm when it was safe to go outside again. The next day we moved up our schedule. My alarm went off at 4am, we were on the road an hour later, and my afternoon nap started at 9am. It's awkward checking into a hotel at 8:30am, but we had no alternatives. The heat was suck-

ing the life out of us. In Myanmar, the next country on our route, limited hotel access most likely meant we'd spend the nights in local monasteries, away from the protective calm of cool air. Our trip quickly
unraveled.

A couple of days later, I wrote the following in our blog:

"TheTouringTandem is winding down. We're getting
old. Our days of *international* bike touring are over. (At least
until we gather up a couple of kids and come back out in ten
years.) It's sad, and it happened unexpectedly.

The other day we checked into our hotel room at
8:30am. After my cold shower, I got in a three hour nap before noon. Katy fuddled around on her Kindle and then we
got to thinking: *What are we doing? It's too hot out there.* In the
words of Hamilton "the Ham" Porter, "This pop isn't
workin', Benny. I'm bakin' like a toasted cheez-it. It's so hot
here!"

We decided to change things up. After a scurry of online
planning, we got in bed at 7:50pm. But as is never the case,
neither of us could sleep. I laid in bed and lived through the
memories of the road. They are good memories. Ones we
will relive again and again. Often we will turn to each other
and say, "Remember that ice cream shop in Ljulbljana? Remember the tea in Ayder? Remember Dartmoor? Or the
Po? Wadi Rum? The sunset in the Kaçkars? Swimming
north of Vang Vieng? The baklava in Trebinje? The plum
crumble? Remember the guy with his sheep in the hills above
Srebrenica? The furniture stores in Tirana? Remember that
slice of pepperoni on our way out of Udine? The free dinner
in India on Thanksgiving? My barber? Rebuilding our wheel
in Kathmandu? The glorious sunshine on the banks of the
Rhone? Lost in the rain in search of 8 Chapel Lane?

I tried to sleep that night, but my mind raced.

At 1am my alarm went off and I shot out of bed. The sun
would be up in five and a half hours, and that meant
heat. Lots of it. Gotta get moving! We raced off to the twenty

four hour 7-Eleven to stock up on water and sugar, but found the morning market just starting to set up. *Who sets up a market at 2am?* We grabbed four khao lam, jammed them in our panniers and got on the road.

As we rolled out of the parking lot a lady waved. It was a unique wave, and I waved back.

"Goodbye," she shouted.

How does she know? I thought to myself. *How does she know we're leaving?*

Three minutes later we hit a fork in the road and had a choice to make. It was a choice we made the night before, but now we had to make the decision for real. Turn left and stick to our new plan or go straight and continue on to mar. More than anything, I wanted to stay on our bike and enjoy three more weeks in Southeast Asia. I wanted to explore the small towns of rural Myanmar. But more than I wanted to stay, I wanted to leave. We wanted to leave. The heat was unbearable. Why finish a fantastic trip hiding inside, underneath the air conditioning? I wasn't ready to go home, but we couldn't stay. We turned left.

We rode from 2:30am until 11:30am. It was a solid 9 hours in the saddle, 182km and our longest day of the trip. When I wanted to quit, I told myself, "If Katy's still out here, surely I can toughen up."

We hit a steep climb early that morning, before my legs could warm up, and my quads ached. Then it was a gradual roll until 8am when the headwind picked up. It was a hot and muggy, ride through the smoke of the crop-burning mountainside, munch on khao lam, kind of day. At 9am, when the sun was raging and our butts were sore, we turned to each other and smiled.

"I can't believe our cycling in Asia is over," Katy declared.

"I know. It's so sad. And it happened so suddenly."

"Here's to our final two hours!"

We rode those last 20 kilometers nice and slow. The heat

was wonderful. It cooked into our skin and we poured sweat from every pore. We soaked up every ray.

Katy's tough. I don't know many other people who can jump on a bike at 2am and ride hard for 9 straight hours. She's also very optimistic. At 10am I pulled off the road and into the shade because I wanted to die. It was so hot. As we shared a couple of ice cold Diet Cokes from a roadside stand, I glanced back at Katy and it looked like she'd just gotten out of a swimming pool. Sweat ran down her face, and over her giant smile. Who smiles on a day like this?

We arrived in Phitsanulok that afternoon and spent eighteen long hours at a WS host's home without air conditioning and with mosquitoes galore. We spent most of the night packing our tandem into some cardboard boxes, and then attempted to fall sleep on the floor of his house. In the morning we boarded a train for Bangkok. Just like that, our across the world bike tour was over.

S'MORE

The Southeast Asian heat kicked us out of Thailand earlier than we had expected, but our trip wasn't over. We weren't finished yet. We still had a month before school would call us home to Ann Arbor, and 587 kilometers to go for a nice and even 10,000 kilometers, so we decided to move our cycling to a cooler climate. Vying for the top of the list of "now where should we go?" were the Gold Coast of Australia, the south of Spain, Ireland or anywhere in Central America. We also contemplated flying to a beach, where we could kick off our shoes and dance in the ocean. The beach was hard to pass up: Katy and I make great beach bums. But this trip began on our bike and it only made sense to end it on our bike. After some deliberation, we decided to end our journey in our own backyard – to compare the great state of Utah to the many places we'd been, and visit Southern Utah's National Parks – after a week on the beach.

We left our bike and belongings in Bangkok and flew down to Krabi, where we swam at a different beach every day for a week and ate all the som tum – Thailand's low-calorie, intensely flavorful green papaya salad – we could get our mouths on. Cycling through the dense smoke of crops burning in the furnace of Northern Thailand: not that cool. Putting on a swimsuit and flip flops every day for a week, and cruising around sunny islands on a scooter, with mango smoothies in hand: very cool. It was just what the doctor (or fugitive medical student) ordered.

Our flight back to the States first landed in Los Angeles, where we spent another day at another beach, and then we connected to Las Vegas, where Katy's grandparents picked us up and drove us to their home in Toquerville, Utah. Culture shock. It's really the only way to describe it.

Throughout our trip we had experienced many different cultures: the peculiar language spoken in England, our first meal with a French family, a lesson on pasta from Roberto and Davida on the Simplon Pass. These cultures were fascinating. Also, the overwhelming friendliness of the Turks, the housewarming parties in Laos, and basically everything that had happened in India, were wonderful and unexpected. People on our planet live such different and fascinating lives.

The greatest shock of our trip, however, didn't come from exposure to other cultures, but from re-immersion into our own. After nine months on a bicycle, while traveling through twenty six different countries, America had stayed exactly the same, but it looked and felt so different. I expected coming home would feel normal or familiar or even comfortable, but it didn't. America is so much different than the rest of the world. From a global or holistic perspective, the countries we visited are not that unique or that odd. In fact, just the opposite. It is America that is the great outlier.

The typical American life is often influenced by the simple idea that more is better. Bigger is better. It starts with a big house. Big houses have big walls, which require big flat-screen TVs. It feels strange to live in an oversized home, but drive a small practical, economical vehicle, so we prefer SUVs and pick-up trucks. It seems strange to me that so many people require four wheel drive to commute through crawling rush-hour traffic on well paved roads, especially after having pedaled many, many kilometers over all sorts of roads, carrying everything I needed on bicycle tires not even two inches thick.

If rush hour traffic is bad or we get held up at work, we pick up dinner on the way home. We prefer Super Size Me menus, Biggie Meal options and Grande Meals. We like buffets and all-you-can-eat. Mmm. Overeating. If the sodium and saturated fat makes us thirsty, we can swing by 7-Eleven for a Big Gulp. In the world of American Cuisine, you really can't argue against the notion that bigger is better.

We shop at huge stores like Costco and Wal-Mart, and having placed too many items in our giant shopping carts, we stash the pre-packaged and frozen foods in our six-foot tall refrigerators. When our first refrigerator fills up, we put an extra freezer in the basement for backup, because transient hunger is America's greatest fear. It is a strange country we live in.

The first thing that shocked me in Southern Utah was that no one was outside. No one was walking around. The sidewalks were empty. In Europe and Asia, people were always outside. Whether on foot or on bike, at the local market or the town square, people were out and about. Life existed outside. But America seemed to exist indoors.

Why are we always inside? Because what do people do with their big homes and their big cars? They sit in them. This might seem like a small or trivial or maybe even an insignificant difference, but it's not. It's a fundamental difference in how our society functions. Stuck inside the doors of our possessions, people cut themselves off from each other. We are no longer connected. We don't spend our evenings in our front yards or walking through the town square. We don't wave to our neighbors or to strangers on the way to work. More often, we get home from a long day of work and plop down at the kitchen table for dinner, or maybe in front of the TV – often with our increasingly larger smartphone and tablet screens in our face – and don't even talk to the people having dinner with us.

The American Medical Association recommends all Americans get 30 minutes of exercise (and walking can count as exercise) a day, most days of the week. The vast majority of Americans fail. We fail. We don't even walk around. Instead, we sit. And because of this, medical experts have warned that sitting is the new smoking. In essence, sitting around is killing America.

The next thing I noticed was the food disaster. Europe and Asia overflow with authentic, delicious, local cuisine. Most of it is fruit and vegetables. They have food pride. Americans lack food pride. We'll eat anything that comes in a wrapper. Throughout Southern Utah, Katy and I were often forced to stop at gas stations to get food, because nothing else was available. What can you find to eat at a gas station? That's a scary question. I will say that Corn Nuts come in Original, BBQ, Nacho, Chile Picante con Limon, Ranch, Ultimate Heat and Jalapeño Cheddar options and Lays Potato Chips now come in New York Reuben, Southern Biscuits and Gravy, Greektown Gyro and West Coast Truffle Fries flavors. But those are just the "new" flavors, the flavors we already have include Barbecue, Cheddar and Sour Cream, Deli Style, Dill Pickle, Hmmm Hot, Honey Barbecue, Lightly Salted, Lemon, Pico de Gallo, Salt and Vinegar, Sour Cream and Onion, Sweet Southern Heat Barbecue, Tapatio, 15 Kettle Cooked varieties, 12 Stax varieties and 6 Wavy varieties. (Warning: they all taste bad.) But just because you can eat it doesn't mean its food. Do they sell any actual food in a gas station? Or anything that at one point was growing in the dirt? I'm not sure, but they do have a measly basket at the check out counter with some over-priced bananas that scream, "I've been sitting here for a hell of a long time – eat at your own risk."

We were in culture shock. The two things that I came to love on our trip – great food and greeting friendly strangers on every street corner – suddenly disappeared. *I can't believe Americans live like this.*

* * *

We spent the weekend in Toquerville with Katy's mother and grandparents, Cherrie and Than Naegle. Cherrie is a genealogy fanatic. If she has a distant relative who lived or died within the last two hundred years, or a thousand miles of her home, then Cherrie knows about them. When Katy and I asked how to get to a bike shop in a nearby town, her answer went something like this: "Go down the highway and after the second light turn right at Wells Fargo. Do you know who used to live on that land before they built the Wells Fargo?"

"Actually I don't."

"That plot belonged to the Johnson family. They bought it from the Dickson family, who moved here in 1855 when . . ."

At that point we knew we wouldn't make it to the bike shop that evening, so we checked what time they opened in the morning and sat down to another family history lesson. Cherrie is wonderful.

Katy's grandfather, Than, is Cherrie's perfect complement. He fixes the computers at the genealogy center, works for the town council and has completed various construction projects around town. He's often interrupted by Cherrie's stories of grandparents, great uncles and uncles' cousins, but he listens patiently and doesn't complain. After each morning's prayers and hugs he gets started on his to-do list and if he finds a little free time he'll wander down to the hangar and continue the ongoing construction of his two-seater airplane. A man needs a hobby, and he has one.

We rode east out of Toquerville, with a planned route to Zion National Park, Bryce Canyon, Escalante and Boulder, a sidetrack along the Burr Trail, then southeast to Blanding via Hite and Fry Canyon, before heading north to Moab. As a kid, my family road-tripped all over Southern Utah and I had been to most of these places many times. But those trips were usually crammed into the backseat of "the Tony" (our Toyota van), fighting with my siblings for "space," with my mother yelling at us to be nice while she made sandwiches and cut up apples, as my Dad listened to the Grateful Dead. Hours later we would magically arrive at our destination and I had no idea where we were or how we had gotten there.

This time we would visit these places on our bike and on our own terms. We'd see familiar sites, but through a different lens. We would create Southern Utah memories of our own.

We hadn't gone far before that first semi flew past us. It must have been going 70mph. It was terrifying. Absolutely terrifying. For the first time on our trip, I thought to myself that if that driver was twelve inches to the right, our lives would have ended in an instant. In Asia, I was never afraid of getting in an accident, because drivers over there never go above 40mph and focus 100% of their attention on the road. The symphony of obstacles and distractions that just might appear on an Asian road at any second requires that drivers don't let their concentration lapse, not even for a second.

Drivers in the States, however, have it much easier. Roads are well paved, and for the most part, reserved just for vehicles. First, this allows drivers to move at reckless speeds of 70mph, and second, when driving in the open country gets "boring", people pull out their cell-ones and pay less attention to what's happening on the road in front of them. As the semi passed, our tandem swerved down the road in its wake. If that driver happened to be text messaging one of his buddies, someone would have had to peel us off the highway. Cycling in India was hectic, but cycling in Southern Utah seemed to be an ongoing near death experience. Ten minutes after the first semi passed, the terrifying process repeated itself.

As we continued north on Highway 89, I thought of the many times I've driven back and forth between Salt Lake City and St. George. But I've never driven the entire way on Highway 89. I've always taken I-15, and always at 80mph. It's always a race to get home, because it's not enough to just get there, you gotta make great time.

Just east of the blazing corridor of I-15, however, are so many beautiful roads. I-89 used to be Utah's main thoroughfare, and it had given life to the small towns of Glendale, Spry, Junction and Maryvale. These towns used to be vibrant and full of life, but now they're quiet and dying. Almost half of the towns that once existed in Southern Utah are now ghost towns. The hustle and bustle of I-15 stole their commerce and charm. It sucked the life out of them.

If I were to drive the entire way home on I-89, I'd get a little glimpse of what Utah used to be like, back in the good old days. I'd meet real Utahns who prefer the mom-n-pop shops to Subway and Maverick. If I were to drive home "the real long way," I'd loop around on Highway 12 through Escalante and Boulder and Torrey and Bicknell. No one ever goes that way, and they're missing out. Highway 12 is the prettiest paved road in Utah.

The highest elevation we reached on our bike trip – while actually cycling – wasn't crossing the Swiss Alps. It was at 7,600 feet, fighting the high altitude desert along Highway 12 between Panguitch and Cannonville. The air was a little thinner up there. Climbing that pass gave us a little insight into the life of Ebenezer Bryce, an early Mormon pioneer from Scotland, who homesteaded the area in the 1860s and frequented the nearby canyon. It wasn't named Bryce Canyon for nothing.

Just north of Glendale, Utah, we approached what appeared to be an auto junkyard. Rows and rows of 1970s or earlier vehicles, rusting, with missing wheels and windshields, covered the desert hills of sagebrush. A thin, robust man in a black cowboy hat and blue jeans approached us. He came down the hill on his four wheeler with his German Shepherd riding on the back. He offered us a firm handshake and then his business card:

William D. (Bill) Spencer

D7e Cat, Backhoe, Old Cars, Classic Chevs, Tree Falling

Bill grew up on that property and so did his parents. He's worked for the family business since he was tall enough to reach the pedals.

"Have a look around," he offered. "Let me know if you see anything you like."

I looked at all his Fords and Chevys and VW Beetles and I suppose if you took the working parts of ten of those junkers then maybe, just maybe, with a little bit of luck and some skill with a wrench you might be able to get one of them up and running. Bill is a Southern Utah man. He didn't say much, but his life exemplifies the difficulty of running a business in the wake of the hustle and bustle of I-15. He was also an optimistic man and content to make do with his plot in life. At first glance, his plot happens to have a lot of rust in it, but surely some fine engines are buried in there somewhere.

We left Bill's auto yard and spent a couple days at Bryce Canyon before continuing to Cannonville, Escalante and Boulder. Boulder is a great town of about 200 people. A nice little sign out front says: Tree City USA. I was skeptical, because one, it's in a desert and two, everyone knows that Ann Arbor, Michigan is Tree Town. Most folks only stop in Boulder for a meal at Hell's Backbone Grill. It's the best restaurant within a hundred miles and draws young folks with young energy to give Boulder enough of a heartbeat to make the town interesting. We rolled into town, made the sweeping left turn at the Burr Trail cutoff, blinked . . . and the town disappeared. The idea of, if you blink you'll miss it, holds true. We circled back around and a small sign in front of the Anasazi State Park caught our attention: Street Food. *Street food? Here in Utah?*

Magnolia's Street Food operates out of a funky teal-colored trailer, and serves up some of the best carne asada tacos and pumpkin with roasted chile quesadillas, ever. The meat was tender, the flavors were potent, and it was spicy – a drastic improvement from the overwhelmingly mediocre Mexican food we choked on at Café Adobe in Hatch, Utah. Also a welcome change from the PB&Js we'd been eating around the clock. Don't get me wrong, I like a nice PB&J as much as the next guy, but to be completely honest, it's a rather bland sandwich that doesn't compete well against actual food with actual ingredients.

Magnolia is the name of the business, and also the daughter of Hailey and Garrett. To stay afloat, Garrett is also a dessert chef for the Hell's Backbone Grill, and Hailey is a hairdresser, working out of her clients' homes. It can be tough trying to run a business you love in a place that you love. But it is possible, and refreshing to see Magnolia and her parents doing just that.

Exactly one and a half miles north of Hell's Backbone Grill, just inside the Dixie National Forest, a dirt turnoff on the east side of the road leads to a secluded campsite. We unloaded our stuff – it's scary how fast our panniers can explode into a mess of belongings strewn across branches and picnic benches – and Katy set up the tent, while I scavenged for wood and built a fire. With dinner behind us, we only had one thing on our mind: roasted marshmallows. Katy and I aren't your average marshmallow fans, we're enthusiasts. Maybe even connoisseurs. A regular sized Kraft Jet-Puffed Marshmallow has 25 calories. A minute of cycling burns about 10 calories. We crunched some numbers and decided we were each allowed to eat half a bag.

After a couple mallows, just to test out the flames, it was time for s'mores. Everyone knows (or should know) that your typical Hershey's chocolate and Honey Maid graham cracker s'mores are lacking. Hershey's chocolate is miserable, doubly so having just biked through Europe, and graham crackers without milk are way too dry, maybe even arid. After a regular s'more my mouth begins to dry out and after half a dozen it feels like the carcass down the road that was picked clean by the vultures a week ago. When I eat regular s'mores, I'm never left wanting s'more. I'm left wanting a glass of water.

Fortunate for us, Katy and I have been tweaking and fine-tuning our s'more recipe since our very first bike tour – a week on carbon fiber frames with huge backpacks in the San Juan Islands during the summer of 2008. We weren't too bike tour savvy, but we were campfire savvy. The Hershey's chocolate was the first to go (thank goodness) and replaced by a Reese's Peanut Butter Cup. The Reese's is best warm and gooey, so we fashion a smooth piece of wood near the flames, and then place the Reese's Cup on a graham cracker and slide them near the flame until the Reese's gets all melty. The next change was the removal of half of the graham, making it an open face s'more. This was Katy's idea, and initially done for carb-counting purposes, but it also cuts down on the dry mouth factor and I approve. Finally, to justify eating s'mores until the bag is empty, we add a couple slices of banana, for a nice flavor fusion, but also so we get our potassium and Vitamin B6, and pretend the whole thing is healthy. It might not be an absolutely perfect recipe, and I'm open to suggestions, but the s'mores go down sticky and delicious, and when we finish the bag of Jet-Puffed Mallows I'm always left wanting s'more.

The simple things in life bring the greatest joy. Shooting the breeze with Bill, listening to stories about how Magnolia's Food Truck was born, securing the elusive, but perfect campsite, collecting firewood all evening instead of resorting to Netflix, and staring into the dying coals of another campfire with my wife as I construct, and consume, another s'more. It's nice to be outside. It's nice not having a home, or a car. None of the day's simple pleasures would have occurred if we had drove off to our reservation at Pole's Palace Motel, flipped on the TV and asked for the WiFi password.

On the way out of town the next morning, we stopped at the gas station to stock up on food and water. We planned to venture onto the Burr Trail and camp at the Cedar Mesa campground that night, which meant we wouldn't see any towns or running water for 36 hours. We packed two gallons into our rear panniers, just to be safe. Before leaving the gas station, we came across some young travelers from the Czech Republic.

"What's the most interesting thing about the United States?" Katy asked, curious to see our country from a foreigner's perspective.

"We went to the Wal-Mart. Have you been there?" one of them asked, genuinely excited about what he had to say.

"Yes. I've been to Wal-Mart," Katy answered.

"Have you seen the fat people, driving around in the little cars?"

"Little cars?"

"Yes, in Europe we have them at the hospital for people who can't walk. But America has them at the grocery store. Some of these people were the really fat people we've heard about. I think you call it obese."

* * *

The Burr Trail gets under your skin, in the way that the desert sand gets under your fingernails. It's a you-have-to-go-there-for-yourself adventure, diving deep into the heart of some of our country's most rugged terrain. The road is relatively untraveled, which makes a casual visitor feel like an explorer. The road is named after John Atlantic Burr, who was born somewhere in the Atlantic Ocean, hence his middle name. It's called a trail and not a road, because Mr. Burr would have wanted it that way. The trail zigs and zags and twists and turns through the most beautiful red rock and white volcanic hills. It's a desert terrain you don't want to miss. The height of the adventure is the dozen switchbacks that traverse the Waterpocket Fold, which allowed Mr. Burr to move his cattle between winter and summer ranges.

To descend the steep switchbacks, Katy hopped off the bike and ran, while I clenched the brakes with all my might and kept my eyes on all the rocks and potholes racing toward my front tire. In the distance, we could see the Henry Mountains, or the Unknown Mountains as they were once called, because they were the last mountains in the lower 48 to be completely explored and mapped. It's beautiful, inhospitable country. At the bottom of the switchbacks, we hit a triangle in the road: we could go south to Ticaboo and Bullfrog, or north to Hanksville. To quote the lady at the Boulder gas station, "you won't find much in Ticaboo, not at this time of year." We went north.

The dirt road quickly turned into sand. *Shit.* Sand is not a bike's best friend. Have you ever ridden a beach cruiser on the beach? I didn't think so. Beach cruisers are for boardwalks, not beaches, because bikes and sand are enemies, maybe even archenemies, and sand almost always wins. A loaded tandem with only 35mm wide tires made our battle near impossible.

"We can do this Katy, only 11 miles until the campground," I encouraged myself as much as I encouraged her.

Eleven miles is just over half an hour on a road bike, or the better part of a day if you're backpacking. We anticipated something in between. When the road ran on the valley floor the sand got too deep to pedal and our tires slid all over the place. And then got stuck. We fell over a few times.

Katy decided that running wasn't much slower than dealing with our bike getting stuck in the sand again and again, so she got off and ran. Without Katy the tandem was a bit lighter, but pedaling still wasn't easy. When the road crested the occasional hill the sand disappeared for a moment, blown away by the desert wind, and Katy got back on. When the sand got really deep, we both got off and pushed together.

The sun and the sand made us thirsty. Really thirsty. On top of that, we knew we only had a limited water supply, which is psychologically dehydrating. The only thing I could think about that afternoon was water, so I sang the lyrics to one of my favorite songs, "Would you care for a glass, when the sand fills up your throat. Water. Water." And then we saw a trail of dust rising into the air in the distance and ten minutes later a friendly young girl in a Subaru Outback pulled up.

"Hey, y'all look tired. Do you need anything?" she asked.

"Do you have any water?"

"Sure, I've got some. Anything else?"

"Nope, just water."

She opened her trunk and pulled a five gallon jug of water to the rear of her car. We drank and drank. Water had never tasted so good. We reached our campsite that night with enough time to scavenge for wood, build a bonfire, wait for the coals to be just perfect, and resume our s'mores routine. The desert air was cool, but the fire was warm. When the fire died, I darted into my sleeping bag with my straight-from-Istanbul purple leggings on, which not only kept me warm, but prevented my dirty, sweaty legs from sticking to each other all night. I love my sleeping bag, but not with sticky, uncovered legs.

The next day the sand continued. I decided to run and let Katy ride the bike. It was slow going. Then, just like magic, the pavement returned and we were cruising. Cruising with one caveat, Katy remained in the captain seat and I was forced onto the back seat. Me in the back seat. It was awful back there. Sure I could lollygag and sightsee, but there was no legroom, the pedals started and stopped without my control. I couldn't steer. The list goes on. But more than these inconveniences, I was a bit fearful of Katy's steering and breaking abilities. What if we crashed? It's scary surrendering all of your cycling independence.

"I can't believe you've been back here this whole time?" I half shouted, half laughed as the awkwardness of riding across the world on the back of a tandem started to set in.

"Tell me about it."

"How in the world have you sat back here this whole time?

"Tell me about it."

"Going down the Simplon Pass? Traffic jams in India? Weren't you terrified?"

"Exactly. I'm glad you realize that."

I didn't last back there for more than 45 minutes, and we never dealt with any traffic or went above 20mph. Katy managed ten months. I don't know anyone else who could have done what she did.

Two days later, we rolled out of our sleeping bags at another makeshift campsite, this one across the street from the Fry Canyon Lodge which had closed decades ago. There was a bit of excitement in the air that day, because yesterday's ride had brought us to 9,957 kilometers. Today we'd reach five figures on our odometer.

Three hours later, we reached Mile Marker 88 on Highway 95, somewhere west of Blanding, Utah, and all those 9s rolled over to 10,000 kilometers. We leaned the bike up on the side of the road and celebrated. We did a little dance. Made a little love. Got down . . . that afternoon. (Not really.) After a song and a dance we looked at each other and said, "Keep cycling?"

We did what we do best and continued the 33 mile, 2,000 foot climb of the day. It was exhausting, as all climbs are. But as opposed to England, where we had often complained, "How many more hills?"

we now wondered, "Do you think this will be our last climb?" As we crested the summit, an aluminum can sitting upright on the white line caught my attention, so I abruptly pulled over.

"What are you doing?" Katy asked.

"Did you see that?"

"No what?"

"There's a can over there on the white line. I think that Subaru left something for us."

Sure enough, a Lava Lake beer was sitting on top of a nicely folded $1 bill right on the white line. People always look out for bike tourers. We passed the same Subaru a couple miles later, and when the thirty year old male driver realized that my ponytail and 7-Eleven tank top belonged to a man, we got an interesting double take and never saw the driver again.

Our good luck continued. On the main highway in Blanding, a lady in an SUV drove up alongside us, shouted some friendly words neither of us could understand and then pulled over before the next intersection. She hopped out of her car and started hollering so we pulled over.

"Thank you so much for advertising for us," she hollered, looking closely at the 7-Eleven tank top I had picked up in Bangkok.

"Umm, advertising?" Katy asked.

"My name is Shelly Martinez. I'm the new 7-Eleven Field Supervisor for the Southeast Utah Region, and we just opened three new stores in the area."

"Of course, anything we can do to help out," I replied.

She looked us over for a moment and when she realized we weren't the average bike commuters on our way home from work she asked, "By the way, where are you guys going?"

"We rode across Europe, and some of Asia. Now we're riding through Utah on our way home to Salt Lake City."

"Really?"

"Yep. I bought this tank top in Thailand. They're crazy about their 7-Elevens over there."

"Thailand? I had no idea. Hold on a second."

She ran back to her car and came out with a stack of coupons: three 1/4 lb. Big Bite Hot Dogs, seven Medium Slurpees (any flavor), seven small coffees or other hot beverages and seven Big Gulps. All for free. Our first sponsorship deal was finally pulling through, and in a big way.

It was just in time too, because the next day we would reach Moab and possibly the end of our trip. Why Moab? and why possibly? Our family was coming down from Salt Lake to visit, and we weren't sure if we would have enough time to cycle home to Salt Lake City after they left, or if we'd hang up our cycling shoes, burn our spandex and call it a trip.

Moab isn't the place we had imagined our trip would end. Start in London, end in Moab? It doesn't really fit. When we left Thailand, however, an email landed in my inbox that brought us to Moab. It was the right thing to do. The email reads:

> Hi Clayton,
>
> You don't know me, and I only discovered your blog a couple of weeks ago through an article about you two in the Deseret News, but your experiences resonated deeply with me because my wife and I have also done some long distance touring on a tandem. We zig-zagged our way across the USA in 2004. While Iowa and Idaho don't sound as exotic as some of the places you've ridden, our experience was still otherworldly. I'm sure you'll agree that it doesn't matter where you're riding your bike; it's the people you meet along the way that make the best memories.
>
> With that in mind, I'd like to invite you to come stay with us in Moab while you're visiting Arches and Canyonlands. We'd love to hear your stories and offer you a hot meal, a warm shower and a soft bed. Maybe we can also dust off our tandem and join you for a ride or two.
>
> Please come!
>
> Chad Harris

Chad is exactly right. I couldn't have said it any better myself. It doesn't matter where you're riding your bike; it's the people you meet along the way that make the best memories. We were fortunate to meet friendlier, more generous, more wonderful people than we ever could have imagined.

The final stretch into Moab, if you're approaching from the south, is a long gradual downhill. It's mild enough to feel like the road is flat, but downhill enough to let you pick up a decent pace. With five miles left, Katy and I shook off the 10,000 kilometers from our legs and hammered away at the pedals, for one last time. I pedaled my heart out, and let my lungs race and my quads burn. Memories of the year floated through our minds.

When we landed at the London Heathrow Airport and assembled our tandem, we had no idea what we were getting ourselves in to. We took it one pedal at a time. We got tired and lost. Our butts grew sore and our necks ached. Katy's fingers tingled. Sometimes it rained and sometimes it poured. Sometimes there were stunning vistas and magical moments, other times were just good old life in the saddle. We ate the best food our planet has to offer, and a lot of it. We learned a thing or two about ourselves and each other and when we were feeling beaten and down on our luck, generous strangers put a smile on our faces and pushed us down the road. The generosity and goodness of strangers, was without a doubt, the best part of our life on the road.

That weekend, we sat down on Chad's couch and looked over our budget and our calendar. We had $41 left and school was starting soon. I turned to Katy and said, "I'm pretty tired. I think I'll go home now." It was time. We said our thank yous and good byes and packed our tandem into the back of our Prius (driven down to us by my dad).

Five hours later we entered the Salt Lake Valley and got onto I-215. It looked familiar, but it felt so different. It was our home, or at least it used to be. Our 28 country, 280 day, 10,000 kilometer adventure was over. I cranked up the volume to that excessively loud level that might blow the speakers and Katy and I sang our hearts out:

Sometimes the lights all shining on me.
Other times I can barely see.
Lately it occurs to me, what a long strange trip it's been.

EPILOGUE:
ANN ARBOR, MICHIGAN

A few weeks later, on the first day of my third year of medical school, I rolled out of my bed, took a shower, dressed up real nice (pants, shoes with laces, that sort of thing) and stood in front of the mirror in my bedroom to tie my necktie. It was a horrifying morning at the end of a wonderful year. As I stood in front of the mirror that morning, I was nervous. Nervous that in a couple of hours I'd be expected to perform physical exams on toddlers to ensure that these 6 or 15 month olds were reaching their developmental milestones, discern between viral versus streptococcal pharyngitis, recommend antidepressants to new mothers with postpartum depression (and warn them about the possible side effects specific to their medication) and counsel middle aged, obese, hypertensive diabetics that unless they improved their diet and started exercising then they would have to increase their metformin dose and potentially begin insulin injections.

My mind was a loose conglomeration of medical knowledge that I didn't quite remember. Words like hemoglobin A1c, selective serotonin reuptake inhibitors and palatal petechiae were phrases that used to make sense, but that seemed like another life of mine. A different life that was going to start in half an hour. I was supposed to be a medical student that day. *A medical student? Me? Oh, I don't think so!*

I stared into the mirror, unhappy about my recent haircut and new professional dress code, and I couldn't concentrate on the task at hand. During the past year, not only did I forget how to tie a necktie, I also forgot most of what I had learned in medical school – and although that knowledge would eventually come back, there was little chance of remembering it before I arrived at the Briarwood Family Medicine clinic at 8am. But that anxiety could wait.

I stared into the mirror, and as I fuddled with my tie and Katy fixed my hair for the third time, thoughts of the past year raced through my mind. It felt like yesterday when I had burst out of my school counselor's office and told Katy that I was free to take a personal leave from school. The images of leaving Heathrow International Airport, summiting Simplon Pass, cruising along the Adriatic Coast, crossing into Turkey, navigating India and the mountains of Laos flashed through my mind. They felt like yesterday. I wanted to relive one more day on my bike. Just one more day.

If I could, I would love to wake up again in the fields of Melrose, Scotland, to the barking of the bulldog Buzz tearing through the fields after rabbits. It would be refreshing to wake up in the open air, and then go for a morning swim (and bath) in the River Tweed. Then, we would instantly be in Sarajevo, Bosnia and sit down to breakfast at Buregdzinica Bosna and have another plate of borek, the Ottoman's Empire world-renowned pastry. Mmm. To officially start our day, Katy and I would get on our bike and climb the last half of Simplon Pass, dodging in and out of tunnels under construction, while motorists hung their heads out the window and cheered us on our ascent. I miss the cool crisp air of the Swiss Alps and the sound of cattle bells echoing off the mountains. At the top we would look for our Italian friends, Davida and Roberto, and tell them about our journey.

For lunch we would enter the streets of Old Delhi, and eat samosa after samosa, washed down with a nice glass of chai. Crispy, spicy, triangular magic. The chaotic, bustling India would shock me at first, but then we would land in the middle of conversations with strangers and I would feel right at home, buried deep inside the madness and love that is India. After samosas and chai, I'd take an afternoon nap in a park near Lac Leman in Geneva, Switzerland and return to the

Rhone for an hour of swimming in the river. We would then climb back on our bike and cycle through Austria, somewhere between Wiesmath and Bad Tatzmannsdorf where those magically green, rolling hills seem to continue forever. Midway through our ride, we'd pull up to a French bakery for another pain au chocolat, or a gas station in Turkey for a cup of tea, or maybe Thailand for another som tum.

After a long day's ride, we would arrive at any of the wonderful Warmshowers hosts that we met along the way. Each of them were so great. After a warm shower, we would walk over to Etno Dinar House in Vrsac, Serbia for an appetizer of kajmak and cured meat, and then through the old city of Dubrovnik and along the outer walls while the giant sun drops into the Adriatic Sea before an Indian dinner at the Hotel Vivek in Gorakhpur.

Our day would end in the Bourgogne region of the French countryside, sitting in the small garden of an old farmhouse overlooking the town of Marmagne. We would sit down with Monsieur and Madame Bourtheir, share stories about the past year and all the wonderful people we met along the way, and enjoy one last bite of her very delicious plum crumble. *C'est tres acidique!*

Made in the USA
Charleston, SC
21 January 2017